W9-ASG-589

Dr. Charles VanEaton
670 Wright Street
Jonesville, MI 49250

ECO-SCAM

A Cato Institute Book

ECO-SCAM

THE FALSE PROPHETS OF ECOLOGICAL APOCALYPSE

RONALD BAILEY

ST. MARTIN'S PRESS
NEW YORK

ECO-SCAM: THE FALSE PROPHETS OF ECOLOGICAL APOCALYPSE.
Copyright © 1993 by Ronald Bailey. All rights reserved. Printed in the
United States of America. No part of this book may be used or reproduced
in any manner whatsoever without written permission except in the case of
brief quotations embodied in critical articles or reviews. For information,
address St. Martin's Press, 175 Fifth Avenue, New York, N.Y. 10010.

Production Editor: David Stanford Burr

Design by Dawn Niles

Library of Congress Cataloging-in-Publication Data

Bailey, Ronald.
    Ecoscam : the false prophets of ecological apocalypse / Ronald
Bailey.
       p.   cm.
    "A Thomas Dunne book."
    ISBN 0-312-08698-9
    1. Environmental degradation.   2. Environmentalists—Attitudes.
I. Title.
GE140.B35   1993
363.7'00973—dc20   92-36035
                                                   CIP

First Edition: February 1993

10 9 8 7 6 5 4 3 2 1

DEDICATION

Traditionally an author dedicates his book to one person. I must break with this tradition because, unworthy as I am of their affection, I have unaccountably been blessed with good friends. So to my friends who have supported me emotionally, intellectually, and yes, to their dismay, even financially over the years I dedicate this book. In no particular order: David and Joan Burr, Steve and Leslie Frantz, David Ridgely, Victoria Heard, Stuart and Brock Lending, Pamela Friedman, Michael Barry, Anne Camper, Lance Landers, Steve and Barbara Huntoon, Arthur Pearlstein, Chris and Sandi O'Connor, David Patton, Melinda and Greg Sidak, Martin and Cindy Cross, Paul Baker, John Lawson, and Philippe Rheault.

CONTENTS

ACKNOWLEDGMENTS

I am very grateful for the encouragement and financial support given me by the Atlas Economic Research Foundation and its gracious president, Alejandro Chafuen. Without Atlas's generosity I might never have had the time to reflect on the issues considered in this book and it may well never have been written. I also want to thank Ed Crane and David Boaz of the Cato Institute for providing me the office space, the computer, and unflagging moral support for far longer than they had planned. I am proud to be associated with the Cato Institute. In addition, John Blundell's efforts to round up the money and the necessary infrastructure were invaluable. I also want to thank Jean Briggs and James Michaels of *Forbes* for taking a chance on a not-so-young journalist at a crucial stage in my career. The good humor and sage advice of *Reason's* editor Virginia Postrel were also greatly appreciated.

Finally, I owe an especially huge debt of gratitude to Marty Zupan of the Institute for Humane Studies. Marty gave me the opportunity years ago to write about some of these issues before anyone else realized their significance. Everyone needs a guardian angel like Marty.

INTRODUCTION

I read *The Population Bomb* and *The Limits to Growth*, two of the three seminal texts of modern environmental apocalyptics, my first year at the University of Virginia in 1972. The third text, *Silent Spring*, I read while in secondary school. These books profoundly disheartened me and many of my generation because they painted the near future—our future—in hopelessly bleak terms.

These gloomy books sold in the millions, and they have dramatically skewed public policy for the past two and a half decades, slowing economic growth and unnecessarily increasing human misery. Even now a new generation of doomsters is flooding our schools and universities with more dire predictions of imminent global disaster. For example, neo-Malthusian Lester Brown's annual *State of the World* is used in more than five hundred college courses, and our primary and secondary schools are being flooded with Environmentalist propaganda.

In this book I hold those environmental alarmists strictly accountable for their faulty analyses, their wildly inaccurate predictions, and their heedless politicization of science, in the hope that the next generation will not grow up feeling that their future is dismal and blighted. This book demonstrates the reality of human progress, and I hope it will thereby help restore the next generation's belief in its future. I do not counsel mindless boosterism or Panglossian optimism. The world faces some real problems, but those problems do not portend the end of the world. And yes, there are sometimes unintended consequences to human actions. However, human history shows that our energy and creativity will surmount whatever difficulties we encounter. Life and progress will always be a struggle and humanity will never lack for new challenges, but as the last fifty years of solid achievement show, there is nothing out there that we cannot handle.

RONALD BAILEY
Washington, D.C., April 25, 1992

ONE

THE IMAGINATION OF DISASTER

The whole aim of practical politics is to keep the populace alarmed (and hence clamorous to be led to safety) by menacing it with an endless series of hobgoblins, all of them imaginary.
—H. L. Mencken

Doom haunts the end of the twentieth century. Millenarian predictions of impending global disaster are heard on every side. The fast-approaching year 2000—the end of the Second Millennium A.D.—is the benchmark date for all kinds of dire predictions, prophecies, and fears. *Fin-de-millennium* blues also afflict the intellectual and policy elites, and, increasingly, the citizenries of the industrialized nations.

Soothsayers once sought the portents of doom in the livers of sheep, in the flight of geese across the sky, and in the patterns of juggled bones. Modern seers examine the entrails of equations, measure molecules in the air, or conjure with computer models looking for signs of the impending apocalypse.

In the last twenty-five years, the modern age has been besieged by a constant litany of dreadful prophecies:

- "The battle to feed all of humanity is over. In the 1970s the world will undergo famines—hundreds of millions of people are going to starve to death in spite of any crash programs embarked upon now."[1]
- "The limits to growth on this planet will be reached sometime in the next one hundred years. The most probable result will be a rather sudden and uncontrollable decline in both population and industrial capacity."[2]
- "In the case of recombinant DNA, it is an all or none situation—only one accident is needed to endanger the future of mankind."[3]
- "Global warming, ozone depletion, deforestation and overpopulation are the four horsemen of a looming 21st century apocalypse."[4]
- "The threat of a new ice age must now stand alongside nuclear war as a likely source of wholesale death and misery for mankind."[5]

Prophets proclaiming imminent catastrophe are nothing new in the history of Western culture. However, at no time in the past have predictions of global disaster achieved such wide currency and been given so much respectful attention by policymakers and the general public. The approach of inevitable doom has become the conventional wisdom of the late twentieth century.

In contrast to our gloomy century, nineteenth-century Europe and America celebrated a robust faith in human progress. And why not? The nineteenth century saw great strides being made in human knowledge and the advance of political liberalism. This faith in progress was shattered by the slaughter of World War I. Subsequently, a sense of cultural disarray and cynicism provided fertile soil for the growth of the twin totalitarian political faiths—fascism and Marxist communism. The worldwide Great Depression accelerated the loss of faith in progress in the United States. The horrors of total war during the Second World War—forty-five million dead, the saturation bombing of cities, and

2

the Holocaust in the concentration camps, ending with the flash of the atomic bomb—further eroded confidence in a better future.

Consequently, nostalgia for a simpler time, when humanity purportedly was not confronted with complex and apparently intractable political, economic, and social problems, powerfully attracted some segments of the West's intellectual castes. Rousseau's romantic notion of the innate goodness of primitive, "natural" man distorted by the temptations of civilization gained favor. Some radical environmentalists, inspired by Rousseau, now literally urged modern mankind to return to a hunter-gatherer existence. The ostensibly more "natural" lives of the earth's remaining tribespeople are used to reproach a corrupt modern society, as in Margaret Mead's biased and misleading accounts of sexual practices and morality in Polynesia.[6]

"The apocalyptic myths of the last several decades have been cast on a global scale: world depression, world war, nuclear holocaust, overpopulation, ecological disaster . . . the imagination of disaster has become fixated on worldwide catastrophe,"[7] Michael Barkun observed in *Disaster and the Millennium*.

Modern ecological millenarians, impatient with waiting for the flash of a thermonuclear doom, now claim there is a "global environmental crisis" threatening not just humanity, but all life on earth. A cadre of professional "apocalypse abusers" frightens the public with lurid scenarios of a devastated earth, overrun by starving hordes of humanity, raped of its precious nonrenewable resources, poisoned by pesticides, pollution, and genetically engineered plagues, and baked by greenhouse warming. The new millenarians no longer expect a wrathful God to end the world in a rain of fire or overwhelming deluge. Instead humanity will die by its own hand.

In Christian eschatology, the "Millennium" denotes specifically the thousand-year kingdom to be established after Christ's Second Coming as prophesied in the New Testament's Book of Revelation (20:4–6). Following Christ's

3

thousand-year reign comes the Last Judgment, and the creation of "a new heaven and a new earth" (Rev. 21:1).

The expectation that the end of the world was imminent has spawned numerous Christian millenarian sects, such as the Anabaptists and Hussites in Central Europe, the Rappites and the Millerites in nineteenth-century America, and more recently the Jehovah's Witnesses. Millenarian movements tend to arise in periods of great social and political turmoil, and this is especially true where modernity begins to undermine traditional institutions and established ways of life.

The Millerites of upstate New York were one fairly typical millenarian sect. In 1818, William Miller, the group's founder, calculated that Christ's Second Coming would take place during the next twenty-five years. Spectacular meteor showers and a huge comet were taken as unmistakable portents of impending disaster. After several missed dates, Miller finally predicted that the end would definitely come on October 22, 1844. On the appointed day many believers, dressed in white robes, climbed nearby hilltops to await the apocalypse. "The Great Disappointment" is how the Seventh-Day Adventists, the modern successors of the Millerites, characterize Miller's prophetic failure.

Millenarian aspiration is not confined to Christianity and Western societies. Traditional societies stressed by contact with modern Western culture are particularly prone to outbreaks of millennialist enthusiasm. For instance, in the late 1880s, Native American tribespeople on the Great Plains and in the West joined the Ghost Dance cult. Ghost Dance ceremonies were supposed to resurrect ancestral warriors who would destroy the expanding white settlements.

Similarly, "cargo cult" rituals in Polynesia sought to lure ships and airplanes filled with Western goods to poor islanders. In one case, natives actually constructed a dummy runway and mock air-control tower to welcome the long-anticipated cargo plane. They even made an aircraft out of sticks and leaves in an effort to woo its mate to the ground.[8] With the advent of apocalyptic environmentalism and the rejection of science and technology, it now seems Western civilization may join the Ghost Dance.

The great medieval millenarian Joachim di Fiore propounded the doctrine that history is divided into stages. For him history was a march from a previous golden age to the present corrupt society whose evil would imminently be swept away by a major cataclysm and replaced by a purified society. Joachim exhorted the faithful to smash their decadent society and thus help bring history to fulfillment. In Joachim's new age, all hierarchies would be eliminated, harmony established, and poverty abolished.[9] This notion that history proceeds in discrete stages toward final perfection profoundly influenced many later thinkers including Rousseau, Hegel, and Marx.

In the nineteenth century, millenarian aspirations, originally spiritual and religious in character, became secularized and were incorporated into the doctrines of radical and utopian politics. The greatest millenarian political faith is Marxism and its more temperate social democratic sects.

"Marx, with his highly detailed and imaginative presentation of the eschatology of capitalism, can be described as the last of the Judeo-Christian prophets, or the first of the secular ones," wrote British social critic Paul Johnson.[10] Like the religious millenarians who preceded him, Marx believed that a corrupt society—in his case, capitalism—would collapse in a massive crisis ushering in a golden age of egalitarian harmony.

According to orthodox Marxist eschatology, the internal class contradictions of capitalist production doom that hateful form of society to inevitable destruction. The proletariat led by the Marxist avant-garde will overthrow the exploiters and topple capitalism into well-deserved oblivion. Now, with Marxist class warfare relegated to the dustbin of history, capitalism can no longer be counted on to self-destruct. Marxist communism's recent disintegration leaves contemporary radicals with an "agency problem."

"Ecological alarmism . . . incorporates many aspects of Marxist theology, especially the idea that capitalist society . . . is ultimately self-destructive," writes Johnson.[11] For many modern leftists the "global environmental crisis" is the new "agent" of history which will eventually destroy capitalism. In the reinterpreted radical vision, capitalism, instead of strangling itself to death on its class contradictions, will choke to death on its own wastes. Radical environmentalists are now the earth's vanguard class who will lead the struggle to bury capitalism and Western materialism.

Self-described "revolutionary leftist" and founder of the Institute of Social Ecology Murray Bookchin flatly declares that "the immediate source of the ecological crisis is capitalism," which he pointedly calls "a cancer in the biosphere."[12] He adds, "I believe that the color of radicalism today is not red, but green."[13]

According to Michael Barkun, the social visions of modern secular millenarians embrace "the disappearance of want and hierarchy, the leveling of distinctions, the elevation of the downtrodden."[14] Like the followers of earlier millenarian movements, both spiritual and political, radical environmentalists stress egalitarianism, the special insight of adherents, the imminence of the apocalypse, and the salvation of the faithful after the cataclysm.

The modern environmental movement strongly attracts "radical egalitarians," says University of California at Berkeley political scientist Aaron Wildavsky. "Radical egalitarians view environmentalism as the best thing that they've got going to attack corporate capitalism."[15] He adds, "Egalitarians believe that the environment is threatened by man-made things, just as man is. Humanity's institutions, in the egalitarian view, are no less the source of inequalities among humans than they are the source of destruction for the environment. To defend the environment is therefore to erode inequalities."[16]

For example, social ecologist Bookchin argues that we must change our repressive industrial capitalist society into "an ecological society based on non-hierarchical relationships, decentralized democratic communities, and eco-technologies like solar power, organic gardening, and humanly scaled industries."[17] In 1976 arch-environmentalist Barry Commoner concluded in *The Poverty of Power* that "it may be time to view the faults of the U.S. capitalist economic system from the vantage point of a socialist alternative," while the "deep ecologist" Arne Naess calls on humanity to adopt a much lower material standard of living.[18]

Ecological mystic and founder of the radical group Earth First! David Foreman asserts that Western society is "rotten to the core" and says he plans to help build "an egalitarian, decentralized, ecologically sound" society that will "emerge out of the ashes of the old industrialized empire" after the ecological apocalypse.[19]

Environmental millenarians, like their medieval forebears, declare that humanity can only avert total ruin if society repents and quickly adopts their sweeping proposals for radical social restructuring and economic redistribution.

Richard Hofstadter tagged this type of apocalyptic demagoguery the "paranoid style" of politics. Political paranoids believe that all of humanity's ills can be traced "to a single center and hence can be eliminated by some kind of final act of victory over the evil source. . . . the world confronts an apocalypse of a sort prefigured in the Book of Revelation."[20] As we have seen, the contemporary focus of evil is the "global ecological crisis."

The political paranoid, like the modern radical environmentalist, "traffics in the birth and death of whole worlds, whole political orders, whole systems of human values."[21] Environmental doomsters believe themselves uniquely capable of seeing the impending catastrophe while the rest of humanity remains stubbornly blind to the danger. "Ecologists are the saved" who believe that they "are better able to plan man, space, and the environment than existing institutions," concludes historian Anna Bramwell.[22]

Predictions of doom have become more numerous in recent years for a more mundane reason as well—they work. Fears of ecological collapse motivate voters and political institutions to adopt environmentalist policies. Environmental

7

scientist Fred Singer notes that the first Earth Day in 1970 "showed that frightening the public gets results. We have been hit by one doomsday prediction after another ever since."[23]

Bill McKibben, an environmental writer, lets the cat out of the bag in his overwrought rendering of the alleged global crisis, *The End of Nature*: "The ecological movement has always had its greatest success in convincing people that we are threatened by some looming problem. . . ."[24] Essentially apocalyptics threaten, "If you don't do what I tell you to do, the world will come to an end."

Wildavsky calls the use of doomsday predictions a form of political pressure, the "Armageddon complex." He notes that apocalyptics "bring all the dangers of the future into the present, hold them over people, and say the most terrible things will happen unless [their] views are accepted. If we are not freezing to death from nuclear winter, for instance, then the greenhouse effect is going to fry us to a crisp. The solution, of course, will be local, state, national, international, and intergalactic regulation to prevent these awful things from happening."[25]

A sizable portion of the contemporary environmental movement has goals far beyond merely preserving wilderness, protecting endangered species, recycling garbage, or even trying to prevent global climate change. American "Green" political activists are building "support for a political outlook that merges ecological and social activism, with a strong emphasis on participatory democracy and political and economic decentralization. The Greens have helped sustain a hopeful alternative voice in a period characterized by a distinct shortage of idealism on the left."[26]

In fact, "social justice" has long been on the agenda of environmental egalitarians. Paul Ehrlich wrote more than twenty years ago: "Many of the suppressed people of our nation consider ecology to be just one more 'racist shuck.' . . . Slums, cockroaches, and rats are ecological problems, too. The correction of ghetto conditions in Detroit is neither more nor less important than saving the Great Lakes—both are imperative."[27]

As recently as 1991, Ehrlich reaffirmed that the "environmental crisis" can only be resolved through the "creation of a new civilization" which will deal with "the inequitable distribution of wealth and resources, racism, sexism, religious prejudice, and xenophobia."[28] In 1970, Denis Hayes, chief organizer of the first Earth Day, forthrightly declared, "We demand a lower productivity and a wider distribution." He argued that the growing environmental movement shared "a single unified value structure" which stood against "exploitation, imperialism, and the war-based economy."[29]

The editors of the influential leftist magazine *The Progressive* warned in their special 1970 Earth Day issue that the "new Four Horsemen—Overpopulation, Pollution, the Famine of Resources, and Nuclear War—are riding relentlessly on their mission of destruction."[30] *The Progressive's* editors added, "The true ecological crusaders and the peace crusaders have a common objective—a world to save from war, poverty, racism—and pollution."[31] Twenty years later, the peace movement and the environmental movement are now virtually indistinguishable.

The environmental movement's widening social justice agenda includes not only preventing the construction of incinerators and nuclear power plants, fighting over landfill sites and recycling campaigns, but also opposing the Persian Gulf War, supporting native treaty rights, and organizing the inner city poor to demand more public housing.[32]

The largest student-run political organization on America's campuses, the Student Environmental Action Coalition (SEAC), calls for a "broader definition of environmentalism," and issues of social justice, recast as "environmental equity," dominated the group's 1991 national conference in Boulder, Colorado. Randolph Viscio, SEAC's national coordinator, declared: "Poor housing is an environmental issue. Fighting for equality in an impoverished community where a company wants to put a toxic waste dump. Building coalitions with labor and minority groups.

9

It's not that these are very new issues. They just haven't been given the attention they deserve."[33]

In response to these social justice concerns, the U.S. Environmental Protection Agency has begun to broaden the scope of its regulatory activities by focusing on "environmental equity." For example, the EPA plans to analyze how the siting of environmental nuisances like landfills and incinerators specifically affects poor people and minorities.[34]

An increasingly influential wing of the modern environmental movement consists of the adherents of the religio-mystical worldview known as "deep ecology." Deep ecologists are even more radically egalitarian than those environmentalists whose roots are in a social justice tradition. They urge us to shun a narrow ethical focus on humanity and adopt a "biocentric" view which treats humans and all other species as morally identical. "Man is no more important than any other species," concludes Earth First! founder Dave Foreman.[35]

Calling for "greater environmental humility," many deep ecologists are frankly antihuman. Foreman says, "We are a cancer on nature."[36] And the highly regarded "eco-theologian" Reverend Thomas Berry doesn't mince words either: "We are an affliction of the world, its demonic presence. We are the violation of Earth's most sacred aspects."[37] Some deep ecologists welcome the AIDS epidemic as a means of population control,[38] while others, like Christopher Manes, shout the slogan "Back to the Pleistocene," and urge us to tear down modern civilization and become tribal hunter-gatherers as our ancestors were ten thousand years ago.[39] This strong antihuman and anticivilization inclination has caused some friction between "deep ecologists" and environmentalists who stem from the more human-centered social justice tradition.

Unlike secular millenarians who express their utopian hopes in political rhetoric, deep ecologists do not shrink from using frankly religious and salvationist language. "If we seek only personal redemption we could become solitary ecological saints among the masses of those we might classify as 'sinners' who continue to pollute," writes Bill Devall.[40] Devall, a professor at Humboldt State University in California, wants to organize society along explicitly egalitarian and communitarian lines.

The environmental problems of "technocratic-industrial societies" are "coming to be understood as a crisis of character and of culture," he writes.[41] What is needed is a "new ecological sensibility."[42] There is a chilling similarity between the old Marxist aspiration of molding a "New Soviet Man" and the deep ecologist's desire to create a "New Ecological Person."

Devall adds that "deep ecology goes beyond the so-called factual scientific level to the level of self and Earth wisdom."[43] Less generously, one critic fumes that environmentalism has become "like a new religion, a new paganism, that worships trees and sacrifices people."[44]

Millenarians, both secular and religious, look forward to a transformed humanity, and radical environmentalists also wish to remake a flawed human race. In his seminal article "The Historical Roots of Our Ecologic Crisis," historian Lynn White, Jr., blamed environmental degradation on Judeo-Christian teleology, which he decried as having instilled in Western culture a "faith in perpetual progress." In 1967, White asserted, "More science and more technology are not going to get us out of the present ecological crisis until we find a new religion, or rethink our old one."[45] And this call to "rethink and refeel our nature and destiny"[46] has not gone unheeded. Environmentalist Victor Scheffer believes that "if religion can be defined simply as a binding philosophy, the start of environmentalism was a religious reformation."[47] Another advocate declared that "environmentalists are the lay priests of a different gospel that can help save us."[48] We are bombarded by demands that we must convert to the new environmental gospel.

In this vein, Paul Ehrlich writes that we must undergo a "revolution in attitudes" leading to a "transformation in human thinking comparable to the one that accompanied the agricultural revolution and in a much, much shorter

11

time."[49] Similarly, eco-doomster Lester Brown is calling for an "Environmental Revolution" in the 1990s. He adds, "The Agricultural Revolution began 10,000 years ago and the Industrial Revolution has been under way for two centuries. But if the Environmental Revolution is to succeed, it must be compressed into a few decades."[50] "Our world," he warns, "faces potentially convulsive change."

The environmental movement also offers a congenial home to many neo-Luddites, that is, modern antitechnology zealots. The term *Luddite* is derived from the name of the apocryphal leader of nineteenth-century England's machine-breakers, Ned Ludd. Gangs of traditional weavers outcompeted by modern looms smashed thousands of the offending machines in the English Midlands in the early nineteenth century. Today many environmental radicals, like the Luddites of old, yearn to smash industrial capitalism. Neo-Luddites like Jeremy Rifkin and Dave Foreman oppose nuclear power, private automobiles, pesticides, automated manufacturing, and biotechnology. Some neo-Luddites literally engage in machine-breaking. The radical group Earth First! uses "ecotage" or what it calls "monkeywrenching" to destroy developers' bulldozers by putting sugar in their fuel tanks or spiking trees with nails so that they shatter saw blades at lumber mills. Flying debris from the shattered blades have maimed several lumberyard workers.

Less militant neo-Luddites have adopted E. F. Schumacher's slogan that "small is beautiful" and urge humanity to adopt "appropriate technologies." Deep ecologists seek technologies which they deem to be "simple in means, rich in ends." These neoutopian platitudes beg the question of just what constitutes "appropriate technology." As Witold Rybcyznski points out, "appropriate technology" usually boils down to labor-intensive low technology or at best some vaguely defined form of "intermediate" technology.[51] Recently the clamor for "appropriate technology" has been repackaged as a generalized demand that we reduce the "scale of human activity."[52]

What makes a technology "appropriate" or "inappropriate"? Deep ecologists Devall and Sessions suggest that in order to determine whether a machine is "appropriate" or not people ask: "Does this technological device or system foster greater autonomy of local communities or greater dependency on some centralized 'authority'?"[53] (Fostering greater autonomy is, of course, "appropriate.")

Just how nonsensical this question is becomes immediately apparent when one considers the case of computers. Early in their history computers were expensive behemoths which social critics almost unanimously predicted would foster highly centralized and regimented organizations. The critics (along with everyone else) completely failed to foresee how personal computers and dispersed networks would eventually emancipate people from central control and put ever greater computing power in the hands of millions of individuals.

It probably would have been impossible to develop liberating personal computers without first building mainframes. And how about automobiles? Certainly cars foster "autonomy," but few environmentalists would deem them "appropriate." It is simply unwarranted, but completely characteristic, hubris for radical environmentalists to think that they can determine with any degree of certainty the future benefits and costs of a new technology.

Modern environmentalism shares the belief—typical of earlier millenarian cults—that we live in the time immediately before the end, that our age is special, and that the final battle between good and evil will culminate during our lifetimes. "We just happen to be living at the moment when the carbon dioxide has increased to an intolerable level. We just happen to be alive at the moment when if nothing is done before we die the world's tropical rain forests will become a brown girdle that will last for millennia," writes Bill McKibben.[54]

"Never in the course of history has humankind been faced with so many threats and dangers," declared the Club of Rome in 1991.[55] Others warn that "we are the last generation on Earth that can save the planet."[56]

Like earlier millenarians who saw signs and portents of the end in comets, meteors, plagues, floods, and droughts, contemporary enviro-prophets see confirming proof of their worst fears wherever they turn. "The signs are there for those who can read them," declares Paul Ehrlich.[57] He points to hurricanes, heat waves, unseasonal cold snaps, depleted oil wells, and local famines, along with the traditional floods, droughts, and epidemics, as portents of the coming global catastrophe—literally anything bad indiscriminately counts as evidence of impending doom.

Millenarians like Ehrlich do not accept the culturally transmitted notions of reality. They selectively fix their attention on information that confirms their strongly held beliefs. They ignore information that does not fit or twist it so that it confirms their views. Even apparently good news is artfully reinterpreted as a bad omen. For example, the fact that worldwide farmers grow far more food per acre now than two decades ago is bad news in the exegesis of the doomsters. They claim that more intensive agriculture means greater soil erosion and groundwater depletion; consequently, more people who are temporarily sustained by the extra agricultural bounty will later die in misery when the earth's fertility is exhausted and the long-predicted global famine finally strikes.

Sad to say, many prominent modern millenarians misuse their scientific credentials to lend authority to their policy pronouncements. They claim certain factual states of affairs necessarily call for specific ethical and policy responses. Thus, they try to make the philosophically illegitimate leap from an "is" to an "ought," from the domain of facts to the realm of values.

Modern doomsayers typically furnish some very qualified scientific data as evidence for the imminence of the crisis and then strike out boldly to reorganize society completely to meet the alleged challenge. In addition, apocalyptics claim our predicament is so perilous that we do not have time for further study of the situation. Despite enormous uncertainties about the seriousness of the alleged

problems, they insist that we must act immediately to radically transform our society, economy, and values. Or else.

These "apocalypse abusers" typically extrapolate only
the most horrendous trends, while systematically ignoring
any ameliorating or optimistic ones, offering worst-case scenarios in the guise of balanced presentations. Ehrlich recently dropped all pretense to scientific objectivity and
endorsed the "quasi-religious" deep ecology movement. He
commended deep ecologists for eschewing "scientific nonsense."[58]

"Normally scientific research leads to scientific conclusions, not to metaphysical manifestos, prophetic outbursts,
utopian reorganizations of society, and political positions,
let alone to a set of internationalist positions on the redistribution of wealth from rich to poor nations, which are clearly
identifiable as positions taken by the far left portion of the
political spectrum," observed Edith Efron in her ground-
breaking *The Apocalyptics*.[59] Physicist Edward Teller
declared, "Highly speculative theories of worldwide destruction—even of the end of life on Earth—used as a call for
a particular kind of political action serve neither the good
reputation of science nor dispassionate political thought."[60]

However, radical environmentalists have become very
skilled at portraying scientific findings as part of a "global
ecological crisis." Consequently, politicians and other policymakers are often forced to respond to the illegitimate
fears fostered by apocalyptic environmentalists. Political
leaders must make decisions—often far-reaching ones—
based on very uncertain, and sometimes deliberately distorted, scientific findings. Some environmentalists are not
above lying in what they believe is a good cause.

What about John and Betty Smith who earnestly recycle
their soda cans and newspapers, east fast-food hamburgers
served in cardboard—not Styrofoam—cartons, and carpool
to work? Surely the Smiths are not apocalyptic egalitarian
environmentalists? They are just trying to do their little bit
to "save the earth."

The Smiths' modest "light green" environmentalism is

an echo of the radical agenda set by millenarians in the "dark green" environmentalist movement. The Smiths and their neighbors are motivated by the relentless drumbeat of fears and millenarian environmental predictions tapped out by apocalypse abusers.

There are more than 450 national organizations, and countless ones at the local level, promoting environmentalism.[61] While certainly not all of these organizations are radical, they all share an institutional imperative to find and publicize an endless series of crises and disasters, since without calamities to combat, they have no reason to exist. Consequently, many of these groups have become quite skilled at mass-marketing doom.

Leading environmental organizations, including the Sierra Club, Greenpeace, the National Wildlife Federation, and the Natural Resources Defense Council, pulled in more than $400 million from a contributor base of nearly four million in 1990.[62] Four hundred million dollars is ten times the amount of money that Republican and Democratic parties *together* raised in 1990. "Ecology is now a political category, like socialism or conservatism," says historian Anna Bramwell.[63] Indeed, in 1970 Marion Edey, a founder of the League of Conservation Voters, argued that environmentalists "must stop acting like a small pressure group and become more like an unofficial political party. . . ."[64]

And the "unofficial" environmental party has been very effective in disseminating its message. When 74 percent of respondents to a *New York Times* poll agree with the statement, "Protecting the environment is so important that the requirements and standards cannot be too high, and continuing environmental improvements must be made regardless of cost,"[65] radical ideas have surely taken hold among average Americans.

Four hundred million dollars also buys a lot of influence in the halls of the United States Capitol. George Mitchell, U.S. Senate Majority Leader, warns in unmistakably apocalyptic tones in his book *World on Fire: Saving an Endangered Earth* of an impending "ecological holocaust" in which "we risk turning our world into a lifeless desert in the coming century, and bringing to pass the grim final judgment of a world on fire."[66]

Meanwhile, Vice-president Albert Gore, who, for more than a decade and a half, was the leading Congressional backer of environmental causes, is now calling on his fellow citizens to "become partners in a bold effort to change the very foundation of our civilization."[67] He urges us "to make the rescue of the environment the central organizing principle for civilization,"[68] offering "a global Marshall Plan" to drastically reorganize the American and world economies along environmentalist lines.[69]

Since the 1960s the United States has adopted scores of new environmental laws and thousands of environmental regulations. Some have been beneficial and necessary. But environmental regulation has been expensive, costing the economy $123 billion in 1991, with the price tag rising to $171 billion annually by the year 2000.[70] The Environmental Protection Agency's budget has jumped 31 percent since 1989, while its staff swelled by 23 percent.[71]

In June 1992, the global environment rose to the top of the world's agenda when the United Nations convoked its 172 members at Rio de Janeiro for the much-heralded "Earth Summit." Organizers grandiloquently billed Rio '92 as "the most important meeting in the history of humanity."[72]

More than 100 presidents, prime ministers, and princes gathered for the world's greatest-ever photo opportunity. The Earth Summit also attracted diplomats from 172 countries, 9,000 journalists, and 17,000 environmentalists representing more than 1,400 nongovernmental organizations.

The U.N. Conference on Environment and Development, as the Earth Summit was officially called, was not known for understatement. Maurice Strong, the Canadian oilman who served as its Secretary-General warned in his opening remarks that humanity's current path "could lead to the end of civilization" and that "this planet could soon become uninhabitable for people." He concluded that the only hopes for saving humanity are sweeping changes in "global culture and value systems." As we have seen, this utopian call for changes in "values" is a staple of millenarian movements including modern apocalyptic environmentalism.

The most significant agreements reached at Earth Summit were the Convention of Global Climate Change, the Convention on Biological Diversity, and Agenda 21. Even before Rio, the nations of the world had signed some 170 international treaties dealing with environmental concerns.[73]

The more interesting event—from a psycho-social-cultural point of view—was the parallel "Global Forum." The Forum, held in a park near downtown Rio, was advertised as the "world's fair of environmentalism." At the Forum, radical environmentalists and their allies in the New Age Spirituality movement hawked their solutions to the global ecological crisis they believe is looming. These nongovernmental organizations hammered out a series of "treaties" among themselves designed to monitor and pressure their countries' governments to comply with the official treaties signed at the Summit.

The most surprising thing about the Earth Summit was how little the natural world and the environment were actually mentioned. Usually, the alleged environmental crises were simply stipulated and the conversation and speeches turned quickly to outlining schemes for drastically redistributing the world's wealth in order to achieve "global equity."

The U.S. and many other nations signed Agenda 21, the ambitious 800-page blueprint for global environmental regulation and economic planning for the twenty-first century. To implement Agenda 21 programs, the developed countries are expected to give the Third World $125 billion annually. At the Summit, one got the impression that many poor countries anticipate the arrival of Western aid much the same way that Polynesian "cargo cults" wait for goods-laden ships to dock.

Agenda 21 is the Mother of all Five Year Plans! A U.N. Sustainable Development Commission will be established by the General Assembly under the authority of the

Secretary-General to oversee Agenda 21. The spectacular failure of Soviet economic central planning has not dimmed the enthusiasm of environmentalists for global ecological central planning.

To ameliorate or prevent impending doom, apocalyptics simultaneously recommend the creation of a huge coercive international bureaucracy while promoting decentralized "participatory democracy" at the local level. They wish to turn the whole world into one gigantic "commons." The notion of a "global commons" is akin to the old-fashioned Marxist demand for the abolition of private property.

Historian Anna Bramwell notes the contradiction between the radical environmentalists' "small is beautiful" values and their belief in global planning. "Their method of returning to the natural world involves mass planning and coercion," she notes.[74]

As the United Nations Conference on the Environment and Development showed, the doomsters reflexively turn to the international control of whatever they deem the problem to be—population, food, climate, or carbon dioxide. Not incidentally, international regulation of the problem would also enhance the doomsters' own power and prestige.

Another disturbing and disheartening aspect of the rise of radical environmentalism is the growing pressure on scientists to manipulate research findings in order to attract funding. "It is well known that Congress has a short attention span—so short that it often appears capable of dealing only with crises. Because everyone else is crying 'crisis,' responsible scientists are forced to join the chorus or risk losing their research programs," avers Harvard University researcher Peter Rogers.[75] He adds that the phony crisis atmosphere engendered by this dismal process causes environmentalists, politicians, and citizen's groups to demand immediate action, which is not what most scientists had in mind at all.

The father of the atom bomb, J. Robert Oppenheimer, appalled by the devastating power of nuclear weapons, once declared that scientists had now "known sin." Scientists have indeed "known sin" in the last fifty years, but not the

19

sin of eating of the fruit of the Tree of Knowledge as implied by Oppenheimer. Instead their besetting sin is far more mundane—greed.

After three years and two billion dollars, Manhattan Project scientists succeeded in making three atomic bombs. The project's two billion dollar budget would add up to more than $16 billion today.[76]

At the dawn of the atomic age, the physicists were the first scientists to enjoy vast government largesse. The great national laboratories like the Argonne National Laboratory outside Chicago and Lawrence Livermore near San Francisco were built and funded as technical citadels devoted to the struggle against Soviet communism. "Government was evidently to be a far more benign and generous patron than most scientists had believed possible," concluded Alice Kimball Smith, in her history of the Federation of American Scientists.[77]

Indeed, federal research spending has now ballooned to more than $76 billion annually,[78] and scientists at government and university laboratories have become a powerful political lobby. The ideal of the dispassionate and objective analysis of the natural world has sometimes been thrown aside in favor of naked interest-group politics and the scramble for funds.

Climatologists are fairly recent entrants to the government science funding frays. In the 1970s, the $50 million Climatic Impact Assessment Program (CIAP) was the first intensive scientific study of humanity's impacts on climate. In the 1980s, some climatologists began warning against an eroding ozone layer and catastrophic increases in the earth's average temperature. Subsequently, they have been rewarded with new grants of federal monies; the climate change research budget, for example, climbed to $1.1 billion in 1992 and will increase by 24 percent in 1993.[79]

Of the scores of scientists interviewed in the course of researching this book, nearly every one of them mentioned, unprompted, how scarce research funds are and how they need more money for their work. Most of them believe in good faith that their work is important and possibly even vital for the future well-being of mankind. Therefore it is not surprising that some are tempted to try to attract more money by linking their efforts to whatever the latest crisis is. Thus the politicization of science has led inexorably to interest-group lobbying and to the erosion of the standards of objectivity, threatening the very foundations of the scientific enterprise.

This intense competition for funding has also led to a steep increase in "science by press release." Scientists working on environmental problems have been particularly prone to issuing their results without the normal benefit of having their work reviewed by their scientific peers. For example, Ehrlich popularized *The Population Bomb* by making several appearances on Johnny Carson's "Tonight Show." The publication of the classic eco-doom study *The Limits to Growth* was orchestrated by a public relations firm. "Nuclear winter" first came to the public's attention in an article by astrophysicist Carl Sagan in the popular newspaper Sunday supplement *Parade,* and was also handled by a public relations firm.

Science by press release has also been used to publicize lesser "crises" such as the carefully choreographed Alar scare in which the Natural Resources Defense Council used a public relations firm to promote the bogus "story" of poisoned apples to CBS's "60 Minutes." In each case, the public was alarmed and new enduring environmental myths were added to the accumulating conventional wisdom of doom, but later scientific analysis severely weakened the original catastrophic claims. The problem of science by press release has become so bad that the National Academy of Sciences issued a report in 1992 calling on scientists to stop the "questionable research practices" of misrepresenting speculations as fact, and releasing research results, especially to the popular press, that have not been evaluated by fellow scientists and judged valid.[80]

Unfortunately, not only do scientists have an incentive to cry "crisis," so too do the environmental advocacy groups

21

need crises. Without them, how could advocacy groups justify their pleas for donations? Nearly every American gets bulk quantities of junk mail warning of ozone depletion, topsoil erosion, resource depletion, diminishing biodiversity, and global warming. The money the advocacy groups collect is spent on lawyers, lobbying, propaganda, and the salaries and perquisites of the headquarters staffs. The media also have a strong incentive to report "crises"—they must sell newspapers and airtime after all. So there it is—an iron triangle of scientists pleading for research funds, interest groups who need crises to justify their existence, and a press that needs to sell papers. It's no wonder people are frightened.

It is, however, far easier to raise fears than to allay them. The apocalyptic factoids manufactured by radical environmentalists develop a life of their own once they are fixed in the popular imagination. Who does not still hear the "facts" of overpopulation, impending global famine, and resource depletion discussed at cocktail parties and congressional hearings?

The hallmark of a truly scientific statement is that it must be made in a way that permits experiments to reveal that it is false. It is also logically impossible to prove a negative. For example, just as it is impossible to prove that there are no unicorns, so too it is impossible to prove that the world will not come to an end imminently.

On the other hand, pseudoscientific claims can never be proved wrong. For instance, we will see in a later chapter that it is difficult to imagine what evidence would ever convince population alarmist Paul Ehrlich that global famine will not occur in the next three decades. Ehrlich and Lester Brown have time and again predicted that world food prices will soon skyrocket and hundreds of millions starve in massive famines. Like earlier millenarians they insist the catastrophe is imminent, predicting global famine beginning in 1975, 1980, etc. Yet world food prices continue to fall and global famine recedes ever further into the hazy future. Unfazed, the gloom peddlers simply postpone doomsday, claiming that humanity has somehow gotten a temporary reprieve. How many times can doomsday be delayed before the soothsayers of doom admit that perhaps their prophecies are wrong?

Half a century's woeful experience indicates, however, that crying wolf never erodes the popularity of the frightful predictions. "One clearly wrong prophecy, or even a whole string of them, rarely discredits the prophet in the eyes of those who believe in prophecy," notes Daniel Cohen in *Waiting for the Apocalypse.*[81] And this is especially true for contemporary environmental predictions of doom.

Nevertheless, the conventional wisdom of doom is simply wrong. Humanity is not running short of food or minerals, and in fact life for most human beings has dramatically improved over the past half century.

So why do so many people in the developed world believe in apocalyptic environmentalism? The attraction of apocalyptic thinking is strong. One survivor of millenarian environmentalism, Eric Zencey, recalled, "There is seduction in apocalyptic thinking. If one lives in the Last Days, one's actions, one's very life, take on historical meaning and no small measure of poignance. . . . Apocalypticism fulfills a desire to escape the flow of real and ordinary time, to fix the flow of history into a single moment of overwhelming importance."[82]

Daniel Cohen believes that every generation grows up convinced that it is the last generation in history. However, the method by which the end is to be brought about changes. For Cohen's generation nuclear war was the agent of the apocalypse. "We believed passionately that there would be such a war, and like the early Christians we were sure that this Judgment Day would come within our own lifetimes," he writes.[83]

The glare of the atomic explosions at Trinity and Hiroshima still illuminates all the subsequent prophesied dooms that have so beset the last melancholy half century. So, let us turn now to the beginning of doomsday—July 16, 1945.

TWO

THE COUNTDOWN
TO DOOMSDAY
BEGINS

"Suddenly the day of judgment was the next day and has been ever since," said physicist I. I. Rabi of the first explosion of an atomic bomb.[1] The mushroom cloud rising over the Trinity nuclear test site in the New Mexico desert in 1945 not only ushered in the Atomic Age, but also the modern Age of Doom. All the apocalyptic fears of thousands of years were focused in that moment of blinding light, and we have lived with nuclear doom hanging over us every day for the past half century.

The vast destructive power of nuclear weapons naturally inspires apocalyptic thoughts. "The atomic bomb was a bridge over which the phantasies ordinarily confined to restricted sections of the population,—hole-and-corner nativist radicalism, religious fundamentalism and revolutionary populism—entered the larger society.... The phantasies of apocalyptic visionaries now claimed the respectability of being a reasonable interpretation of the real situation," wrote sociologist Edward Shils in 1956.[2]

The Trinity explosion moved the director of the Alamogordo Laboratory, J. Robert Oppenheimer, to quote Hindu scripture: "I am become Death, the Shatterer of worlds."[3] God or the gods would no longer be humanity's destroyers when annihilation lies forever in our own hands.

Make no mistake about it, the detonation of even a small fraction of the more than fifty thousand thermonuclear bombs in the world's arsenals would spell disaster for humanity. Those arsenals contain the force of 3.2 tons of high explosives for every human being alive. No sane person can contemplate nuclear war without feeling horror.

At the beginning of the nuclear age, many scientists, activists, politicians, and intellectuals succumbed to a pessimistic version of the technological imperative—merely to have the weapons meant that they would necessarily be used. Nuclear war was inevitable and imminent.

Consequently, the years since Trinity have been filled with dark nuclear prophecies. Albert Einstein declared, "We drift toward unparalleled catastrophe."[4] In 1945, British philosopher Bertrand Russell predicted an atomic war lasting thirty years which would "leave a world without civilized people, from which everything will have to be built afresh—a process taking (say) 500 years."[5]

In 1946 Bernard Baruch, head of U.S. negotiations at the United Nations, asserted that the world faced a "choice between the quick and the dead" and warned, "Let us not deceive ourselves: We must elect World Peace or World Destruction."[6]

In 1961, C. P. Snow warned that if international control over nuclear weapons was not soon established, "within, at most, ten years, some of those bombs are going off. I am saying this as responsibly as I can. *That* is the certainty."[7]

New Yorker writer Jonathan Schell passionately declared in his 1982 bestseller *The Fate of the Earth*: "Unless we rid ourselves of our nuclear weapons a holocaust not only *might* occur but *will* occur—if not today, then tomorrow; if not this year, then the next. We have come to live on borrowed time: every year of continued human life on earth is a borrowed year, every day a borrowed day."[8] And as recently as 1985, the former editor of the *Bulletin of the Atomic Scientists* said, "It is quite likely that a nuclear weapon will be used in a conflict before the end of this century."[9]

Despite these stark and gloomy predictions, no nuclear weapons have been exploded in war since Nagasaki was bombed. Instead it appears that Winston Churchill's judgment in 1955 that "safety will be the sturdy child of terror, and survival the twin brother of annihilation"[10] is the accurate assessment of nuclear deterrence. The "long peace" between the world's leading powers has endured for more than forty-five years.

In his brilliant book on the consequences of nuclear war, *Thinking about the Unthinkable*, Herman Kahn noted in 1962 that many intellectuals and policymakers "believe that the current system must inevitably end in total annihilation. They reject, sometimes very emotionally, any attempts to analyse this notion . . . They want to make the choice one between a risk and the certainty of disaster, between sanity and insanity, between good and evil."[11] He also identified the tendency on the part of antinuclear activists and pacifists to have "a fanatic desire to concentrate all our energies—material and intellectual—on a single 'approved' approach."[12] This proclivity of framing policy debates in stark terms of total ecological annihilation versus some form of drastic and immediate action would later become a hallmark of radical environmentalism. Discussions of shades of gray or varying levels of risk are simply dismissed as quibbling in the face of a global emergency. Ecological absolutists would later insist that the planet can only be saved by immediately banning the bomb, pesticides, babies, biotechnology, chlorofluorocarbons, or carbon dioxide.

Enraged peace activists and self-styled nuclear moralists heaped opprobrium on Kahn for daring to think about nuclear war strategy and about how the United States might recover should the "unthinkable" happen. Similarly, skeptics of ecological apocalypses, like economist Julian Simon and climatologist Richard Lindzen, would later be demonized by radical environmentalists.

The millennial dread inspired by Trinity is the wellspring of the numerous doomsday predictions that have afflicted this past half century. The exponential chain reaction of nuclear fission resulting in a vast explosion often serves as a powerful metaphor for many modern doomsday scenarios, for example, population growth, accelerating resource depletion, increasing global temperatures, and pandemics of bioengineered diseases.

The panacea for stuffing the evil genie of atomic weapons back into its bottle has been the international control of nuclear research and development. One popular book posed the choice starkly, *One World, or None*.[13] Some form of world government was seen by leading politicians, intellectuals, and scientists as the only means of restraining the horrific power unleashed by nuclear physics.[14]

Radical environmentalists, who would later ceaselessly make the facile comparison that ecological problems were as threatening as nuclear war, are today forceful advocates for developing strong international institutions and controls to halt human activities they believe menace the earth. "On ecological grounds, the case for world government is beyond argument," succinctly concluded Amherst College professor Leo Marx in 1970.[15]

"When the late war ended in a thunderclap, it left two noteworthy developments in its wake. Science had become politically interesting and scientists had become interested in politics," said Manhattan Project physicist Joseph H. Rush in 1947.[16] Since then, scientists and politicians have only grown more infatuated with one another.

The Manhattan Project was born from an appeal to President Roosevelt to fund research into nuclear weapons by the world's most famous scientist, Albert Einstein, in 1939. The world's leading physicists—J. Robert Oppenheimer, Leo Szilard, Enrico Fermi, Richard Feynman, Edward Teller, John von Neumann, Eugene Rabinowitch, Eugene

Wigner—were gathered at top-secret laboratories scattered across America. Fearful that Nazi scientists would beat them in the race to construct an atomic bomb, Manhattan Project scientists worked at breakneck speed to create the most destructive weapon ever known.

The world was violently introduced to the Atomic Age by the explosion of an atomic bomb two thousand feet over the Japanese city of Hiroshima on August 6, 1945. The flash killed seventy thousand people in an instant. Three days later, another bomb killed forty thousand in Nagasaki. One hundred thousand more died of injuries by the end of 1945.[17] Japan surrendered on August 14, ending the war whose carnage reached 45 million lives.

Within weeks after the bombs burst over Japan, many younger Manhattan Project scientists, stricken with remorse over the destruction that resulted from their research, formed organizations dedicated to educating the public to the dangers of atomic weapons and to lobbying for international control of the new weapons. By the end of 1945, Manhattan Project scientists had merged their groups into the Federation of American Scientists (FAS).[18] The founding of the FAS marks the beginning of the first of three waves of anti–nuclear weapons activism that have swept the United States since World War II.

The new FAS's goals included persuading the United States government to "help initiate and perpetuate an effective and workable system of world control based on full cooperation among all nations."[19] Also the FAS would act "to safeguard the spirit of free inquiry and free interchange of information without which science cannot flourish."[20] The atomic scientists found ready allies in world-government advocates. One indefatigable spokesman for the international control of atomic weapons was Norman Cousins, a leader of the United World Federalists and editor of the *Saturday Review*.[21]

In the spring of 1946, the FAS launched a public education program sending scientist members to everything from Kiwanis clubs, town meetings, and church socials to the National Council of Churches, union leadership conferences, and congressional hearings.

A closely allied organization called the National Committee on Atomic Information enlisted the help of church groups, labor unions, and the League of Women Voters in the campaign for international control of atomic weaponry. Foreshadowing later civil rights, antiwar, and environmental coalitions, NCAI's leaders were drawn from the National Education Association, the American Association of University Women, the United Council of Church Women, and the Catholic Association for International Peace.[22]

The FAS strongly backed the State Department's Acheson-Lilienthal Report which recommended the creation of an international atomic development authority under the auspices of the United Nations' Atomic Energy Commission. Under the plan, the development authority would monitor all stages of atomic manufacturing from raw materials to fabrication of weapons.[23] The United States plan was submitted to the United Nations in June 1946. After some initial dickering, the Soviet Union's UN ambassador Andrei Gromyko rejected the proposal in March 1947.[24] The world-government and atomic scientists' movement began fading in the face of aggressive and brutal Soviet expansion in Eastern Europe and Korea.

However, even at the outset of the Atomic Age, some observers questioned scientists' claims to have some special wisdom about what U.S. atomic policy should be. *The New York Times* in October 1945 noted that when a "scientist emerges from his laboratory he is no more disinterested than a businessman or politician, having like them his own beliefs, aversions, his own creeds and biases."[25] This statement is as true now as it was then. Rarely do many scientists, politicians, or journalists note today when scientists make the leap from investigating the realm of facts to advocating policies and remedies that embody their personal beliefs, values, and ideological commitments.

In the mid-1940s, many cocky American scientists thought that the Soviets would need at least ten years to develop their own bomb. Others, who believed Soviet totalitarianism posed a grave danger to the West, recommended that the United States should take advantage of its nuclear monopoly and launch a "preventive war" to forestall eventual Soviet atomic ascendancy. Among those urging preventive war was Bertrand Russell.[26] Strangely, Russell would later become a leading figure in Britain's Pacifist Campaign for Nuclear Disarmament.

The leading forum for the discussion of atomic energy and weapons issues was the *Bulletin of the Atomic Scientists*, which began publication in December 1945.[27] For nearly fifty years, humanity has been stuck at the Beginning of the End, watching anxiously as the hands of the famous doomsday clock on the cover of the *Bulletin* inched ever closer to the midnight hour. In 1953 after the U.S. successfully tested the hydrogen bomb the clock moved to only two minutes before midnight. The minute hand of doom swayed back and forth during the next three decades, registering the waxing and waning of superpower tensions. In 1984, the clock hands stood only three minutes from Armageddon. After superpower tensions thawed, the *Bulletin* in 1991 moved the minute hand to seventeen minutes before nuclear midnight, the earliest it has ever stood. As of July, 1992 Armageddon is still seventeen minutes away.

The nuclear arms race took off in earnest after the Soviets detonated their first atomic bomb in 1949. American politicians, military officials, and atomic scientists fiercely debated whether the U.S. should respond to the Soviets by building the immensely more powerful hydrogen bomb. The "father of the atomic bomb" J. Robert Oppenheimer advised against taking the next step up the ladder of nuclear escalation. In the McCarthyite atmosphere of the time, Oppenheimer's opposition to the hydrogen bomb led to the lifting of his security clearance in 1954.

On Halloween 1952, the United States detonated "Mike," the world's first hydrogen bomb, at the Eniwetok Atoll. The 10.4-megaton explosion was eight hundred times more powerful than the one that destroyed Hiroshima.[28]

30

But the Soviet Union did not lag far behind the United States, testing its first thermonuclear device in 1953.

Later in the decade, Soviet scientists scored a stunning success by launching Sputnik, the world's first artificial satellite. This dazzling achievement worried American politicians like Senator John F. Kennedy, who charged that the Eisenhower administration had allowed a "missile gap" between the U.S. and the Soviet Union to open, thus making America vulnerable to a push-button attack from the Soviet Union.

The arms race continued and the U.S. nuclear arsenal reached its deadliest extent at 20,000 megatons of explosive force in 1960. Due to improvements in weapons' delivery accuracy, the destructive power of the U.S. nuclear stockpile dropped by nearly three quarters, to 5,500 megatons by the mid-1980s.[29]

The second wave of peace and antinuclear activism mounted in the United States and Britain in the late 1950s when the National Committee for a Sane Nuclear Policy (SANE) began pushing for a nuclear test ban treaty. Norman Cousins was a key figure in organizing SANE in 1957 to face "a danger unlike any danger that has ever existed." He warned, "In our possession and in the possession of the Russians are more than enough nuclear explosives to put an end to the life of man on earth." SANE proposed that all nuclear testing stop under a United Nations–monitored agreement. SANE also wanted the United Nations to be transformed into "an instrument of effective world law."[30] At the same time in Britain, the more overtly pacifist Campaign for Nuclear Disarmament (CND) began its activities.

To drum up public support for a nuclear test ban, SANE launched a series of full-page advertisements to publicize the findings of biologist Barry Commoner. Commoner's work showed that milk contained strontium-90, a radioactive byproduct in the fallout from nuclear testing. Chemically similar to calcium, strontium-90 was being absorbed by the bones and teeth of children.[31] (Commoner would later become one of America's leading environmental activists.) SANE also sponsored a four-week display in Times Square on the dangers posed by strontium-90 to human health.

Cousins, capitalizing on American fears about fallout, argued, "No nation has the right to contaminate or jeopardize the air or water or food that belongs to people."[32] In a refrain that would resonate more strongly in the 1980s during the stratospheric ozone and greenhouse gas controversies, the *Bulletin of the Atomic Scientists* praised SANE's campaign, commenting, "The general agreement that the air we breathe is the common property of mankind and not to be polluted at the will of sovereign nations is a step forward in the education of the human race."[33]

In the late 1950s, Neville Shute brilliantly depicted the slow extinction of human life due to fallout after a nuclear war in his best-selling novel *On the Beach*. Foreshadowing the 1980s and 1990s, Hollywood stars were enlisted in the test ban crusade. Marlon Brando, Kirk Douglas, Gregory Peck, and Henry Fonda all joined the Hollywood SANE chapter.[34]

Nobel Prize–winning chemist Linus Pauling declared that probably not more than one million Americans would survive a nuclear attack,[35] and he persuaded two thousand scientists to sign his petition to ban nuclear testing.[36] Martin Luther King, Jr., signed a number of SANE manifestos in support of an atomic test ban.[37]

The Cuban missile crisis in October 1962 was probably the closest the world ever came to nuclear war between the superpowers, but a year later, the U.S. and Soviet Union signed the Limited Test Ban Treaty prohibiting all nuclear tests in the atmosphere and oceans. The test ban treaty has been since described "not as an agreement which related to the arms race, but as the first international law to prohibit environmental pollution."[38]

The 1960s saw the fusing of the civil rights and peace movements with environmental activism. Environmentalist Victor Scheffer points out that there is a natural affinity between peace and civil rights activists and the nascent environmental movement[39]: Both movements appeal to people with strong egalitarian sympathies.

The first wave of environmentalist (as opposed to earlier conservationist) fervor in the United States emerged from the late 1960s and early 1970s peace and civil rights movements, and the second began in the late 1980s and continues to swell. Many of the more militant environmental lobbying organizations, including Greenpeace, the Environmental Defense Fund, and the Natural Resources Defense Council, were born in the political hothouse of the 1960s. Later, old-line conservation groups like the Sierra Club, the National Wildlife Foundation, and the Audubon Society also became radicalized. In the 1970s, environmental organizations began to pay greater attention to peace and arms-control issues when public interest in specifically ecological problems flagged.

The political activism inspired by the real possibility of a nuclear holocaust served as the training ground for the later purveyors of apocalyptic environmentalism. The politicization of science; the revolving doors between government agencies in charge of environmental affairs and environmental advocacy groups; the symbiotic relationship among activists, the press, and politicians, all of whom thrive on a crisis atmosphere; the massive propaganda campaigns involving public schools, church organizations, and civic clubs; the call for massive government intervention and international control—all were policies and strategies developed and refined first by antinuclear and peace activists.

For instance, New Left peace activism and environmentalism were combined in the Union of Concerned Scientists (UCS). The UCS emerged from a one-day research strike and teach-in at the Massachusetts Institute of Technology in March 1969. During the MIT strike, faculty and students discussed the atomic bomb, the Vietnam War, and the world food crisis. The UCS's founding "faculty document" called on scientists and engineers to "devise means for turning research applications away from the present overemphasis

33

on military technology towards the solution of pressing environmental and social problems."[40]

UCS moved to the forefront of arms control, nuclear power, and environmental activism. In the 1970s, it focused most of its efforts on opposing nuclear power plants. In the early 1980s, it became one of the chief promoters of "nuclear winter," and led the opposition to President Reagan's Star Wars missile defense plan.[41] Recently the UCS has launched a major effort to combat the latest and most fashionable environmental doom—global warming.

In the 1970s, the Soviets and the U.S. signed the Strategic Arms Limitation Treaty (SALT) and the Anti-Ballistic Missile Treaty. Thereafter the superpowers embarked on arduous negotiations aimed at reducing—not just limiting—the arsenals pointed at one another. Some progress was made, but the SALT II treaty was never ratified because President Jimmy Carter withdrew it from consideration to show his displeasure at the Soviet Union's brutal invasion of Afghanistan.

In the 1980s peace advocacy groups were reinvigorated by the hardline anticommunist rhetoric emanating from the Reagan administration. Activist Randall Forsberg's proposal that both superpowers freeze their current nuclear forces seemed like a good simple solution to a complex problem to a sizable portion of the public. The "Freeze" eventually garnered considerable support in Congress. Antinuclear activists also tried to stop the positioning in Western Europe of American Pershing II and cruise missiles. These weapons were designed to counter earlier Soviet deployments of mobile SS-20 missiles in Eastern Europe. Mass demonstrations against the U.S. deployments took place in Western Europe and the United States.

Antinuclear and peace activism in the West reached its high-water mark during the Nuclear Freeze Campaign. On June 12, 1982, some 700,000 people crammed into New York City's Central Park to rally against the nuclear arms race. It was the largest political demonstration in U.S. history. Eventually voters in nine states passed referenda approving a nuclear freeze. Scores of towns and cities also passed resolutions supporting the Freeze campaign and declared themselves to be "nuclear free zones."

By 1984, the number of disarmament and peace groups in the U.S. blossomed from eight to thirty-nine and their membership rolls swelled to over a million. The core of the peace advocacy community consisted of the Federation of American Scientists, the National Committee for a Sane Nuclear Policy (SANE), the Union of Concerned Scientists, the Council for a Livable World, Physicians for Social Responsibility, and the National Nuclear Freeze Campaign (Freeze). Prominent environmental organizations like Greenpeace, the Natural Resources Defense Council, and Friends of the Earth also strongly came out in favor of the Freeze.[42]

In 1982, Jonathan Schell explicitly called on environmentalists to join forces with the peace/antinuclear activists in his portentous *The Fate of the Earth*. He reminded environmentalists that nuclear holocaust, which "might render the biosphere unfit for human survival, is, in a word, an *ecological* peril. The nuclear peril is usually seen in isolation from the threats to other forms of life and their ecosystems, but in fact it should be seen as the very center of the ecological crisis."[43]

Cornell University astrophysicist Carl Sagan and his colleagues, at about the same time, unveiled their "nuclear winter" doomsday scenario (see Chapter Seven). Environmentalists, inspired by Schell's urgent call to abolish nuclear weapons, quickly offered to help promote and publicize Sagan's new version of nuclear doomsday.[44] Sagan claimed that the detonation of thousands of nuclear bombs would loft megatons of smoke high into the stratosphere, blocking the sunlight from the surface. Temperatures would plunge by more than 25C degrees, killing crops and freezing the hapless human survivors to death. Sagan asserted that the nuclear arsenals of the Soviet Union and the United States had already far exceeded the threshold for triggering nuclear winter in the event of war.

Meanwhile, the Soviets huffed out of nuclear disarmament talks in Geneva, hoping that Western public opinion would force the United States to make concessions at the negotiating table. Instead, in 1983 President Reagan announced his controversial Strategic Defense Initiative (SDI, often referred to as "Star Wars"). Reagan proposed to build an antimissile shield to protect the United States and its allies from Soviet ballistic missile attacks.

In 1985, the Soviets, apparently worried by the prospect that the U.S. might succeed in building a missile defense system, returned to the negotiating table. At the Reykjavik summit meeting in 1986, Reagan startled Soviet President Mikhail Gorbachev by proposing the complete abolition of nuclear weapons.[45] By 1987, the two rival nations signed the Intermediate Nuclear Forces Treaty (INF), the first agreement ever to scrap any type of nuclear weapons system.

"Most disarmament groups merely hoped to stop deployment of new Western missiles in Europe," acknowledged one chagrined German peace activist. "We never hoped to get the Soviet Union to remove all of its SS-20s and we should criticize ourselves for that."[46] In 1989, historian John Gaddis ruefully admitted in the *Bulletin of the Atomic Scientists*, "During his eight years as president, Ronald Reagan has presided over the most dramatic improvement in U.S.-Soviet relations—and the most solid progress in arms control—since the Cold War began." Gaddis concluded, " 'Hanging tough paid off.' "[47]

Later, Presidents Bush and Gorbachev reached an agreement to reduce strategic nuclear weapons by 30 percent. After the failed Soviet coup in August 1991, Gorbachev and Bush participated in an astonishing bidding war to further reduce strategic weapons. In January 1992, Bush in his State of the Union address proposed deeper cuts in the superpower arsenals, and Russian President Boris Yeltsin upped the ante, suggesting still larger reductions. In fact, the cutbacks proposed by the U.S. and Russia are now approaching those made by proponents of "minimum deterrence."

The unforeseen dissolution of aggressive Soviet communism, not the protests and activities of the Western peace movement, has led to the end of the Cold War. The historic events of the past five years have now made it clear that disarmament intellectuals and activists were wedded to a false doctrine of technological determinism, to wit, since nuclear weapons exist, they will necessarily be used. They failed to put other countries' nuclear arsenals in their proper political context.

According to defense analysts Theodore Reuter and Thomas Kalil, "A nuclear-armed, democratic, market-oriented Soviet Union with a foreign policy committed to international peace and international law and a defense policy strictly limited to defense is different from a nuclear-armed, non-democratic, command economy Soviet Union committed to hegemonic domination and a defense policy oriented toward nuclear preemption. The United States worries little about a French or British nuclear arsenal of several hundred nuclear warheads; an Iraqi or Libyan nuclear arsenal of several hundred warheads is another matter entirely."[48]

At the end of the Cold War, foreign policy expert Owen Harries finds the attitude of leading peace intellectuals toward nuclear weapons highly ironical. Nuclear weapons

were supposed to make the "balance of terror" so delicate, and scribes like the scientist-novelist C. P. Snow solemnly and fatuously demonstrated the inevitability of nuclear war in a matter of a few years in the absence of a general nuclear disarmament, while the aged philosopher Bertrand Russell sat on cold pavements to dramatize the cause. All in all, no other issue was given as high a priority by intellectuals during the cold war as "banning the Bomb." And yet it is surely true that it was only the existence of nuclear weapons that kept the cold war cold. Certainly it is difficult to think of another case in history where such a level of intense hostility, backed by massive and growing stocks of arms and sustained for such a lengthy period, did not result in active warfare; and it is also difficult to identify any factor other than the existence of nuclear weapons that can explain why this conflict was the exception.[49]

With the advent of superpower comity, peace activist organizations were dealt a severe setback—donations and membership rolls plummeted. *Nuclear Times* editor John Tirman admitted, "Fear is a better motivator than hope."[50] *Newsweek* reported that "groups like SANE/Freeze are retrenching as members gravitate to environmentalism or other causes."[51]

By 1992, peace advocacy groups had all but stampeded away from a singular focus on arms control and were prominently incorporating environmental issues into their programs. For example, more than fifty environmental and peace organizations, including the American Peace Network, Campaign for the Earth, Energy and Environmental Study Institute, Environmental Action Foundation, National Mobilization for Survival, Nuclear Free America, Peace Links, Physicians for Social Responsibility, SANE/Freeze, and the World Federalist Association, have formed the Alliance for Our Common Future.

The Alliance created a media campaign aimed at pushing President Bush into personally leading the U.S. delegation to the Earth Summit in Rio de Janeiro, Brazil. This peace-environmental alliance wanted the U.S. to make specific commitments to reduced emissions of greenhouse gases, to perfect and sign a new convention on global climate change, and to create new United Nations agencies in charge of transferring technical and financial aid from industrial counties to the developing world.[52]

A psychology of apocalypticism, which animated many peace activists, is now firmly lodged in the minds of today's radical environmental activists. The legacy of technophobia that pervades modern environmentalism can be directly traced to the fears engendered by the atomic bomb and the dark prophecies of the peace activists. Science and technology, which had long been the sturdy handmaidens of progress, came to be seen as a threat to all future progress. In one remarkable and dismaying exercise in technophobia, molecular biologists, self-consciously imitating Manhattan Project physicists, debated at the historic Asilomar conference in 1975 whether their new ability to manipulate genes should be exploited. Just as Manhattan Project physicist Leo Szilard once argued that atomic technology should be kept secret, so later did biologist George Wald contend that biotechnology was too dangerous for humanity to handle (see Chapter Six).

Now the specter of imminent nuclear destruction vanishes, only to be replaced by a variety of environmental dooms. Dr. Robert Jay Lifton, head of the Center on Violence and Human Survival, says that among his patients in 1987, "the fear of nuclear war we encountered was fairly widespread." He added, "They spoke of holocaust, the end of the world."

But by 1990 fashions in apocalyptic imagery were changing. According to Lifton, "Rather than fear of nuclear war, people began offering environmental images, fear of the greenhouse effect, the ozone layer and Chernobyl as dangers to the future."[53]

Given the symbolic power of nuclear bombs, it is not at all surprising that one of the first of many subsequent environmental dooms was styled as a "bomb." In 1968, Stanford University entomologist Paul Ehrlich unleashed his Malthusian enthusiasms on the public in *The Population Bomb*.

THREE

THE END OF HUNGER

Most convincing as evidence of populousness, we men have actually become a burden to the earth, the fruits of nature hardly suffice to sustain us, there is a general pressure of scarcity giving rise to complaints, since the earth can no longer support us. Need we be astonished that plague and famine, warfare and earthquake come to be regarded as remedies, serving, as it were, to trim and prune the superfluity of population.
—Tertullian, A.D. 200[1]

Famine is the fiercest of the biblical Four Horsemen of the Apocalypse. Hunger has stalked humanity from our beginnings on the savannahs of Africa 250,000 years ago. Today, television pictures of children, bellies distended by hunger, rend our hearts. Now at the end of the twentieth century, we are on the verge of eliminating hunger. Yet despite massive amounts of evidence to the contrary, some still predict that a global famine, killing hundreds of millions, will soon sweep the planet.

The two leading prophets of famine are Dr. Paul Ehrlich and Dr. Lester Brown. Both are adherents to the doctrine first propounded by the Reverend Thomas Robert Malthus in his *An Essay on the Principle of Population*, first printed in 1798. Malthus asserted that "Population, when unchecked, increases in a geometrical ratio. Subsistence increases only in an arithmetical ratio. A slight acquaintance with numbers will show the immensity of the first power in comparison of the second." Thus, Malthus concluded that some portion of the population would always be condemned to starvation.

Although his latter-day disciples do not acknowledge it, Malthus amended his views. He decided that humans could control the number of offspring they engendered and thereby avoid perpetual famine.[2]

However, Malthus's original doctrine appealed especially to nineteenth-century "radical critics and antagonists of capitalism. The Malthus of the first edition could be used to demonstrate that *under capitalism* the grim ratio between population and food would inevitably prevail, leaving the working class in a permanent straitjacket of poverty and unemployment. . . ."[3] Nineteenth-century egalitarians argued that only a postcapitalist, non-hierarchical society could equitably provide for the needs of humanity. This conviction remains a staple of contemporary environmental millenarianism.

Malthus was a victim of fascination with exponential growth rates—a fascination which would later mesmerize many twentieth-century doomsters including Ehrlich, Brown, Jay Forrester, and Dennis and Donella Meadows. What worries them is that more babies are being born than old people are dying. Let's say for every thousand people, 30 new babies are born each year and 10 people die, yielding a net annual population increase of 20. This yields a 2 percent compound growth rate, doubling the population every 35 years. If this situation were to continue indefinitely, the earth would eventually drown in people. This image of a standing-room-only world mesmerizes modern Malthusians. They focus solely on one exponential trend, population growth, while ignoring other even faster positive trends in economic growth and food production.

Stanford University entomologist Paul Ehrlich is the

most famous population alarmist alive. He has tirelessly promoted his millenarian predictions in a torrent of best-selling books and articles for a quarter of a century. In 1968, he published the sensational The Population Bomb.

Ehrlich is a master of sketching out imaginative doom-fraught future scenarios. His role as a population doomster has brought him considerable renown and financial security —in 1990 he won the prestigious Craafoord Prize from the Swedish Academy and a MacArthur Foundation "genius grant." All this recognition notwithstanding, the fact is that not one of Ehrlich's many frightful predictions has ever come true.

Ehrlich succeeds by making himself a rapidly moving target, following the old political adage, "Never apologize and never explain." He makes a prediction, and when refuted by scientific evidence or events, he simply makes another assertion incorporating the latest apocalyptic fads. Being proved wrong apparently never bothers him, and he has great faith that his population predictions must eventually come true. Like earlier millenarians whose prophecies failed, he serenely defers doomsday.

Also like religious millenarians who claim that doomsday was averted on account of their prayers, Ehrlich is not above taking credit for the postponement of the end either. He modestly suggests that the steep decline in American birth rates in the 1970s may be due to the publication of The Population Bomb and the work of his Zero Population Growth lobbying organization.[4] He also takes credit for the regulations on pesticides and for the improvement of water quality in the United States.[5] In Ehrlich's own self-estimation, the world would be in much worse shape if he weren't in it.

Let's take a stroll down memory lane.

"The battle to feed all of humanity is over. In the 1970s the world will undergo famines—hundreds of millions of people are going to starve to death in spite of any crash programs embarked upon now" is the arresting way Ehrlich began The Population Bomb.[6] Twenty-two years later we hear again the old familiar refrain in *The Population Explosion*: "One thing seems safe to predict: starvation and epidemic disease will raise the death rates over most of the planet."[7]

Rather than make specific predictions, Ehrlich prefers to use "scenarios" which he disingenuously calls "devices for helping one to think about the future." The three scenarios outlined in *The Population Bomb* feature atomic war, killer smogs, massive famines, food riots, poisoned water, and global epidemics. The most optimistic scenario ends with the death of only half a billion people in a major "dieback" by 1985.[8] Ehrlich intends to scare the hell out of his readers as a way to get them to adopt his coercive population control policies.

In 1968, Ehrlich agreed with an expert who predicted India couldn't "possibly feed two hundred million more people by 1980." Furthermore, he claimed, "I have yet to meet anyone familiar with the situation who thinks that India will be self-sufficient in food by 1971." In the revised *The Population Bomb* in 1971, he evidently recognized that his predictions about India had already been proved wrong because he discreetly omitted them. In fact, India became more than self-sufficient, exporting surplus grain in the early 1980s to the Soviet Union.

In 1969, Ehrlich pumped up the volume in an article entitled "Eco-Catastrophe!" for *Ramparts Magazine*: "Most of the people who are going to die in the greatest cataclysm in the history of man have already been born."[9] He added: "By that time [1975!] some experts feel that food shortages will have escalated the present level of world hunger and starvation into famines of unbelievable proportions. Other experts, more optimistic, think the ultimate food-population collision will not occur until the decade of the 1980s."[10]

In "Eco-Catastrophe!" Ehrlich outlined his most lurid scare scenario: the oceans died of DDT poisoning by 1979; crops failed due to air pollution blocking sunlight; the "much ballyhooed" Green Revolution collapsed; 200,000 people died of "smog disasters" in New York and Los Angeles in 1973; and U.S. life expectancy dropped to only forty-two years by 1980 owing to epidemic cancer caused by pesticide use. The scenario ended with the beginning of World War III on October 13, 1979. (Recall that the Millerites thought the world would also end in October, only 135 years earlier in 1844.)

Ehrlich particularly savored the part of his scenario where he portrayed "cornucopian" economists, his perpetual nemeses, as humiliated in congressional hearings on resource depletion. Ehrlich acknowledged that he offered a "pretty grim scenario," but concluded that "Unfortunately, we're a long way into it already . . . much of [it] is based on trends already appearing."[11]

In 1970, for the first Earth Day issue of the leftist journal *The Progressive*, Ehrlich painted yet another gruesome picture in which sixty-five million Americans died of famine and worldwide a total of four billion people perished in "the Great Die-Off" between the years 1980 and 1989.[12]

The massive famines killing billions of people predicted for the 1970s and the 1980s never happened, of course. Instead of the death rate going up, life expectancy sharply increased worldwide. Too many people did die of starvation, especially children in the developing world, but on nothing remotely like the apocalyptic scale predicted by Ehrlich.

For millenarians like Ehrlich, the world is filled with portents of the apocalypse. He uncritically jumps on board any doomsday train at the station. In the 1960s, as evidence of the coming cataclysm, Ehrlich cited air pollution, pesticide poisoning, and the then-fashionable notion of global cooling, which was going to bring on a new ice age and severely shorten growing seasons in the world's breadbaskets. He foresaw pesticide-resistant insects gobbling up what little grain farmers were able to coax from their severely eroded land, and flatly dismissed the enormous success of the Green Revolution that swept the Third World in the late 1960s and early 1970s. He also foresaw massive deaths from pollution.

Later when pesticides turned out not to be such a mortal danger, air pollution began to abate, and global cooling turned to global warming, Ehrlich smoothly switched to promoting other dooms (including global warming). Ehrlich also coauthored an article in *Science* on the biological effects of nuclear winter in the early 1980s. Now he believes that the thinning ozone layer, topsoil erosion, and the depletion of groundwater will give humanity the coup de grace. In the meantime, he published a new book in 1991, *Healing the Planet*, in which he once again predicted the deaths of billions in the early years of the next millennium. He went to all this effort despite the fact that he told *Look* magazine in 1971, "When you reach a point where you realize further efforts will be futile, you may as well look after yourself and your friends and enjoy what little time you have left. That point for me is 1972."[13] Twenty years later Ehrlich continues his campaign.

Ehrlich claims in his 1990 book, *The Population Explosion*, that global food production peaked in 1986 and that global food production per person peaked in 1984."[14] In a kind of "you scratch my back, and I'll scratch yours" technique commonly used by environmental millenarians, he apparently cribbed this information from fellow Malthusian Lester Brown. The small cadre of influential millenarians constantly cite each other's work as evidence for the truth of their assertions. Unfortunately for the gloomy professors, it's not true.[15]

The career of Lester Brown closely parallels Ehrlich's. In the 1960s, Brown hit upon an arresting public relations formula when he joined claims of environmental degradation to fears of imminent global famine. He, like Ehrlich, has been very successful at peddling millennial doom. He is now the president of the notoriously gloomy Worldwatch Institute, which publishes each year the self-styled *State of the World Report*.

Predictably the "state of the world" in this volume is always just *terrible* and rapidly getting much worse. The book is also a wonderful propaganda tool for apocalyptic environmentalism. Available in 27 languages, the first print run of the 1992 edition in English is 100,000 copies. In 1991, it was used as a text by more than 1,300 professors at 633 colleges and universities in the United States.[16]

Brown's divinatory powers have proven to be no better than Ehrlich's, however. In each of the last three decades he proclaimed that world food production had peaked and food per capita would henceforth decline, leading to inevitable widespread famines.

In 1967, when Brown was the administrator of the Agriculture Department's International Agricultural Development Services, he asserted, "The trend in grain stocks indicates clearly that 1961 marked a worldwide turning point . . . food consumption moved ahead of production." In his view, increased food consumption in the 1960s was compensated by a one-time drawing down of world food stores, which had been built up in the 1950s.[17]

Again, in 1974, Brown predicted in his *Not by Bread Alone* that the end was nigh after world food stocks were drawn down following bad harvests in 1972 and 1974. Brown again saw the transition to the end when he spoke at the Earth Island Institute's *On the Fate of the Earth* conference in 1984: "If we go back to 1950 and look at the economic, agricultural, and social trends, we can see a clear breaking point somewhere around 1973."[18]

In 1989, Brown once again keyed into reductions in the world's grain stocks and declared that global food shortages were at last at hand.[19] His record remains unbroken; he has been wrong every time—world food supplies continue to grow while prices steadily decline.

In the 1960s, Brown pointed to stagnant crop productivity and the lack of new cropland on which to grow additional food as support for his predictions of impending famine. However, the "Green Revolution" came along and dramatically boosted crop productivity. Both Brown and Ehrlich, like the heirs of Malthus they are, paint a picture of developing countries rapidly running out of arable land and blame deforestation on poor people who are desperately seeking more land for crops. But this picture too is wrong.

Nearly all of the increase in grain production in the developing countries over the past two decades has been from higher yields rather than from expanding crop area.[20]

Rather than admit error, Brown joins fellow doomster Ehrlich in adopting whatever is the latest fad in cataclysm to support his faltering predictions. Brown jumped on the resource depletion bandwagon in the early 1970s, praising *The Limits to Growth* as a "remarkable achievement." In the late 1970s, Brown coauthored a book, *Running on Empty*, which predicted that oil supplies would soon diminish sharply "with production peaking around 1990." The depletion crises he has lavished most of his attention on are the alleged loss of topsoil, the "mining" of fossilized groundwater, and the salinization of irrigated land.

Brown, who maintains that topsoil is "more crucial than oil,"[21] is just the latest in a long line of alarmists peddling a "topsoil erosion crisis." In 1928, a U.S. Department of Agriculture bureaucrat, Hugh Hammond Bennett, published an apocalyptic tract declaring that tens of millions of acres of cropland were "devastated" and "totally destroyed" by erosion. Rewarded by being made the chief of the new U.S. Soil Conservation Service, Bennett would later claim almost half of the U.S.'s 415 million acres of cropland were severely eroded.[22]

"It may be accepted that over the past fifty years the threat of erosion to permanent losses of soil productivity was never as great as many people claimed," mildly concludes soil expert Pierre Crosson of the highly respected environmental think tank Resources for the Future.[23] He points out that U.S. crop productivity would be much lower if soil erosion rates were as bad as claimed.

The Soil Conservation Service estimates that topsoil regenerates at five tons per acre per year. By contrast, Crosson cites studies showing regeneration rates of twelve to sixty tons per year are not uncommon. In addition, since plant roots are the main source of organic material in soils, modern high-yield crops with their greater quantity of roots may actually restore productivity.[24]

47

And what does it mean to say that eroded soil is "lost"? The National Research Council of the National Academy of Sciences says the practice of using erosion estimates as measures of "soil loss" is wrong. Soil is moved or displaced, it isn't lost. Soil that leaves one farm is far more likely to end up on another farm than to flow into the ocean.[25]

Crosson concludes that "present rates of erosion throughout most of the next century would pose no serious threat to the productivity of the nation's soils." He estimates that even with no improvements in agricultural technology, crop yields would drop by a minuscule 2 percent over the next century.[26] Of course, one prediction you can bank on is that vast technical improvements in farming will be made over the next one hundred years.

Brown points with alarm to high erosion rates in some parts of the Third World. However, whatever problems do exist can be solved by adapting soil conservation techniques commonly used by Western farmers to Third World farms. Hudson Institute agricultural economist Dennis Avery points out, for instance, that many of the problems associated with soil salinization caused by irrigation can be reduced by new sprinkler, drip, and trailing-tube irrigation systems which also double water-use efficiency.[27] Farmers can also plant new salt-tolerant crop varieties in the future.[28]

"Economic factors will reduce and then eliminate groundwater mining long before the water in an aquifer is exhausted," according to renewable resource director Kenneth Frederick at Resources for the Future.[29] Farmers respond to prices like anyone else: once it costs too much to pump water from a shrinking aquifer, the land is no longer irrigated. Scientists are also in the process of devising ways to recharge aquifers.

Brown also alarmed the public about an alleged "cropland conversion crisis" in which the U.S. was supposedly losing vital cropland to urban uses, especially to suburban housing developments. This illusory crisis was based on a badly flawed federal government survey that in 1977 claimed the U.S. was losing nearly 3 million acres per year to urbanization. Characteristically, Brown uncritically latched on to the study to support his apocalyptic claims about declining food supplies. The crisis dissipated when later studies showed that only as much as 30 million acres of the country's 570 million acres of farmland would be converted by the year 2030.[30]

Like Ehrlich, Brown grasps at each momentary crisis to bolster his famine predictions. He prominently featured global warming and ozone-layer thinning in *State of the World 1989*, suggesting these particular dooms will devastate crops in the United States (see Chapters Eight and Nine).

One reason such apocalypse abusers thrive is that the public has no long-term memory. People are unlikely to remember that a doomster made dire predictions twenty years ago that have since been proved wrong. Brown's food production predictions using the "S-shaped yield curve" are a wonderful example of how this works.

In 1967 he wrote, "As the non-recurring sources of [agricultural] productivity are exhausted, the sources of increased productivity are reduced until eventually the rate of increase in yield per acre begins to slow. This might be depicted by that familiar biologic function the S-shaped growth curve."[31] In 1990, he writes without apparent irony, "Projecting food production was once a simple matter of extrapolating historical trends. But as yields in many countries approach the upper bend on the S-shaped growth curve, this approach becomes irrelevant."[32]

Have farmers gotten, albeit twenty years late, to the upper bend on the S-shaped curve yet? No one can tell for sure since the information that would confirm such a conclusion will not be available for perhaps another decade. This is a variation on a common rhetorical technique used by doomsters. For them, the past is no guide to the future, since they claim we have passed some critical threshold, making past evidence irrelevant. This same rhetorical technique has been applied time and again to alleged crises involving pesticides, air and water pollution, global cooling, ozone depletion, and now global warming. The advantage of such thresholds is that a doomsayer can predict catastrophic changes without having to provide any evidence to back his claims. By the way, Brown never addresses the question of why, if predicting future food production was once a simple matter of "extrapolating historical trends," he has spent the last twenty-five years predicting imminent famine.

Malthusians barrage readers with a torrent of examples, when added up, however, simply do not countervail against the general positive trends that are evident everywhere. Phenomena that have been incorporated into the conventional wisdom of doom—food is getting scarce, millions of tons of topsoil are "lost" each year, the world is running out of oil, global temperatures are increasing catastrophically—are merely asserted on the thinnest of data bases.

Contemporary millenarians are like unsophisticated theologians a couple of centuries ago who attributed hurricanes, lightning bolts, and plagues to the hand of God. As scientific knowledge advanced they could attribute fewer and fewer occurrences in the physical world to miracles. Their god was reduced to living in the gaps of human knowledge; so too today, the doomster's apocalypses live only in the ever-narrowing gaps of our understanding.

Ehrlich, in particular, is firmly in the grip of the biological fallacy. He equates humans and animals, arguing that what is true of animals must also be true of human beings. Consequently, he treats human beings as if we were just a clever herd of gazelles limited by the earth's "carrying capacity."

Naturalist Aldo Leopold devised the concept of "carrying capacity" after studying the famous population explosion and subsequent crash of the Kaibab Plateau mule deer in the 1920s. The systematic destruction of predators like mountain lions and wolves allowed the Kaibab deer population to drastically increase, leading to severe overgrazing and massive starvation. Leopold concluded that any given ecosystem can only support a limited number of a single species.[33]

Ehrlich simplemindedly applies this useful zoological notion to human beings: "To ecologists who study animals, food and population often seem like sides of the same coin. If too many animals are devouring it, the food supply declines; too little food, the supply of animals declines ... *Homo sapiens* is no exception to that rule, and at the moment it seems likely that food will be our limiting resource."[34]

Harvard Population Center demographer Nick Eberstadt disagrees strongly. "One of the reasons that Ehrlich's been so wrong is that he has no understanding of or sympathy for the economic process that human beings engage in."[35] In nature, gazelles uncontrolled by predators do occasionally overrun their pasturage and then starve when they run out of grass—that is, exceed their carrying capacity. But humans, unlike gazelles, have proved extraordinarily proficient at expanding the pasturage. Humans are uniquely productive creatures; unlike other species, we can increase the supply of resources available to us. And we have done a magnificent job of it: since 1750, the gross world product has grown more than 1,700-fold while the world's population has risen only sixfold. Let's see a gazelle herd do that!

Before being seduced by the attractive, but misleading, notion of carrying capacity, recall that the carrying capacity of the American continent north of the Rio Grande before 1600 without modern agriculture and technology was only six to twelve million people, most of whom lived only slightly above subsistence level. Now our continent supports three hundred million people in what two centuries ago would have been unimagined luxury.

In 1968, Ehrlich asserted that most of the developed countries, "are overpopulated by the simple criterion that they are not able to produce enough food to feed their populations."[36] The sheer arbitrariness of this criterion is immediately made plain when one asks why would Ehrlich not require New York City to produce all its own food? Is he somehow likening national borders to the boundaries of animal habitats? And how far does this criterion apply? Besides food, would each country have to produce all its own steel, cars, stereos, refrigerators, drugs, televisions, clothes, shoes, and wine? For that matter why not require every person to produce his own food, weave his own cloth, build his own house, butcher his own meat, and manufacture his own curatives? This requirement would quickly reduce humanity to the grinding poverty our ancestors knew and no doubt eliminate much of the "excess" population.

This definition of "overpopulation" is manifestly absurd, yet twenty years later, many environmentalists advocate a form of environmental feudalism called "bioregionalism." Bioregionalists would draw human community boundaries along habitat and climatic zones and require people to live only on the resources found within their bioregion.[37]

Ehrlich acknowledges the evolutionary breakthrough that humanity achieved through its ability to pass cultural information from generation to generation. However, he evidently thinks culture is a dangerous evolutionary mistake since it allows humanity to keep too many children alive. He really doesn't appreciate just how radical a break the cultural transmission of information is, and thus his simple-minded reductionism analogizing us to other species is wrong. Unlike most other species, we modify the world to suit our needs; we don't have to adapt to its given constraints. Human intelligence usually breaks the bonds that "carrying capacity" imposes on other species. This is why economics, the science of human interaction, is more relevant to the study of human beings than is ecology.

Ehrlich, however, dismisses economic information out of hand. Ecology is, in his view, the most encompassing of sciences. A hallmark of true science is that it can be used to make predictions. Given Ehrlich's and Brown's predictive failures, one would have to conclude that ecology as they practice it is far from achieving scientific status. Of course, like any millenarian scavenging for signs to bolster his case for the coming apocalypse, these doomsayers rely on economic statistics when they confirm what they wish to believe—when food prices temporarily increase, they rush into print more claims that the end is near. However, when food prices decline, that is simply reinterpreted as evidence that humanity is overstressing its resource base, pillaging its past and mortgaging its future.

One of Ehrlich's more disturbing personal characteristics is his relentless attempts to shut off all public and scientific debate on population issues. Generally, the search for scientific truth allows for the airing of all views, a process of which he is utterly contemptuous. Typically he dismisses contrary views with sharp *ad hominem* attacks, attempting to brand opponents as part of an uninformed fringe. Two particular targets of his venomous attacks are American Enterprise Institute Fellow Ben Wattenberg and University of Maryland economist Julian Simon.[38]

Ehrlich's attacks on Simon and Wattenberg are far from being isolated incidences. At the beginning of his crusade in the 1970s, he tried to silence fellow environmental activist Barry Commoner. Ehrlich wanted to cut a back-room deal to suppress Commoner's conclusion in his book *The Closing Circle* that pollution rather than population was relatively the greater cause of damage to the environment. A furious Commoner concluded, "Ehrlich is so intent upon population control as to be unwilling to tolerate open discussion of data that might weaken the argument for it."[39]

Ehrlich's failure as a prophet of environmental doom was publicly highlighted in 1990 by the embarrassing loss of his bet with cornucopian Julian Simon. In 1980, Simon challenged Ehrlich to put his money where his mouth is. Simon bet that the real price of any raw material would indefinitely decline. In October 1980, Ehrlich and Simon drew up a futures contract obligating Simon to sell Ehrlich the same quantities which could be purchased for $1,000 of five metals (copper, chrome, nickel, tin, and tungsten) ten years later at 1980 prices.[40] If the combined prices rose above $1,000, Simon would pay the difference. If they fell below $1,000, Ehrlich would pay Simon. Ehrlich mailed

Simon a check for $576.07 in October 1990.[41] Simply put, the combined real prices of the metals selected by Ehrlich fell by more than 50 percent during the 1980s, confirming cornucopian claims that the supply of resources is becoming more abundant, not more scarce.

As the global famines he predicted fail to materialize, Ehrlich becomes ever more frantic in trying to shut off discussion. He urges journalists not to report the findings of his opponents since these will, in his own narrow view, only serve to mislead the public. He dismisses the relatively optimistic conclusions of economists and demographers who, unlike Ehrlich, are trained in analyzing and predicting the development of human societies. The fact is that the despised "cornucopian" economists like Simon have been proven right while Ehrlich has been consistently wrong. Perhaps in time the media will finally realize that it is Paul Ehrlich who is the real fringe player.

To anyone who has not been mesmerized by the chorus of predictions of imminent famine, it is clear that humanity has made enormous strides in feeding the world's hungry since the Second World War. While the world's population doubled, food production tripled and the real price of wheat and corn fell steeply from $365 and $281 per ton to only $144 and $105 in 1989, a drop of more than 60 percent.[42] The real price of rice has been halved.[43]

University of Chicago agricultural expert D. Gale Johnson's work shows that the simpleminded biological model of "carrying capacity" which claims to demonstrate "the relationship between more people and per capita food supplies based upon the concept of diminishing returns and a fixed supply of land has little or no predictive value."[44] He adds, "Except where civil wars exist or despotic governments prevail, there has never been a time during the last two centuries when the people in the developing world were better fed or when their food supply was more secure." He concludes, "The scourge of famine due to natural causes has been almost conquered and could be entirely eliminated by the end of the century."[45]

Plummeting death rates in the developing world strongly contradict assertions that starvation is increasing. Worldwide life expectancy at birth rose from 47.5 years in 1950 to 63.9 years in 1990 while the world infant death rate dropped from 155 to 70 per 1,000 births.[46] Even in the poorest countries, those with per capita incomes under $400, average life expectancy rose spectacularly from 35 years in 1960 to 60 years in 1985.[47]

In fact the so-called "population explosion" is more a result of falling death rates, not burgeoning birth rates. "Artificially lowering the death rate" is the way Ehrlich describes this remarkable achievement! He cruelly implies that the industrialized nations should let hunger and disease *naturally* keep the developing world's population in check.

How were the world's farmers able to more than keep pace with population growth? And how could Ehrlich and Brown miss the truth in their predictions? Typically, the two avoided the good news because they were too busy fitting miscellaneous facts to their gloomy theories, focusing singlemindedly on information that supports their assertions that the end is nigh.

"I underestimated the speed with which the so-called Green Revolution's technologies would be deployed," admits a rueful Ehrlich.[48] Actually, Ehrlich did more than "underestimate" the Green Revolution. For years, he belittled and denounced it as "drivel" and an "illusion," even as it was massively increasing food production, especially in the developing world.

The Green Revolution was born in a network of agricultural research laboratories in the 1960s. After World War II, plant breeders, led by Nobelist Norman Borlaug, developed new high-yielding fertilizer-responsive dwarf varieties of cereal grains. Wheat yields in England that used to be 9 bushels per acre are now 100 bushels and rice yields of 2 tons per hectare are now up to 13 tons in Japan.[49] The Green Revolution enabled India to double its wheat yields within a few years, and China now supports 22 percent of the world's population on 7 percent of its arable land.[50] China's farmers also increased food production by more than 50 percent in only six years once the Communist government began allowing them to grow crops on private plots.[51]

In the past forty years, corn, wheat, soybean, and sorghum yields per acre in the United States have increased 220 percent, 107 percent, 60 percent, and 275 percent, respectively.[52] Since the 1970s, world wheat yields are up 36 percent, rice up 38 percent, and coarse grains, e.g., corn and sorghum, are up 30 percent.[53] Wheat and rice production in the developing world doubled, with rice production tripling in Indonesia.[54] And the Green Revolution rolls on—Third World grain and oilseed yields continue to grow at a remarkable 3 percent annual rate.[55]

The steady progress in plant breeding undercuts the doomsters' assumption that humanity has reached the end of its technological tether. Nevertheless, in 1991 Brown incredibly claimed "the backlog of technology available for farmers to raise food output is shrinking."[56] In 1971, Ehrlich made the absurd assertion, "Diminishing returns are . . . operative in increasing food production to meet the needs of growing populations."[57] Neither man provided any evidence to back up these ominous claims.

In fact, even more fruitful varieties of cereal grains are already on the way. For example, Veery wheats, which are particularly suitable for subtropical Africa, will increase yields up to 15 percent. New Chinese hybrid rice increases yields up to 30 percent. Gurdev Khush, chief plant breeder at the International Rice Research Institute, believes that rice production can be boosted an additional 25 to 30 percent in the 1990s. Khush is developing new rice varieties that will increase yields from 8 or 9 tons up to 15 tons per hectare.[58] Also, acid- and salt-tolerant plant varieties are being developed that will thrive in areas where crops cannot currently grow, such as Brazil's vast Cerrado Plateau.[59]

The Hudson Institute's Dennis Avery also applauds the development of bioengineered pork growth hormone. Hogs treated with growth hormone produce low-fat pork using one-fourth less feed grain. "In effect, the growth hormone will manufacture 30 million to 40 million tons of feed corn a year from laboratory bacteria," crows Avery.[60]

The leftish World Resources Institute notes that current levels of food production could feed more than an extra billion people. Robert Kates, director of the Alan Shawn Feinstein World Hunger Program at Brown University, believes that world hunger can be cut at least in half by the year 2000.[61] Avery points out that the world's massive increase in animal feed grain stocks can be easily converted to feed human beings in the event of an unprecedented crisis. The problem is not a lack of food, but inadequate distribution and poverty. Sadly, many of the world's poor simply lack the income necessary to buy the copious quantities of food available in world markets.

Perhaps as many as half a billion people are undernourished. But this is a far cry from global famines killing hundreds of millions, as predicted by Ehrlich and Brown. Only a tenth as many people died of starvation in the third quarter of the twentieth century as in the last quarter of the nineteenth, despite the fact that the world's population is vastly larger.[62]

Also, defining malnutrition is much more difficult than apocalyptics would have laymen believe. One World Bank economist applied the United Nations Food and Agriculture Organization's nutritional standards to the United States. According to the FAO standards, 67 percent of American males and 80 percent of females were malnourished in 1980.

Similarly, using the statistical techniques of the International Food Policy Research Institute, the World Bank once concluded that 40 to 50 percent of the people in Hong Kong and Taiwan lived on inadequate diets. However, citizens of Hong Kong and Taiwan have life expectancies matching U.S. standards and exceeding those of some European countries.[63] Perhaps the standards are skewed? Like all bureaucracies, the FAO was set up to solve a problem, so its bureaucrats will always hunt around for a problem in order to justify their jobs.

Once again, worldwide increases in life expectancies strongly indicate that global hunger is lessening. Even the best medical care and community sanitation cannot keep people alive unless they have food to eat. Declining global infant mortality rates are an especially good indicator of improving nutrition since children are more vulnerable to poor diets.[64]

Not only has nutrition for poor children in developing countries improved, but they are also benefiting from a simple and effective medical treatment for diarrheal diseases. Diseases like cholera strike poor people in the developing world because they lack potable water or proper sanitation. Oral rehydration therapy, an easy-to-prepare solution of salts and sugar, now saves millions of lives annually. Curing a case of diarrhea can save a child as much as five hundred calories worth of food per day.[65]

Actual starvation has been relegated to a few isolated corners of the globe usually beset with civil strife. Deliberately created famines have been used several times as a weapon in this century; for example, Stalin starved the Ukraine in the 1930s, Ethiopia's General Mengistu halted food aid to rebel regions of his country in the 1980s, and war lords in Somalia created famine throughout that country in the 1990s. But these tragedies must not be confused with apocalyptic claims that humanity is about to overrun its carrying capacity.

However, the ability of despotic governments, such as those in Sudan and Ethiopia, to use food and medicine as a weapon against their own peoples may be coming to an end. In 1991, the United Nations adopted, at the insistence of the United States and other Western nations, a policy calling for food relief to be provided to people without requiring their government's approval. Relief agencies one day may be able to intervene on behalf of afflicted people wherever they are.[66]

Africa is most often cited by population alarmists as a continent that has reached its carrying capacity. But the Hudson Institute's Avery replies, "Africa is a vestige of the hunger problem which once faced all of the Third World—it is not the forerunner of impending famine for the Earth."[67] D. Gale Johnson writes, "It is generally conceded that Africa is much better endowed with natural resources per capita than Asia and is as well endowed as Latin America."[68] Africa has up to 760 million hectares (1 hectare = 2.47 acres) of cultivable land, more than three and a half times the amount currently cultivated in the United States. Only 160 million hectares are presently being farmed.[69] Africa could easily produce more than enough food to feed its people, so why don't Africans have enough to eat? Often, because Africa's governments swindle their farmers. Deliberate government policies impoverish the rural sectors at the expense of the urban centers.

When an African farmer realizes that he will receive only a fraction of the real value of his crops, he has little incentive to grow more than his family needs. This leaves African farmers in the precarious position that subsistence farmers have endured since time immemorial. With no surplus to fall back on and no money earned from the sale of earlier crops, if something goes wrong, then the farmer's family will go hungry.

Full participation in the world food market is the best guarantee of food security for the poor in the developing world, yet government policies often discourage this trend. Recently, several African governments achieved astonishing results by liberalizing their agricultural policies. In Ghana, corn production has tripled, while in Togo cotton production doubled and Zambia saw a 20 percent increase in agricultural output. "If all black African leaders were to . . . lift price controls to permit their peasants to sell their produce in open, free markets, there would be no food crisis in the continent," concludes Ghanaian economist George Ayittey.[70]

Had African farmers been paid world prices for their produce while paying world prices for inputs like fertilizer and improved seeds, they would have dramatically raised crop yields during the last two decades. For example, Ghanaian farm output would be 87 percent higher than it is now. Owing to bad government policies, African farmers are, on average, producing 30 percent less food than they otherwise would have.[71] Thus, proper policies would have turned Africa's current 15 percent deficit in food production into a 15 percent surplus. Eliminating these injurious policies would allow African farmers to adopt the more efficient agricultural methods which have been sweeping the globe in the last two decades.

Ironically, just as Ehrlich was setting the fuse to his population bomb, "a contraceptive revolution" was beginning. The fall in Third World fertility is "as impressive as agriculture's Green Revolution," according to population experts Steven Sinding of the Rockefeller Foundation and Sheldon Segal of the Population Council. They note that the "global population's growth rate has declined faster than many experts thought possible."[72]

World population growth peaked at a 2 percent growth rate in the 1960s. Global population growth stands now at 1.7 percent annually and is steadily declining. The United Nations expects the world's population to peak sometime late in the next century at between ten and twelve billion.

Instead of Brown's spurious "S-shaped curve," for agricultural production, there is a real S-shaped curve for the populations of the industrialized countries. This curve clearly shows that the United States, Japan, and many European countries have already undergone the "demographic transition" to relatively stable populations. This situation contradicts biologist Garrett Hardin's assertion in his famous "The Tragedy of the Commons" article that "there is no prosperous population in the world today that has, and has had for some time, a growth rate of zero."[73] Perhaps the most spectacular decline in fertility occurred in Japan, which dropped to replacement level in only ten years during the 1950s.

Recent years have seen more and more couples eager to use contraception in Thailand, Indonesia, Mexico, Colombia, Brazil, and Bangladesh. Increased contraceptive use in these developing countries was achieved voluntarily without resorting to forced sterilizations or spiking food aid with sterilants as once suggested by Ehrlich.

Demographic and health surveys conducted by the Institute for Resource Development (IRD) for the U.S. Agency for International Development in twenty-five developing countries in Africa, Asia, and Latin America show that fertility rates are dropping rapidly in nearly all of them. The steepest declines have occurred in Thailand, Sri Lanka, and Indonesia, where fertility rates declined by 46 percent, 28 percent, and 39 percent respectively over the past fifteen years.[74] Thailand's birth rate has fallen to just above replacement level.[75]

Fertility rates have also declined by 24 to 34 percent in Colombia, Brazil, Peru, and Mexico over the past fifteen years. Fertility rates fell at lesser rates for all other Latin American and Caribbean countries.[76] Africa, too, is experiencing fertility declines. Rates in Kenya, Botswana, and Zimbabwe dropped 18 percent, 25 percent, and 23 percent respectively. Of the African countries IRD surveyed, only Mali and Liberia show increases in fertility.[77] India's fertility rate fell by more than 25 percent during the 1980s,[78] and between 1970 and 1990, China's fertility rate plunged by 60 percent.[79]

The remedy for population growth is more economic growth, not less as recommended by Ehrlich, Brown, and their sustainable-development disciples. From the foregoing data it is clear that many developing nations are now in the beginning stages of their "demographic transition." As people become wealthier, and medical care improves, they choose to have fewer children. For instance, in India, farmers who have adopted Green Revolution technologies have fewer children and give those they have more schooling.[80]

A truism fiercely peddled by the apocalyptics is that economic development and rapid population growth are incompatible. Apocalypse abusers implicitly assume there are ever more people exploiting a fixed supply of land while using unchanged technology, yielding diminishing returns for their efforts. But this elegant and simple formulation is wrong.

"The rate of population growth has little or no observable effect upon the rate of growth of real per capita incomes in the developing countries," concludes D. Gale Johnson of the University of Chicago.[81] Since 1965, economic growth consistently outpaced population growth in the developing world, raising per capita incomes at an annual rate of 2.5 percent.[82]

The industrialized nations' own histories contradict the facile population/income ratio posited by apocalyptics. While they were industrializing and vastly increasing per capita incomes their populations were growing at unprecedented rates. On average this has also been true of today's developing nations (see Chapter Four).

Once again, Ehrlich typically ignores the lessons of history: *"Most people do not recognize that, at least in rich nations, economic growth is the disease, not the cure"* (emphasis his).[83]

Paul Ehrlich is by no means alone in his opposition to economic growth. In 1972, another group of particularly influential apocalypse abusers came forcefully to public attention when they published the notorious tract *The Limits to Growth*. We turn in the next chapter to this extraordinary document and the notion of the imminent depletion of "nonrenewable resources" which it popularized.

FOUR
THE DEPLETION MYTH

"A world where industrial production has sunk to zero. Where population has suffered a catastrophic decline. Where the air, sea, and land are polluted beyond redemption. Where civilization is a distant memory" read the ominous introductory blurbs in the best-selling *The Limits to Growth*. The apocalyptic motifs drummed on: "This is the world that the computer forecasts. What is even more alarming, the collapse will not come gradually, but with awesome suddenness, with no way of stopping it."[1] *Limits* project leader, MIT professor Dennis Meadows, simply told *Time*, "All growth projections end in collapse."[2]

At about the time that Ehrlich began preaching population doom, a group of international businessmen and academics styling themselves the Club of Rome set themselves the task of pondering the "predicament of mankind." The group turned for help to MIT management professor and computer genius Jay Forrester. In 1970, using his "systems dynamics" approach, Forrester whipped up a quick computer model for the Club which purportedly proved that the "predicament of mankind" was just terrible and the end nigh.

Forrester left the popularization of his ideas to two acolytes, Dennis and Donella Meadows, whose gloss on Forrester's own *World Dynamics* became the bestseller *The Limits to Growth*. This spectacularly wrongheaded book popularized the notion of nonrenewable resources. With a boost from the temporary success of the Arab oil embargo, *The Limits to Growth* sold more than ten million copies in thirty languages. The antigrowth ideology which infects modern environmentalism is amply reflected in this book. Its dire forecasts were the precursors of further gloomy studies, such as President Carter's Global 2000 report and more recent efforts by champions of "sustainable development."

Later environmental radicals, like Lester Brown and his Worldwatch Institute, and the prime minister of Norway, Gro Brundtland, are the direct intellectual heirs of *The Limits to Growth*. Brown and Brundtland, now advocates of so-called sustainable development, have simply repackaged the old depletionist myths for the 1990s.[3]

"Much of the moral idealism which in earlier times found expression in various movements of social reform appears now, particularly in the USA, to seek an outlet in the environmentalist movement. It is this environmentalist critique of industrialism, rather than the socialist critique of cupidity, which finds explicit representation in the MIT model," concluded economist T. C. Sinclair shortly after *Limits* was published.[4]

The Limits to Growth was launched amid enormous ballyhoo at a widely reported conference held at the Smithsonian Institution in February 1972. Eduard Pestel, a leading figure in the Club of Rome, averred that "policy decisions can now be derived from what has been worked out. There is no need to wait to start action." Lester Brown hailed the model as a "remarkable achievement."[5]

Holding an urgent press conference to announce grim "scientific" findings before other scientists can review the work on which the claims are made would later become standard operating procedure for environmental apocalyptics, especially for proponents of climate catastrophes. This public relations ploy achieves maximum public impact while doing an end run around potential critics.

And it worked. *The New York Times* heralded *The Limits to Growth*'s publication with a front-page article entitled "Mankind Warned of Perils in Growth." It reported, "A major computer study of world trends has concluded, as many have feared, that mankind probably faces an uncontrollable and disastrous collapse of its society within 100 years unless it moves to establish a 'global equilibrium' in which growth of population and industrial output are halted."[6] *Time*, citing *The Limits to Growth*, described the collapse of civilization as "a grim inevitability if society continues its present dedication to growth and 'progress.' "[7]

The publication of *The Limits to Growth* was not, however, greeted by universal acclaim. One anonymous MIT professor told *Science*: "What they're doing is providing simple-minded answers for simple-minded people who are scared to death. And that's a dangerous thing . . . it's not that *they* want publicity, or a grant, but they want to save the world. This messianic impulse is what disturbs me." *Science* went on to make a prediction that has turned out to be a vast understatement: "Thus ends the first but probably not the last act of a remarkably successful venture in the mass marketing of neo-Malthusian economics."[8]

The Limits to Growth specifically concluded, "If the present growth trends in world population, industrialization, pollution, food production, and resource depletion continue unchanged, the limits to growth on this planet will be reached sometime within the next hundred years. The most probable result will be a rather sudden and uncontrollable decline in both population and industrial capacity."[9] Translation: Billions of people will die horribly in a massive famine and/or epidemic bringing about the collapse of civilization sometime during the next century.

The book's predictions, although tarted up in the latest

computer jargon, really boil down to plain old-fashioned Malthusianism. In fact, Forrester explicitly acknowledges his debt to Malthus in his earlier book *World Dynamics*: "The Malthusian thesis has been true and at work at all times. Population is regulated to food supply."[10]

Forrester saw the study as a call to begin the slowdown of economic growth to global economic equilibrium. The idea of equilibrium, of balance, harks back to romantic characterizations of feudal society. Progress is seen as causing all kinds of stresses which will lead humanity to an apocalyptic end unless stopped. Nothing less than "a Copernican revolution of the mind" involving "fundamental changes in laws, values, religious attitudes, and expectations" is required to save humanity from catastrophe. *The Limits to Growth*, like earlier millenarian tracts, foresaw that "a society based on equality and justice, is far more likely to evolve in a state of global equilibrium than it is in the state of growth we are experiencing today."[11] Sounding familiar millennialist egalitarian motifs, this theory posits that a utopian postgrowth society will distribute wealth equally to all citizens, who will devote themselves to such gentle "sustainable" pursuits as art, music, religion, basic scientific research, athletics, and socializing.[12]

According to Forrester and his two disciples, Dennis and Donella Meadows, economic growth is forever circumscribed by the Four Horsemen of the New Age apocalypse: depletion of nonrenewable resources, decline of food supplies, pollution, and overcrowding. If one limit doesn't stop growth, then surely another will.

Forrester's computer model looks at how feedback loops affect several interlocking, highly aggregated variables. Feedback loops are circular flows in which changes in one variable provoke changes in a second which in turn alters the first one. For example, the feedback loop of perennial concern to environmental millenarians supposes that the production of more food induces an increase in population which provokes greater food production which supports a greater population, ad infinitum. Forrester claimed his computer model is superior to the mental models most of us use because it supposedly clarifies how major components of the "world system" interact to impose limits on growth.

Twenty years later, how are the predictions of Forrester's model standing the test of time?

"I think *The Limits to Growth* was an excellent piece of work that is becoming more true every day," he unblushingly declares. He adds, "It really casts doubt on the underlying theology of growth."[13] But is it true? Let's look at each of the "limits" posited by Forrester and associates.

On nonrenewable resources, they have been proven to be spectacularly wrong. In 1972, *The Limits to Growth* predicted that at exponential growth rates, the world would run out of gold by 1981, mercury by 1985, tin by 1987, zinc by 1990, petroleum by 1992, and copper, lead, and natural gas by 1993.[14]

Not quite. The U.S. Bureau of Mines estimates that at 1990 rates of production, world reserves of gold will last 24 years, mercury 40 years, tin 28 years, zinc 40 years, copper 65 years, and lead 35 years.[15] And these estimates do not take into account that modern manufacturing techniques are coming to rely less and less on such minerals. After all, tiny optical fibers and telecommunications satellites transmitting thousands of telephone calls have now largely replaced huge copper cables which transmit only scores of calls. Also, telecommuting saves millions of barrels of oil.

The World Resources Institute estimates that between 1970 and 1988 the average price of all metals and minerals fell by more than 40 percent.[16] This means that world supplies of minerals and metals are more abundant than ever. Proven reserves of petroleum are now expected to last 46 years,[17] and natural gas will last 58 years at 1988 production rates.[18] For all these minerals, new reserves are being added each year. Even the alarmist Worldwatch Institute admitted in 1992 that "recent trends in price and availability suggest that for most minerals we are a long way from running out. Regular improvements in exploitative technology have allowed the production of growing amounts at declining prices."[19] Asked about these figures, Forrester dryly noted, "I think in retrospect that *The Limits to Growth* overemphasized the material resources side."[20] Indeed.

Yet most of the public still believes that the world is rapidly running out of resources. Most people hold to a buried-treasure theory of resources in which minerals are thought of as a sort of pirate's hoard of doubloons. The obvious notion that there is a finite quantity of anything is intuitively attractive. It seems clear that there can only be so much of something in the world.

Like all depletionists, Forrester assumed that natural resources are a fixed quantity. Imagine for a moment an ancient Egyptian bronze manufacturer worrying about the exhaustion of Nubian tin mines leading to an impending bronze crisis. Then along comes iron ore. University of Georgia economist Dwight Lee estimates that before 1000 B.C. iron cost eight thousand times more than bronze to produce. As tin became scarce, ancient metalsmiths developed new techniques which resulted in a ten thousand–fold collapse in the cost of iron, making it ten times cheaper than bronze by 700 B.C.[21] Perhaps in the near future the transition will be from steel to organic composites?

The nineteenth century saw a number of serious resource crises which led many to predict that economic progress would soon grind to a halt. For example, the extensive harvesting of whales created a shortage of whale oil, which was widely used for artificial lighting and lubrication. The price of whale oil more than doubled in less than ten years.[22] In 1865, the eminent economist Stanley Jevons predicted that Great Britain would soon run out of coal, bringing its factories to a standstill.[23] In 1877, U.S. Secretary of the Interior Carl Schurz warned of an imminent "timber famine," predicting shortages within twenty years.[24] Forecasts of looming petroleum shortages have been an apocalyptic staple for more than a century. Between 1866 and 1975, no fewer than ten U.S. government studies predicted impending oil shortages.[25] For example, in 1926, the

Federal Oil Conservation Board predicted that the supply of oil would last only seven more years.[26]

Nineteenth-century depletionists made the same mistake that their intellectual descendants like Forrester continue to make—they extrapolated trends of resource use without making due allowance for technological progress. Absolutely all of the shortages predicted above would indeed have caused disastrous problems, if people had simply continued doing what they had been doing. Machinery lubricated by whale oil would have been paralyzed; coal-powered steam engines would have clanked to a halt; wood cooking fires would have grown cold; and modern automobiles stalled.

Most people are beguiled by the "resource illusion," the notion that physical substances are the chief source of wealth in the world. History clearly confirms that "no exhaustible resource is essential or irreplaceable,"[27] according to economist Gale Johnson. Dwight Lee points out that "The relevant resource base is defined by knowledge, rather than by physical deposits of existing resources."[28] A deposit of copper is just a bunch of rocks without the know-how to mine, mill, refine, shape, ship, and market it.

Impending scarcity provokes people to search for substitutes and to improve technologies used to exploit natural resources. For example, copper reserves are not only expanded through new ore discoveries, but also through technology. Improvements in refining allow humanity to exploit copper ores now that are eight times less rich than those mined in 1900. Meanwhile the real price of copper has fallen steeply.[29] Spurred on by higher oil prices, industrial countries now use 23 percent less oil to produce a dollar of output than they did in 1970.[30]

The whale oil crisis caused people to look to petroleum as a substitute. Higher coal prices provoked the development of more efficient mining methods. Higher lumber prices led to new techniques to preserve wood and to a switch to other construction materials. And new drilling and exploration technologies vastly expanded the recoverable reserves of crude oil. Apocalypse abusers like Ehrlich and Forrester drastically discount human ingenuity and technological prowess. The fact is that technological innovation is on a much faster exponential growth curve than either population or resource use.

While the notion of "nonrenewable resources" remains an orthodox doctrine of millenarian environmentalism, Forrester, the father of the concept, has repudiated it: "There is a structure in *World Dynamics* and I believe also in *The Limits to Growth*, that one would not do again, and that is the assumption of an absolute fixed stock of resources that you're drawing from, which when it's depleted, is gone."[31] In fact, if the rates of technological improvement grow at a modest 2 percent per year, the collapses projected by the Club of Rome are postponed indefinitely.[32]

The next of Forrester's limits to growth is the familiar Malthusian one—famine. His computer model was constructed with built-in Malthusianism: "If all other influences on growth are removed, the population will rise by as much as necessary to generate the degree of food shortage that is needed to suppress growth."[33] If somehow humanity succeeded in surmounting the other supposed limits to growth, famine would finally get us.

In 1971, Forrester believed that the world was already near the limits of our ability to grow food. He wrote, "For the first time demand [for food] is rising into a condition where supply will begin to fall while need increases."[34] He was no better at forecasting food supplies than his fellow apocalypse abusers, Ehrlich and Brown. As was shown in the preceding chapter, food production has been expanding much faster than population, and world food prices have fallen drastically in the last twenty years.

Curiously, in Forrester's *World Dynamics* computer model, "an abundance of food is assumed to raise the birth rate by a factor of 2."[35] Why? The countries with the best-fed citizenries and plentiful food supplies—the United States, France, Germany, Canada, the Netherlands, Japan, etc.—are the ones with the lowest birth rates. Forrester must have known this assumption was nonsense when he made it. If the abundance of food were positively correlated with birth rates, the United States' birth rate would be the highest in the world, instead of one of the lowest. In fact, the knowledge that your children will grow up instead of starving to death allows you to have fewer children.

Forrester's third limit to growth was "overcrowding." In 1970, he estimated the world's population density at 69 people per square mile. By 1989, world population density grew to 97 people per square mile. Let's get some perspective on these figures.

U.S. population density is a spacious 69 people per square mile. Note, however, that the Garden State of New Jersey has a population density of 1,033 people per square mile. India's density is 658 per square mile, while China has less than half that—288 persons per square mile.

The tidy little country of the Netherlands' population density is 931 people per square mile. Japan tallies at 844; Great Britain has 601 people per square mile; Germany, 520; Italy, 493; and France, 252. Clearly these countries are not poor due to overpopulation. Brazil, much poorer, has a population density only two-thirds that of the United States and only 6 percent of Japan's—a mere 47 people per square mile. The average world population density is about one-tenth that of New Jersey or Japan. At a peak world population figure of 10 billion, the average density would be 192 per square mile, far less than the current densities of Japan, France, Great Britain, Italy, Germany, and the Netherlands.

As Harvard Population Center demographer Nick Eberstadt noted: "People are always looking for the Iron Laws of Population. Well, because population means creative active human beings, there's no more of an Iron Law of Population than there is an Iron Law of History. You can't come up with a uniform, univariate theory of population, any more than you can come up with a uniform univariate theory of history." He added, "There is absolutely no content to the notion of overpopulation."[36] If population density had any predictive power, then "underpopulated" Brazil would be a much richer country than "overcrowded" France and Germany.

Forrester's model assumes that "as crowding rises toward five times the present population, the death rate is taken to rise ever more steeply and to reach three times the present rate, for a crowding ratio of 5."[37] Crowding is supposed to increase social violence, enhance disease transmission, and lead to more wars. However, countries whose population densities are already well beyond Forrester's crowding ratio of 5 show no increase in their death rates. Quite the contrary—life expectancies of "overcrowded" countries like the Netherlands, Japan, France, Germany, and Great Britain continue to increase. Also crime rates in those countries are considerably lower than in the much less crowded United States.

Forrester's fourth limit to growth is pollution. If none of the other limits halts a profligate humanity, then we will surely choke on our own wastes. This notion is a perennial favorite of doomsters even though the quality of the air and water in the United States has improved markedly over the last twenty years—while the population and economy have grown, the emissions of the most dangerous air pollutants have declined significantly since 1970.[38] For example, sulfur dioxide emissions are down 25 percent, carbon monoxide down 41 percent, volatile organic compounds—chief contributors to smog formation—have been reduced by 31 percent, and total particulates like smoke, smoot, and dust have fallen by 59 percent. And nitrogen dioxide emissions have dropped 6 percent since 1980.[39]

U.S. surface water quality deteriorated until the 1960s, when pollution control measures began to improve the situation. Today, according to some estimates up to 95 percent of America's rivers, 92 percent of its lakes, and 86 percent of its estuaries are fishable and swimmable, and further progress is being made.[40] Many conventional pollutants such as bacteria and oxygen-depleting materials are diminishing.[41] Higher oxygen levels mean an improved environment for fish and other aquatic life. Also, nutrient phosphorus levels in the Great Lakes have been reduced and are now near or below the targets set by international treaty.[42] As a result, Lake Erie, which both Forrester and Ehrlich pronounced dead, is once again being fished commercially. On a global scale, the World Resources Institute notes that in the industrialized countries "domestic and industrial effluents are now generally controlled."[43]

Strangely, Forrester assumes that as capital investment increases, pollution must also increase. In fact, capital investment can reduce pollution, for example, scrubbers on electricity generation plants to remove sulfur, waste water treatment, recycling programs, improvements in mining and drilling for minerals, etc.

A recent study by two Princeton University economists, Gene Grossman and Alan Krueger, demonstrated that levels of two important air contaminants, sulfur dioxide and smoke, are strongly related to per capita income. Surveying World Health Organization data, the two concluded that as a rule air pollution increases in a city until the average income reaches $4,000–5,000, at which point pollution levels begin to fall.[44] In other words, economic growth leads to less pollution, not more as asserted by the environmental doomsters. This is obvious since the countries with the least pollution today are the wealthy industrialized countries and the very poorest countries whose citizens live on the thin edge of subsistence. Of course, poor countries must still deal with such natural "pollutants" as contaminated foods, raw sewage, and disease-ridden water supplies.

The initial stages of the Industrial Revolution did impose some costs on the natural environment—Britain's "dark satanic mills"—but modern technologies are much less polluting. Since pollution is the loss of expensive materials, entrepreneurs are constantly trying to conserve them through improved technologies. The good news is that developing countries will be able to adopt cleaner manufacturing processes and more efficient pollution control techniques as their economies grow, thus avoiding some of the damage caused by earlier primitive technologies.

73

Forrester believed in 1970 that humanity was at the point where increases in pollution would raise the death rate.[45] Recall that fellow doomster Ehrlich had earlier suggested that hundreds of thousands of Americans would die in massive air pollution crises in the 1970s. Despite the fact that a few premature deaths can be traced to specific acute pollution incidents, there is no evidence that pollution has reduced overall life expectancy worldwide. Life expectancy has been falling in the Soviet Union and some countries in Eastern Europe and pollution cannot be ruled out as a cause, but poor quality food, water, and medical care combined with high rates of alcoholism are more likely contributors.[46]

How could Forrester, the Meadowses, and the Club of Rome be so far off? One answer is that the computer model was designed to confirm what its designers already believed. After demonstrating that "the results of the models can be changed radically by altering a few principal assumptions," one group of analysts concluded that "Forrester's and the Meadows' assumptions are very much a reflection of their generally pessimistic view of the world."[47] Call it "PIPO"— "Pessimism In, Pessimism Out."

In the 1980s, the themes and ideas developed in *The Limits to Growth* were taken up by the proponents of "sustainable development." The notion of "sustainable development" received its most influential endorsement in *Our Common Future*, a report issued in 1987 by the U.N.'s World Commission on Environment and Development, which was chaired by Norway's Gro Brundtland. The report calls on affluent countries to "adopt life-styles within the planet's ecological means."[48] While acknowledging that technological progress and accumulating human knowledge will significantly extend resources, *Our Common Future* adheres to the notion that humanity will run up against some "ultimate limits,"[49] and it continues to peddle the vacuous concept of "environmentally appropriate technologies."[50] Also, while backing some limited economic growth, the report's preoccupation with egalitarian schemes for wealth redistribution establishes it firmly in the tradition of millenarian environmentalism.[51]

Sustainable developers also call for "intergenerational equity." As a way of ensuring that the interests of future generations will be taken into account, some have suggested that we should follow the Iroquois Indian rule that all decisions be taken in light of how they will affect the next seven generations. This rule might be fine for a traditional society which—no matter how admirable or noble—was still using chipped rocks and animal skins as the basis of their material culture. Seven generations is more than 240 years. There is no way that even the most thoughtful and insightful among us can foresee what the state of human knowledge and technology will be at the end of such a time span. Only the deeply ignorant or intellectually conceited think that they can see that far ahead.

Just compare what technology and learning were like 240 years ago—no steamships, no trains, no germ theory of disease, no automobiles, no comprehensive theory of chemistry. Slavery still flourished, women couldn't vote, illiteracy was the rule. No highways, no electricity, and no telephones. The list is endless. The wisest person in 1750 could not have foreseen our modern world of computers, satellites, vaccinations, organ transplants, and universal suffrage.

The plain fact is that true "intergenerational equity" requires us to pass along and add as much as possible to the ever growing store of human knowledge, technology, and material wealth that we have inherited to future generations. We are vastly richer due to the efforts of our ancestors and we owe them a great debt of gratitude. If we wish to pursue *real* intergenerational equity, we have a duty to expand the world's knowledge base and the economy for our descendants instead of ossifying into some form of feudal stasis as advised by radical environmentalists. Although some primitivist deep ecologists may quibble, that we are better off than our great grandparents seven times removed cannot be doubted—just look at our lower infant mortality rates, longer life spans, greater leisure time, and growing abundance of food and resources.

One might have thought, given how far off the mark its predictions were, that the Club of Rome would have disbanded out of embarrassment by now. Instead the Club cheerfully takes credit for the atmosphere of doom that has pervaded policy debates in the last couple of decades in its latest report, *The First Global Revolution*.[52] Undeterred by the massive failure of its first effort to define the "predicament of mankind," the Club has essentially written a job application for the position of planetary savior.

The twenty years since *Limits* have not, however, been completely lost on the Club—its members have learned a bit from mainstream economics. In 1978, the Club repudiated Forrester's notion of resource depletion, admitting that "it is highly improbable that the physical limits to man's existence will ever be reached."[53] Nowadays the Club cautiously favors nuclear power,[54] recognizes that economic "improvement" (let's avoid using the demonized word "growth" by all means) lowers fertility rates,[55] and notes that some Third World governments have starved their people by swindling their farmers.[56]

Nevertheless, like other millenarians, Club members believe that the spiritual transformation of humanity is necessary to save the planet. The Club asserts that society is mired in a "human malaise" which can only be dissipated by "an ethical mobilization worldwide" demanding "sacrifices of all people." To save the earth there must be "a true transformation of mind-sets and behaviour"[57]—a worldwide religious conversion to the gospel of environmentalism.

The Club makes no bones about the fact that it is ready to take up the burden of power. In its lofty opinion, politicians, driven by election-cycle pressures, and businessmen, prodded by the need to keep quarterly earnings high, concentrate too much on the short term. According to the Club the world needs "men and women of the right quality and capacity," evidently an environmental aristocracy or priesthood, to save the planet from shortsighted voters and consumers.[58] Of course, the Club's members have just the "right qualities and capacities," and would offer their expertise to the United Nations, the World Bank, the European Economic Community, and the Japanese government, among others.[59] Like other millenarians, the Club wants to eliminate social and economic inequality and nurture communitarian values. They would enhance the power of the United Nations, and especially recommend the creation of a U.N. *Environmental* Security Council.[60] Essentially, the Club wants to create an international command-and-control bureaucracy to manage the world's environment. The spectacular collapse in Eastern Europe and the Soviet Union of this type of top-down governance does not deter the Club from recommending it as a way to regulate our global environment.

Let's take a brief look now at what happened while the world was supposedly approaching the limits to growth.

The world's total output of goods and services increased 500 percent since 1950.[61] Not everybody got richer, but the vast majority of people did. Those countries that experienced disappointing economic growth did not do so because they ran up against any environmental limits, but because of wars or devastatingly bad economic policies.

Since 1965, in the developing world real gross domestic product grew 4.7 percent annually, while the industrial world's economies grew at an average rate of 3.1 percent.[62] Since 1950, per capita annual income has increased in Asia from $487 to $2,812, in Latin America from $1,729 to $3,164, and in the Middle East and North Africa from $940 to $2,576. Tragically, sub-Saharan African incomes rose from $348 to $558 in 1973, but under the impact of monumental government mismanagement, have fallen back to $513 now. Overall, however, per capita real incomes in the developing world more than tripled from $839 in 1950 to $2,796 in 1989. Meanwhile, per capita real incomes in the industrialized countries also tripled from $3,298 to $10,104.[63]

The rate of economic progress is picking up, too. In the

nineteenth century, it took Great Britain 58 years to double its output per person. The United States took 47 years, and Japan 34 years. After World War II, Brazil doubled its output per person in 18 years, Indonesia in 17 years, South Korea in 11 years, and China did it in a breathtaking 10 years.[64] While China's per capita income is officially just $350 a year, many experts believe that it is vastly understated and is actually above $1,000 per year.[65]

And the future? The World Bank believes, "the opportunity for rapid development is greater today than at any time in history."[66] One of the chief reasons is that policymakers are coming to understand the importance of drastically reducing government interference in the economy and of establishing stable property rights and free markets as the way to create wealth. In addition, new technologies are vastly improving both industrial and agricultural productivity around the world.

The World Bank expects developing countries' economies to expand at an average rate of 4.9 percent per year in the 1990s, while industrial countries will grow at a 3 percent annual rate.[67]

There are no permanent resource shortages—future food supplies are ample, world population will level off before overcrowding becomes a problem, and pollution can be controlled at modest cost. So it appears that the only limit to growth is the human imagination—if we sink back and accept the antigrowth eco-theology we may well condemn our posterity to desperate poverty in a resource-depleted world. Yet this is precisely the world that some radical environmentalists would like us to accept.

FIVE

THE REFRIGERATOR EFFECT

Climatic changes cause massive crop failures in the American Midwest and the grain-growing regions of the Ukraine, millions die of famine, populations migrate from their formerly bountiful countries, sea levels alter, and whole eco-systems begin a forced march to more equable regions. The harbinger of this impending climate disaster was a global trend toward decreasing temperatures that began in the 1940s.

Most of the public has forgotten that just fifteen years ago the eco-doomsayers were frantically predicting the advent of a New Ice Age. In the 1970s, worried scientists pointed to a relentless thirty-year trend toward ever-lower temperatures. Many were sure that they had detected the cooling "signal" which portended the return of the mile-thick glaciers that had covered North America and Europe only eighteen thousand years earlier.

Climatologists theorized that mankind was responsible for this refrigerator effect. Industrial pollution and slash-

and-burn agriculture were the main culprits, injecting dust particles (aerosols) into the air which cooled the earth by reflecting sunlight back into space. In 1971, an atmospheric scientist at the National Center for Atmospheric Research, Stephen Schneider, warned that quadrupling aerosols "could *decrease* the mean surface temperature by as much as 3.5K degrees. If sustained over a period of several years, such a temperature decrease could be sufficient to trigger an ice age!"[1]

Five years later, the scientific consensus held that the earth's climate would certainly change soon, and "a majority believe that the longer trend will be downward," according to University of Wisconsin climatologist Reid Bryson.[2] Bryson made this assertion in his preface to Lowell Ponte's *The Cooling*, one of what has turned out to be a long series of popular doomsday books predicting global climatological disaster. *The Cooling* also garnered the endorsement of U.S. Senator Claiborne Pell (D-R.I.), who called it "as disquieting as *Silent Spring*" and declared that it "could prove to be the most important and prophetic popular science book of the 1970s."[3]

But the 1970s global cooling scare was merely a dress rehearsal for the current apocalyptic hysteria being whipped up over global warming (see Chapter Nine). Some prominent global coolers have adroitly converted themselves fifteen years later into ardent global warmers. No matter, while their opinions on which direction the temperature is going have changed, their solutions remain the same. Freeze or fry, the problem is always industrial capitalism, and the solution is always international socialism.

What is an ice age? The last couple of million years have seen several ice ages come and go. During the last one, the earth's average temperature was 10F degrees cooler, the climate much drier, and some 30 percent of the land area was covered by sheets of ice. Since so much water was locked in ice on continental landmasses, the sea level was hundreds of feet lower than now. Eighteen thousand years ago, glaciers a mile high covered Canada and reached as far south as New York City and Chicago. Herds of woolly mammoths ranged freely from Siberia to Alaska, crossing the land bridge where now the Bering Strait connects the Arctic and Pacific oceans. In Europe the ice spread from Scandinavia to cover most of Britain and Northern Europe. Sea ice reached as far south as Britain. There were mountain glaciers in New Guinea, Hawaii, and Central America.

Paleoclimatologists, scientists who study past climates, are still uncertain why the earth periodically suffers ice ages, though they have identified an apparent 100,000-year cycle of cooling and warming. The last ice age reached its peak 18,000 years ago, and ended 10,000 years ago. Glaciated eras are interrupted by relatively short warm periods, called interglacials, lasting about 10,000 years. Only 5 to 10 percent of the last two million years have been relatively ice-free; thus during this time period the earth's "normal" climate has been an ice age.

In the 1970s, scientists were worried about an impending new ice age because our warm era had already lasted 10,000 years, the average duration of an interglacial period. During the last ice age, winter temperatures in South Carolina and Tennessee were bitterly cold, perhaps 15–20C (27–36F) degrees cooler than now.[4] Because of the arid climate and cooler temperatures, the earth's tropical rain forests, surrounded by dry grasslands, were confined to a few scattered refuges along the equator.[5]

As the last ice age ended, humanity began its ascent toward civilization, shifting from hunting and gathering to farming. In the brief period since the glaciers melted, we have advanced from stone axes to space stations, from cuneiform to computers.

Why do ice ages end? Scientists still argue this question, pointing to variations in earth's orbital relation to the sun, changes in carbon dioxide levels, reversals in deep ocean currents, and fluctuations in the sun's radiance.

As the glaciers retreated toward the poles, the midlatitudes gradually grew warmer until eight thousand years ago, and the earth's average temperature was 2C degrees warmer than now. Climatologists straightforwardly refer to this period of milder weather as the earth's "Climatic Optimum." And with good reason, because rainfall was more abundant and the world's deserts shrank. The Sahara was well watered, supporting large herds of grazing animals and human hunters. Summer temperatures in Canada were 4C (7.2F) degrees warmer six thousand years ago, and the spruce forest boundary pushed much farther north. Then the temperature dropped from this "optimum" by 2C degrees, ushering in a drier climate worldwide.

A period of balmier weather called the "Medieval Optimum" returned between A.D. 900 and 1200. England then supported many vineyards, oats and barley grew in Iceland, wheat in Norway, and hay in Greenland. Eric the Red's Viking colony at Brattalid in Greenland grew to three thousand settlers. Greenland's climate was then mild enough to support farming and livestock such as horses, goats, cows, and sheep.[6]

After 1200, the climate degenerated. Havoc ensued—the inhospitable weather brought on famines and social unrest throughout Europe. Mountain glaciers expanded worldwide, sea ice around Iceland increased, England's vineyards died, the Greenland Viking colony perished, and the growing season shortened by as much as two weeks in Northern Europe.

Temperatures fell further, ushering in the period (A.D. 1400–1890) that paleoclimatologists call "the Little Ice Age." The Little Ice Age was marked by two century-long interludes of especially colder weather. The first occurred in the seventeenth century and the second during the nineteenth century.[7] Then mankind got a reprieve—at the end of the nineteenth century, temperatures began to rise again.

One interesting note—the lower temperatures of the Little Ice Age also coincided with the "Maunder Minimum," a period when sunspot activity was greatly reduced. No one knows if this is more than a coincidence.

The earth can also be significantly cooled when dust and sulfur blasted into the atmosphere by volcanoes block sunlight from reaching earth's surface. The huge eruption of the Indonesian Tambora volcano in 1815 cooled the earth by about 1C degree and perhaps caused New England's Year Without Summer in 1816.[8] In June 1991, the Philippine volcano Mount Pinatubo blasted megatons of dust and sulfur into the atmosphere, which might lower the earth's temperature by as much 0.5C degrees.[9]

Two decades ago climatologists bluntly called the world's warmer weather a "good thing." The climatological consensus was that the twentieth century's weather had been "the warmest and best for world agriculture in over a millennium."[10] "The world's major agricultural areas have enjoyed an unparalleled record of beneficent weather for the past half century," said Time magazine in 1974.[11] The warmer temperatures were also credited with fostering plant growth and helping to shrink deserts through increased rainfall.[12] (Notice the politically incorrect linkage—warm, good; cold, bad.) Then in the 1940s, temperatures began a steep decline. Doomster Lowell Ponte claimed in his popular book The Cooling that humanity, lulled by the deceptively amiable climate of the early twentieth century, had foolishly "created a new, fair-weather world" which was now ending.[13]

Indeed, if a "Little Ice Age" could cause so much misery to humanity, climatologists were right to worry about what the effects of the new cooling trend would be. In 1974, scientists disclosed that the 12 percent increase in the area of snow and ice cover in the Northern Hemisphere had persisted for three years. Snow covered some areas year-round in the Canadian Arctic which formerly were snow-free in the summer. Sea ice around Iceland was thickening and warmth-loving animals like armadillos were retreating to more southerly climes.[14] Even worse, the colder temperatures had shortened the average growing season since 1950 by about two weeks.[15] British climatologist Hubert H. Lamb fretted, "How long the current cooling trend continues is one of the most important problems of our civilization."[16]

Some scientists believed the earth was merely undergoing a return to another little ice age. However, a National Academy of Sciences report in 1975 warned that the earth might be at the end of a 10,000-year warm period and on the brink of a full-blown Great Ice Age.[17] Other meteorologists claimed the cooling since 1940 would not soon be reversed.[18] And if gradual global cooling weren't disastrous enough, some scientists proposed the onset of a new ice age could happen suddenly in a "snowblitz."[19]

In a snowblitz, nature could suddenly cover a large area with enough snow that it would persist through a colder than normal summer. This begins a terrifying feedback loop in which the snow reflects sunlight making temperatures lower, which in turn prevents melting of the snow and encourages earlier snowstorms the following winter. The ever-deeper snow decreases the likelihood that it will melt in the following summers. Inexorably the snow piles up higher and higher, becoming continent-sized ice sheets in only a few centuries. Seven such winters in a row might trigger an ice age.[20]

Like other apocalyptics, global cooling Cassandras couldn't resist making the customary comparison to the danger of nuclear war. "The threat of a new ice age must now stand alongside nuclear war as a likely source of wholesale death and misery for mankind," wrote Nigel Calder, the former editor of *New Scientist,* in 1975.[21]

Global coolers like Reid Bryson, Stephen Schneider, and Lowell Ponte promptly jumped on the millenarian bandwagons then rolling—overpopulation and resource depletion. Worried about crop failures and famines due to the chilling climate, they all approvingly cited Ehrlich's *The Population Bomb* to bolster their own dire predictions. Reid Bryson warned that perhaps a half billion people could soon starve due to climate change.[22] Schneider tried to plumb the "climatic limits to growth"[23] in his first climate doomsday book, *The Genesis Strategy: Climate and Global Survival.* Schneider's book embraced most of the radical environmentalist agenda with concerns about overpopulation and depletion of nonrenewable resources, a rejection of nuclear

84

power, and calls for extensive recycling. He declared that earlier doomsday predictions of impending "Times of Famine" in the 1970s were "extraordinarily accurate."[24] Not surprisingly, fellow doomsters Ehrlich, Brown, and Carl Sagan all praised Schneider's book.

Global coolers predicted colder temperatures would bring droughts to India, the Sahara Desert, and the American Midwest. Fifteen years later global warmers would claim the same regions would suffer droughts as temperatures rose (see Chapter Nine).

Typically, the many global cooling books gloss over the scientific evidence for the purported climatic trends and move quickly to their detailed policy prescriptions on how to deal with the impending crisis. ("The world will come to an end if you don't do what I say.") Schneider's *Genesis Strategy* is a classic of the apocalyptic genre. He cannily hedges his bets, pointing out that while in 1975 the scientific consensus favors global cooling,[25] greenhouse warming may be a threat one day. Schneider apparently wanted the climate to change in some way so that he could get the world to adopt his sweeping proposals for social and economic reform.

Being a mere climatologist is evidently too humble a task—he must be a planetary savior. To save itself, humanity must embrace Schneider's grandly named "Global Survival Compromise" plan to redistribute wealth from the rich nations to the poor.[26] The cooling crisis is so urgent that we must toss aside such inconvenient formalities as democracy, national sovereignty, property rights, and free markets in order to cope with it, he argued. Schneider would institutionalize his global crisis mentality by creating several elaborate "extranational" bureaucracies modeled on the autocratic European Commission.

Schneider's "World Security Institutes" would include an "Institute of Imminent Disasters," an "Institute of Resource Availability," and an "Institute of Alternative Technologies." The institutes would be staffed by unelected experts who, like bureaucrats everywhere, would then have to justify their cushy jobs by finding that there were indeed global crises for them to manage. The Disaster Institute would be on the lookout for impending catastrophes using data collected on carbon dioxide, energy use, food supplies, population, and economic growth rates by its sister Resource Availability Institute. Scarier still, the Alternative Technologies Institute would evaluate new technologies using "small but beautiful" criteria before letting the public and corporations adopt them. All of the information provided by these three bureaus would be coordinated by an "Institute of Policy Options." Schneider's World Security Institutes would not just disseminate information but would also act as "*planning bodies* considering environmental, political, economic, and social aspects of policy options from a global perspective."[27] In the 1970s the massive failures inherent in bureaucratic planning were yet to be made plain by the collapse of the Soviet Union.

For the United States, Schneider suggested the creation of a new fourth branch of government which he called "the Truth and Consequences Branch." Frustrated that newspapers and television had failed to alarm the public about looming global disasters, Schneider designed his Truth and Consequences Branch to disseminate more widely radical environmentalism's agenda. He even suggested that "a fair fraction" of the fourth branch's budget be spent on weekly prime-time television programs and fifteen-minute nightly news segments. He hoped that through repeated exposure, "the public would question present value systems and adopt a new political consciousness. Such a consciousness could move us away from narrow and immediate economic-interest policies and redirect our efforts and resources toward the creation of a stable, equilibrium world order."[28] Schneider, like his fellow apocalyptics, wanted to convert consumerist sinners to the new ecological faith.

This call for economic redistribution is typical of millenarian environmentalism. Like other apocalypse abusers, Schneider is, paradoxically, an elitist egalitarian. Everyone must be equal, but he can level socioeconomic distinctions only through coercive institutions. "Experts" then impose their "egalitarian" solutions on the world.

To climate alarmists, the status quo is always better than any other state of affairs. One can imagine a prehistoric Steve Schneider twenty thousand years ago, when the glaciers covered 30 percent of the earth's land area, worrying about the melting of the glaciers over the future site of New York City. He might have predicted rising seas, flooded wetlands, drastic warming, centuries-long droughts, and the wrenching displacement of fragile tundra ecosystems. Why, the delicate savannahs around the equator would be overrun with dense forests and rainfall would increase flooding in those areas!

Our prehistoric Schneider would have asked, What will happen to the critical mammoth steak supplies? Humanity simply would not be able to adapt. How would we survive in a warmer world? He would intone that there is simply no technological solution available. The critically needed advances in spears, bows and arrows, hunting techniques, and the manufacture of skin clothing simply couldn't be devised in time to save us.

The fact is that humanity adapted beautifully to prehistoric global temperature changes—our ancestors invented agriculture, cities, science, and industry. Climate reactionaries apparently would prefer to be the curators of a Museum Earth where everything is preserved forever as is. But then Nature is not like that; it changes.

Schneider, like Ehrlich, was downright impatient with people who wanted to debate these issues. To them, such cavilers were simply confusing the public and stood in the way of urgent action. The peril was much too great to wait to gather more data: we had to act now![29]

We waited, however, and the cooling ended. But was that cause for rejoicing? No indeed, in the view of the apocalyptics, we avoided the Scylla of global cooling only to confront the Charybdis of global warming.

SIX

DR. FRANKENSTEIN'S DREAM

"I don't think there is any doubt that the biotech industry is going to be as important to this country as the car industry was," declares National Institutes of Health Director Bernadine Healy.[1]

"Biotechnology is going to be the dominant technology of the next 20 years. It is a technology that will save lives, preserve the environment, feed the hungry and revolutionize industries such as the chemical industry, agriculture, and mining. The products and practices will be more environmentally compatible than those that will be replaced," declares Winston Brill of the biotechnology company Agracetus.[2]

Revolutions always spawn reactionaries to oppose them—the biotechnology revolution is no exception, and bio-Luddite Jeremy Rifkin is biotech's leading counterrevolutionary. Like his fellow prophets of doom, Rifkin posits a looming global catastrophe that threatens us all—biotechnology.

"For many years social commentators have looked on nuclear weaponry as the most powerful and dangerous tool at the disposal of humanity. With the development of human genetic engineering, a tool even more awesome is now available," he warned in 1977. He added that biotechnology threatened "a form of annihilation every bit as deadly as nuclear holocaust, and even more profound."[3] In 1983, Rifkin contended that biotechnology "could very well pose as serious a threat to the existence of life on this planet as the bomb itself." One literary popularizer of Rifkin's message, Bill McKibben, denounces biotechnology with characteristic hyperbole as "the second end of nature."[4]

"People want healthier babies, more efficient plants and animals, a better GNP, and more security for their offspring. All of which biotechnology promises," despairs Rifkin.[5] Unlike the prophecies of Ehrlich, Brown, and Forrester, this prediction by Rifkin is likely to come true—humanity will welcome the medical therapies, foods, and materials that the biotech revolution brings.

The scientific discoveries fueling the biotechnology revolution are only a generation old. In 1953, Francis Crick and James Watson first identified deoxyribonucleic acid, better known as DNA, as the substance making up every living cell's genes. They described how DNA's now-familiar double-helix structure unzips into two strands which serve as templates for duplicating its original structure, ensuring genetic continuity when cells divide. The intricate dance of proteins, sugars, amino acids, and enzymes is precisely choreographed by each cell's DNA molecules.

In 1972, Paul Berg, a molecular biologist at Stanford University, made a major advance when he invented a process whereby genetic segments of DNA can be spliced— separated from one another and then attached to other segments of DNA—a technique he called "recombining" DNA. In 1980, Berg won the Nobel Prize in chemistry for his discovery. In 1983, Stanley Cohen of Stanford and Herbert Boyer of the University of California at Berkeley successfully spliced a toad gene into bacterial DNA.

Twenty years later, biotech is flourishing with more than 1,100 biotech companies in the United States employing 70,000 people. Private industry invested $3.2 billion and government $3.8 billion in biotech research and development in 1991. Total product sales exceeded $4 billion in 1991 and are expected to grow to $80 billion by the end of the decade.[6] Applications for more than 40,000 biotech patents have been made, soaring from 30 submitted in 1978 to more than 10,000 in 1991.[7]

Scientists now regularly take DNA from one organism and insert it into another, wholly different organism, where it continues to function. This is how, for example, the gene for human insulin has come to reside in a common bacterium, E. coli. These organisms happily make large quantities of human insulin, which is now commercially available as a nonallergenic replacement for the pig and cattle insulin that diabetics had used for decades.

New medical uses of biotech are among its most wondrous promises. Nearly every day the newspapers announce a new discovery or some advance on the way to curing the ills to which humanity is heir.

Biotechnologists have created a huge array of diagnostic tests for detecting everything from pregnancies to colon cancer using bioengineered antibodies. If Rifkin's fearmongering had succeeded in stopping the development of biotechnology, the biotech AIDS and hepatitis diagnostics which keep the nation's blood supply largely free of these horrific diseases wouldn't have been invented in time to prevent the spread of these diseases via transfusion.

Molecular biologists are also creating new vaccines against dreadful diseases, such as hepatitis B and the malaria parasite which every year afflicts two hundred million people in tropical countries. Biologists are testing a unique biotech rabies vaccine which is administered to wild raccoons and foxes through bait left in the woods. Using biotechnology, doctors are beginning to understand the immunological processes which cause the human body to reject organ transplants, and are testing biotech therapies that show promise of curing diseases like AIDS, cystic fibrosis, hemophilia, and a wide variety of cancers.[8] The U.S. Food and Drug Administration has already approved fifteen biotechnology-based drugs—for example, the heart attack drug Tissue Plasminogen Activator (TPA)—and about a hundred others are in the approval pipeline.[9]

In agriculture, the prospects are equally bright. Biotech can produce food plants and animals that are more nutritious and less costly to raise. Self-fertilizing cereal grains that are highly disease resistant are being developed. Such genetically modified crops would significantly lessen the need for controversial pesticides and expensive fertilizers. Vaccines against the disease "scours," which kills young animals through dehydration, are already in use, and hormones to increase milk and meat production using less feed will soon be available. And ingenious researchers will be able to devise hundreds more applications in the future. Disease- and pest-resistant strains of rice, cassava, yams, and sweet potatoes, crops critical to feeding hungry people in developing countries, will soon emerge from the labs.[10]

Bioremediation is another area in which great strides are being made and which ought to gladden the gloomy hearts of many environmentalists. Companies are currently developing microbes designed to clean up oil spills, treat human sewage, and remove toxic chemicals from groundwater.

Despite the benefits that biotechnology offers, even some molecular biologists were initially uncomfortable with the implications of recombining DNA during the early days of the technique. A letter from a committee of eminent molecular biologists including Paul Berg, David Baltimore, Stanley Cohen, Herbert Boyer, and James Watson appeared in July 1974 in *Science* asking for a worldwide moratorium on certain types of gene-splicing experiments.[11] The moratorium was to last until the hazards of recombinant-DNA research could be assessed. The letter also recommended that the director of the National Institutes of Health (NIH) develop a set of safety procedures for working with recombinant DNA molecules. A worldwide voluntary moratorium by molecular biologists then began and lasted more than two years. This was the first self-imposed ban on basic research in the history of science.

The moratorium was a red flag to a wide variety of activists and critics who predicted that microorganisms modified by this new technology could escape from laboratories, causing "superplagues" or an epidemic of infectious cancer. Some activists even urged that all such research be completely forbidden, and Congress held hearings to consider imposing very stringent regulations on the use of recombinant DNA technology.

In 1975, some 140 molecular biologists, in conscious imitation of Manhattan Project atomic physicists a generation earlier, gathered at the Asilomar Conference Center in Pacific Grove, California, and drafted a set of guidelines to govern experiments with recombinant DNA. In 1976, the NIH's newly formed Recombinant DNA Committee (RAC) issued a set of guidelines that specified four levels of precautionary physical containment for gene-splicing experiments, based on very preliminary assessments of the biological hazards that they might pose. Since then it has been amply demonstrated that microorganisms constantly promote the exchange of genetic material between creatures living wild in nature—a kind of natural bioengineering. Bacteria are particularly eager to exchange genes among themselves. Consequently, the guidelines have greatly been relaxed.

It is now clear that molecular biologists seriously underrated the damage that government regulation can do to a new endeavor. The politically naive scientists selected the NIH as the forum in which to develop safety guidelines for gene-splicing experiments. By involving a federal agency in rulemaking, they caused a whole panoply of governmental procedures automatically to come into play, enmeshing participants in the internecine political and bureaucratic battles between interest groups. During the early hysterical opposition to biotechnology, significant and burdensome regulatory action in Congress (led by Senators Kennedy and Metzenbaum and then-Congressman Albert Gore) was narrowly averted only because biological evidence for the common occurrence of recombinant DNA in nature was demonstrated before the lawmakers could act. Kennedy proposed creating a National Biohazards Commission modeled on the Nuclear Regulatory Commission—presumably such a commission could have done for the biotech industry what the NRC has done for nuclear power. The harsh NIH guidelines just missed being cast in legislative stone.

This rush to regulate was spurred on in the 1970s when the media often uncritically passed along apocalyptic claims, voiced by a number of activists, about the hazards of recombinant DNA research. In 1976, for example, *The New York Times Magazine* published a terrifying article, "New Strains of Life—or Death," written by Liebe Cavalieri, a professor of biochemistry at Cornell University. The professor suggested, among other outlandish things, that recombinant DNA research could lead to accidental outbreaks of infectious cancer. "In the case of recombinant DNA, it is an all or none situation—only one accident is needed to endanger the future of mankind," he warned.[12] In classic apocalyptic fashion Cavalieri argued that biotechnology was more dangerous than the atomic bomb: "The A-bomb, nerve gas, the destruction of the stratospheric ozone layer by fluorocarbon sprays—all have been held up as threats to human existence. But all of these dangers can, in theory if not in practice, be limited or controlled. The threat of a new form of life is more compelling, for once released, it cannot be controlled, and its effects cannot be reversed."[13]

Many scientists immediately condemned the article as being wild speculation and fantasy. Nevertheless, Cavalieri's claims—published, after all, in the staid *Times*—caused a considerable uproar and led to congressional hearings in 1976 and 1977 to consider whether the federal government should slap restrictions on the new technology.

Meanwhile, Alfred Vellucci, the mayor of Cambridge, Massachusetts, guided by the leftist group Science for the

People, was attempting to ban gene-splicing work in that city. "We want to be damned sure the people of Cambridge won't be affected by anything that could crawl out of that laboratory," Vellucci told *The New York Times*, adding, "They may come up with a disease that can't be cured— even a monster. Is this the answer to Dr. Frankenstein's dream?"[14] Amid national media attention, a citizens board evaluated the danger but in the end decided that the NIH guidelines were adequate for regulating experiments.

"Scientifically, I was a nut," succinctly noted DNA co-discoverer James Watson, who initially supported the research moratorium, adding, "There is no evidence at all the recombinant DNA poses the slightest danger." Biophysicist Burke Zimmerman, who was an active participant in the legislative debate over whether to regulate biotechnology, concluded, "In looking back, it would be hard to insist that a law was necessary, or, perhaps, that guidelines were necessary."[15]

The regulatory brawl slowed progress in biotechnology and wasted the valuable time of scientists that could have been productively spent on research. As embryologist Nina Federoff said, "Much of the RAC's time was spent undoing what was done quickly and without adequate analysis."[16] University of Wisconsin biologist Waclaw Szybalski, who helped draw up the NIH guidelines, agrees: "Much blood, sweat and tears went into changing the regulations. The people who undid all that damage should get a monument."[17]

Despite the mounting scientific evidence for the safety of recombinant DNA techniques and the public's acceptance of biotech's manifold benefits, Rifkin still fears that biotechnology could bring about the end of the world and is devoting his life to blocking its development.

Rifkin believes that humanity must reject the alluring benefits of biotechnology on quasi-mystical grounds. His popular books are filled with vague pseudo-profundities like: "[Life] reaches out to and is lured by the totality of mind that pervades the universe. Evolution, then, is seen as a movement striving to complete itself. The goal of evolution is the enlargement of mind until it fills the universe and becomes one with it."[18]

Like fellow millenarian Karl Marx, Rifkin worries about modern man's alleged "alienation," not from himself or his fellow men, but from nature. He asserts, "Humanity seeks the elation that goes with the drive for mastery over the world. Nature offers us the sublime resignation that goes with an undifferentiated participation in the world around us."[19]

Our technologies have set us outside the community of nature, and we ought "To end our long, self-imposed exile; to rejoin the community of life. This is the task before us. It will require that we renounce our drive for sovereignty over everything that lives; that we restore the rest of creation to a place of dignity and respect. The resacralization of nature stands before us as the great mission of the coming age."[20] Rifkin clearly has a strong affinity for the deep-ecology mystics in the environmental movement.

In essence, Rifkin deifies nature, and firmly believes that we sin when we tamper with it. By inducing an organism to produce something of value to mankind, we have, in his view, somehow made life irredeemably artificial. We should not arrogate to ourselves the power of improving human life through biotechnology. Characteristically, he poses a false dilemma when he asks, "Is guaranteeing our health worth trading away our humanity?"[21]

Such a conception of beneficent nature is a romantic fantasy which only a comfortable late-twentieth-century urbanite could believe. Nature, as beautiful as it is, is a dangerous place. It once spawned the Black Plague, which wiped out a quarter of Europe's population in only two years, and has now given us the modern plague of AIDS. Modern civilization protects us against a fickle nature filled with famines, plagues, floods, and droughts.

Rifkin especially fears that molecular biologists may one day be able to repair the defective genes that cause more than 3,500 inherited diseases. Since the repairs would be made to a human embryo's genetic blueprint, an adult would then pass along the repaired genes to his or her eventual offspring, who would also be free from the diseases.

Can Rifkin seriously maintain that children who, through the aid of gene therapies, are spared the agonies of Huntington's chorea, Tay-Sachs disease, or sickle-cell anemia are somehow not fully human? Would it be inhuman and immoral to mend deleterious genes? In fact, wouldn't it be inhuman and immoral *not* to mend deleterious genes in human embryos? Ethicists and the public are now wrestling with these questions. However, many like clergyman and bioethicist John Fletcher have concluded, "We have a moral obligation to learn whether you can insert genetic material in the human embryo early enough; not only to treat the disease, but to transmit prevention to future generations."[22]

What is the ethical status of penicillin? It didn't exist seventy years ago but has since saved millions of lives. Is bioengineered tumor necrosis factor (TNF), which may cure some cancers, more immoral than penicillin? Why? Does the fact that it was produced using human genes inserted into a microbe change its ethical status? What if we insert the gene directly into the cells of patients dying of cancer? Is that wrong? Is that "playing God" as Rifkin insists? Instead of letting God's will be done, we regularly give patients penicillin to cure infections from which they would otherwise die. Why not cure them of cancer? Why ought we sink into "sublime resignation" to our fates, as Rifkin counsels?

What about Rifkin's "ethical" concerns about maintaining "species integrity," that is, not transferring genes between species? Bioethicist Arthur Caplan replies, "I find it hysterically funny that Rifkin wants to ban such transfers." Caplan chuckled. "Three generations hence, people will think that worrying about biotechnology will be akin to our ancestors' worries about flying an airplane."[23]

Rifkin anticipated the deep-ecology ethic of the radical environmental movement, noting in 1977, "The traditional notion of ruthlessly exploiting and controlling nature in the name of progress is being challenged by an environmental-ist creed that emphasizes a reintegration with the ecosystem."[24] He decried "unbridled scientific and technological progress" and creeping "corporate hegemony" and called for a "new spiritual awakening" which would lead to "a fundamental change in the values and institutional relationships of American society."[25]

Like other millenarians, he presents a vision of an egalitarian utopia as our reward for rejecting a wicked technology. If we avoid the snares and delusions offered by diabolic biotechnologists, humanity may reach "the attainment of harmony and enlightenment; feeling a sense of oneness with the world."[26]

Not surprisingly, Rifkin is a longtime radical activist, beginning his career in protests against the Vietnam War. He served as national coordinator for the National Committee for a Citizens Commission of Inquiry on U.S. War Crimes in Vietnam. In 1971, he was a founding member of the New American Movement (NAM), an organization wedding elements of the old hard Left with the New Left. In 1972, NAM created the People's Bicentennial Commission (PBC) with Rifkin at its helm to "promote NAM and other radical activities and demands."[27]

The PBC generated a lot of media attention in the run-up to the bicentennial. For example, it mobilized forty thousand protesters against President Ford's bicentennial "kickoff" speech in Concord, Massachusetts in 1975. The purpose of the demonstration, Rifkin told *Newsweek* at the time, was to "issue an economic declaration of independence calling for a full-scale redistribution of U.S. corporate wealth and power."[28]

In a PBC-sponsored anthology of leftist essays, *How To Commit Revolution American Style* (1973), Rifkin's introduction candidly states: "This book is not about how to counter the Bicentennial campaign; it is about how to capitalize on it by building a mass revolutionary movement for a radically restructured America." In his own contribution to the volume, he argued that "the new American Revolution must bring about fundamental changes in our social, economic, and political institutions." The radical restructuring he envisioned involved the typical indictment of economic freedoms and their attendant prosperity in this century: "Human rights are placed above property values; Personal interests can be identified with the collective interest; Technology is made to serve rather than exploit man and the environment; Control of the economy is taken from the very rich and returned to the worker and consumer."

After the bicentennial passed without any evidence of a "mass revolutionary movement" coming into existence, Rifkin regrouped the PBC as the People's Business Commission, intended to focus on two or three corporate issues per year. As luck would have it, one of the first was the pharmaceutical industry's experiments with DNA.

Rifkin told *Dun's Review* in April 1977, "There must be public control over 'the new forms of life' that might be produced." Rifkin was not a major player in the public debate over the safety of recombinant DNA research that was taking place at the time, but he was finding his issue. That year, the PBC changed its name to its current incarnation, the Foundation on Economic Trends.

Rifkin burst upon the biotechnology scene with a protest at a meeting of molecular biologists at the National Academy of Sciences in 1977. Harvard bacterial physiologist C. Bernard Davis recalled the incident in *The New Republic*. "Just as the session was about to begin, we became aware that Rifkin's people had settled in the audience all around the perimeter. As David Hamburg [then president of the Institute of Medicine] began to speak, they all jumped up singing, 'We shall not be cloned.' Then they unfurled banners and linked them all around the room. We were their hostages. We were being terrorized."

Rifkin insists that the conference participants "knew what was planned and had agreed to allow it."[29] Bioethicist David Callahan, a conference participant, agreed that Rifkin's protest had been previously arranged—although he is not sure that everyone was aware of it. He says that he personally found it to be "more amusing than threatening."[30] Rifkin's subsequent activities leave no doubt that amusement was not his aim.

Charting this intellectual odyssey is interesting. Rifkin, at one time, believed capitalism to be in its terminal stages— a common notion among New Left, Marxist-influenced activists in the late 1960s. After the collapse of the radical movement in the 1970s, hope for the demise of capitalism resided for some in the apocalyptic visions of radical environmentalism, which, as we know, featured ominous predictions about overpopulation and the imminent exhaustion of nonrenewable resources. Either humans would call a halt to "progress," establishing limits to growth, or there would be disaster. In either case, Rifkin, along with other millenarian environmentalists, looked forward to a new age characterized by a simpler, more communitarian society.

When the environmental apocalypse failed to materialize, Rifkin looked to a rather different catalyst for the changes he so desired. By 1979—just when groups like the Moral Majority were attracting a good deal of media attention—he was hailing the upwelling of evangelical Christianity. In his book *The Emerging Order: God in the Age of Scarcity*, he portrayed fundamentalist Christianity as a "liberating force that could topple the prevailing ethos and provide a bridge to the next age of history."[31] In place of "the Protestant work ethic that has dominated the past 600 years of the age of growth," he looked forward to "a new Protestant conservation ethic, ready-made for the new age of scarcity the world is moving into."[32]

Rifkin's history is no better than his biology. He puts the beginning of the Protestant Reformation in the fourteenth century instead of the sixteenth where it belongs. In *The Emerging Order*, Rifkin praises fellow doomsters, Lester Brown and Barry Commoner, and shows his usual public relations acumen by promoting all of the now familiar ecological apocalypses purportedly menacing mankind—the "energy crisis," the soil erosion crisis, nonrenewable resource depletion, overpopulation, ozone layer destruction, global warming, massive pesticide poisoning, acid rain, and even a "timber famine."[33]

In his next book, published in 1980, *Entropy: A New World View*, Rifkin further developed the imminent "new age of scarcity" as a major theme. Of course, the "age of scarcity" never arrived, and it is ironic that these predictions of widescale scarcity may well have been undercut precisely by the advent of biotechnology-based weapons against hunger and disease.

But Rifkin is inspired by a different vision. His antibiotech fervor is fueled by a desire to replace present-day science with what he calls "empathetic science," which could lead an alienated humanity "into a participatory relationship with our environment."[34]

Stephen Jay Gould, the noted Harvard paleontologist, mirrored the opinions of the vast majority of the scientific community in a review in *Discover* of Rifkin's popular book, *Algeny*. (*Algeny* is a coined word standing for "genetic alchemy.")

Gould scored the book "as a cleverly constructed tract of anti-intellectual propaganda masquerading as scholarship. Among books promoted as serious intellectual statements by important thinkers, I don't think I have ever read a shoddier work."[35] *Algeny* neatly fits Richard Hofstadter's description of "paranoid" political tracts.

Rejecting this attempt to condemn biotech as a bourgeois development, Gould also wrote: "If Rifkin's argument embodies any antithesis, it is not left versus right, but romanticism, in its most dangerous anti-intellectual form, versus respect for knowledge and its humane employment. In both its content and presentation, *Algeny* belongs in the sordid company of anti-science. Few campaigns are more dangerous than emotional calls for proscription rather than thought."[36]

Despite Rifkin's muddled thinking and the determined opposition of scientists around the world, he has been remarkably successful in slowing down some aspects of biotechnology. He cares passionately in what he believes in, and the mechanisms of governmental regulation are so intricately intermeshed that one such passionate individual can be a tiny speck of grit that brings the gears to a halt. From years of activist experience, Rifkin has learned well how to manipulate the regulatory and legal systems. This is the tack he took in his next move after the orchestrated protest at the National Academy of Sciences meeting in 1977. Other environmental activists have since discovered the value of tying up opponents in the ponderous and expensive regulatory procedures established under the National Environmental Policy Act and the Endangered Species Act.

In 1979, Rifkin's Foundation on Economic Trends filed a "friend of the court" brief supporting the Office of the U.S. Attorney General in its contention that the federal patent laws should not be extended to cover the new, genetically modified organisms. Rifkin correctly perceived that if genetic engineers could patent their products and techniques and thus obtain property rights to them for a defined period of time, this would be a tremendous incentive for the development of commercial biotechnology—individuals and firms could then put time and money into research and be assured of earning economic rewards for doing so.

In the landmark case *Diamond v. Chakrabatry*, the Supreme Court ruled in 1980 that genetically modified organisms can be patented. Rifkin's fears were justified, and since the *Chakrabatry* decision, there has been an explosion of patents filed for biotechnology products and processes and billions of dollars invested in biotechnology companies.

Rifkin's next attack on biotechnology was aimed at two plant pathologists at the University of California at Berkeley, Steven Lindow and Nicholas Panopoulos, who sought authorization in 1983 to field-test a genetically modified bacterium, *Pseudomonas syringae*.

The *P. syringae* bacteria in the proposed experiment live naturally on the leaves of many plants. When the temperature drops to freezing, the bacteria manufacture a chemical which promotes the formation of ice crystals. The frost kills the plants, and the bacteria can then feast on the rotting remains.

Several points should be kept in mind about this experiment: No *new* genetic material was to be introduced into the environment. Lindow and Panopoulos had simply deleted the gene that made the ice-promoting chemical. Naturally occurring ice-resistant *P. syringae* already live in the environment. And ice-resistant *P. syringae* had been created by other techniques in the 1970s and released into the environment with no ill effects. Moreover, if the experiment was successful, a significant proportion of the $6 billion of crops lost annually to frost damage in the United States might be saved.

Over Rifkin's objections, the members of the RAC unanimously found the experiment to be safe and environmentally benign and authorized the proposed field test. Rifkin persisted, taking the matter to the U.S. District Court. In a major victory for his antibiotech crusade, Judge John J. Sirica issued an order in May 1984 blocking the two scientists from proceeding and barring the NIH from approving any other field tests.

The NIH and the University of California appealed Sirica's decision, and in February 1985, the appeals court upheld the injunction against the "ice-minus" experiment. Nevertheless one appeals court judge castigated Rifkin, noting, "The use of delaying tactics by those who fear and oppose scientific progress is nothing new."[37]

Eventually, the biotech company Advanced Genetic Sciences (AGS) also asked to field-test the ice-minus bacteria, which it labeled "Frostban," to determine its commercial feasibility. Through legal maneuvers and local protests inspired by Rifkin's scaremongering, the tests were delayed until 1987.

The first deliberate release of a genetically modified organism in the United States was a public relations debacle. On the network evening news programs, millions of Americans saw Dr. Julie Lindemann, dressed in a protective "moonsuit," spraying allegedly harmless micoorganisms on a plot of strawberries in Brentwood, California.

"That picture said—'these guys are lying'—this stuff is so goddamned dangerous that you've got to wear moonsuits to use it," despairs Fred Smith of the Competitive Enterprise Institute.[38] By complying with California regulations that unnecessarily required the "moonsuit," the biotech industry furnished antitechnology propaganda worth millions to bio-Luddites like Rifkin. "Either it's safe or it's not safe. If it's not safe then you shouldn't do it, if it is, then you should throw the stuff out while wearing bathing suits," says Smith.[39]

Meanwhile, Lindow ran a similar test on a patch of potatoes in Tulelake, California. Earth First! activists vandalized Lindow's plot while other biotech foes ripped up AGS's strawberries. Both were replanted. A second AGS experiment was delayed in December 1987 when rock salt and ammonia were spread on the test plot by vandals calling themselves "Mindless Thugs Against Genetic Engineering." The tests showed that plants treated with Frostban suffer far less frost damage than untreated plants do. Nevertheless, AGS subsequently dropped commercial development of Frostban.[40] Why? "Come back and talk to us when AGS tries to commercialize Frostban," archly threatens Rifkin.[41]

"Rifkin knows better than anybody how to use the political and legal systems for obstructionist purposes," says science policy analyst Peter Huber, adding, "He is very dedicated. He's got all the passion of a true believer."[42] Albert Heier, a spokesman for the Environmental Protection Agency, notes, "Crackpot or no crackpot, he has the public's ear, and he has to be reckoned with."[43]

In 1984, Rifkin asked the NIH to ban all transfers of genetic material between mammalian species. The NIH's Recombinant DNA Committee voted 22 to 0 against his proposal, noting that the potential benefits—such as more effective treatments of human and animal diseases and the development of more efficient food sources—"make it imperative that we strongly oppose the blanket prohibition of this class of experiments."

During this particular meeting, some members of the RAC "charged Mr. Rifkin with trying to incite fears in the public by using half truths and dubious interpretations of the known facts of genetics," according to *The New York Times*. One speaker argued that adopting his rationales about "species integrity" would call into question the success of the world's health organizations in totally eradicating smallpox—that "might have been a violation of a species integrity, but it was hardly mourned by any except possibly the smallpox virus itself."[44]

Rifkin takes credit for halting a Monsanto field test of soil bacteria designed to protect plants from insect pests and for delaying many other tests. Due to his legal maneuvering, another company, Biotechnica, had to postpone its test of bacteria that make some crops more productive by colonizing plant roots and producing usable nitrogen. Rifkin also worked with North Carolina Congressman Charlie Rose to introduce a bill to establish a moratorium on the patenting of animals.

To gain credibility for his antibiotech crusade, Rifkin invests considerable effort in building coalitions with other organizations and individuals whose interests intersect in the campaign against biotech and industrial capitalism. Rifkin targets "environmentalist groups, animal welfare organizations, the peace community, the women's health wing of the feminist movement, the right-to-lifers, and the evangelical churches" as likely allies in his war against biotechnology. Rifkin has organized coalitions to oppose field tests of genetically modified organisms; the Human Genome Project, which is the $3 billion effort to unravel all fifty thousand to one hundred thousand human genes; and the use of bovine somatotrophin (BST) to increase milk production in cows, among many others.

The fight over BST is vintage Rifkin. Following an activist's career is a lot like following a ballplayer's—one comes to recognize and appreciate the skills and finesse that make them good at what they do. Rifkin is a champ.

In 1989, he launched his campaign to stop the commercialization of BST (sometimes called Bovine Growth Hormone, or BGH). Developed by leading pharmaceutical and chemical companies including Monsanto and Eli Lilly, BST boosts milk production in dairy cows by as much as 25 percent. Milk could be produced using less feed, and consumer prices, in the absence of dairy price supports, could fall. In 1986, the U.S. Food and Drug Administration determined that BST is inactive in humans. "It's 100 percent safe," insists the FDA's Dr. John Augsberg.

Unfazed by scientific evidence, Rifkin sent a questionnaire to leading supermarket chains asking the grocers for their policy on distributing "BGH test milk." He told them that the results of the survey would be announced at a national press conference at which the "anti-BGH coalition" would announce a national education campaign on the alleged dangers of milk from cows treated with BGH. The questionnaire asked stores whether they would refuse to sell milk or meat from BGH test herds and whether they would label products, allowing consumers to "choose between natural or BGH tainted products?"

Already spooked by the earlier Alar and Chilean grape scares, five leading grocery chains including Kroger, Safeway, and Vons, promptly responded to Rifkin's pressure and agreed not to sell products from test herds. If grocers won't sell it, then farmers won't use it and manufacturers won't market it. Rifkin wins through corporate timidity.

"The grocers would probably like to tell you that they're being blackmailed, but I think their lawyers tell them they can't say that," said Karen Brown of the Food Marketing Institute. She added, "The supermarkets have to be responsive to consumers' concerns whether they are real or not."[45] Rifkin's anti-BST campaign embodies the old political rule—once a false charge is made it is never possible to refute it—it lingers forever in the minds of a confused and worried public.

Rifkin also claims some of the credit for getting Wisconsin and Minnesota to adopt a temporary ban on BST. (Wisconsin farmers alarmed at the prospect of falling dairy prices can also claim some credit.)

"It is unfortunate if an anti-science zealot becomes the regulatory process for this country," says Monsanto's Gerard Ingenthron.[46] Eight years after it was submitted for approved, BST's fate remains in the palsied hands of cowed FDA regulators.

"Rifkin has had astonishing success in getting into doors on Capitol Hill," notes Peter Huber.[47] Not only is he influential in the narrow world of Congress and federal regulatory agencies, where he has advised environmentalist politicians like former Senator Albert Gore, but *Vanity Fair* credits Rifkin with sparking the "Great Awakening" to environmental concerns among the anguished of Hollywood.[48] He has traveled to Italy and Germany, where his message of biotechnological doom resonates strongly. Opposition to biotechnology is so fervent in Europe that Denmark banned field tests[49] and German biotech companies are fleeing their homeland.[50]

In his rush to usher in the millennium, Rifkin embraces other environmental dooms. In 1986, after even the Club of Rome repudiated the notion of the catastrophic depletion of nonrenewable resources, he declared that imminent shortages of fossil fuels, metals, and minerals would soon bring the Industrial Age to a close. Mirroring Lester Brown, he also recited the topsoil erosion motif: "We're running out of the nutrients in the soil to sustain life."[51]

In recent years, Rifkin has hopped aboard the global warming bandwagon. "The greenhouse effect may be the most profound environmental threat mankind has faced," he declared.[52] He is now the president of the Greenhouse Crisis Foundation, which "through education, litigation and international organizing . . . is focusing public attention on the threat of global warming and related atmospheric problems, such as ozone depletion and acid rain."[53] An international conference on global warming organized by Rifkin in 1988 was attended by representatives from America's leading environmental, peace, and church groups, including the Environmental Policy Institute, Environmental Action, the National Council of Churches, Friends of the Earth, SANE/Freeze, the Environmental Defense Fund, Evangelicals for Social Action, the U.S. Public Interest Research Group, the United Nations Environment Project, the National Wildlife Federation, the World Resources Institute, Greenpeace, and the Natural Resources Defense Council.[54]

Despite these new side interests, Rifkin's antibiotech crusade continues. Over the years he has gotten a good deal of media attention and has managed to stir up public fears, but has he really been effective in slowing the progress of biotechnology?

The Frostban experiment was delayed four years, and FDA approval for BST has taken eight years so far. In a recent survey of recombinant DNA scientists, 34 percent reported that their research has been negatively affected by antibiotech activism. Sixty-six percent believed that controversy and litigation would cause scientists to avoid certain areas of research, especially research on humans. A majority (54 percent) believe that "federal and industry funding is likely to be reduced by activist-inspired litigation and controversy, such as that mounted by Jeremy Rifkin."[55]

Yet like other apocalyptic prophecies, the biotechnological holocaust predicted by Rifkin has failed to materialize. "No one has gotten even so much as a sniffle from biotechnology," insists bacteriologist Winston Brill.[56] "The more than 140 field tests of genetically modified organisms have caused absolutely no harm to the environment," says Alan Goldhammer of the Industrial Biotechnology Association.[57]

Since 1972, millions of experiments using biotechnological techniques have been performed without a single person suffering any harm. Billions of genetically modified microbes have "escaped" laboratories and greenhouses all over the world, usually riding out on experimenters' clothing, shoes, and hair, causing no damage to the outside environment.[58]

In 1989, a committee of the Ecological Society of America concluded, "most engineered organisms will probably pose minimal ecological risk."[59] Directly challenging Rifkin's quasi-mystical assertions that switching genes between species "violates species integrity" and is somehow dangerous, the ESA argued that how an organism is created is irrelevant. Bioengineered organisms should be evaluated and regulated based on their probable ecological effects.[60]

The National Academy of Sciences found that bioengineered crops pose risks no different from crops developed by traditional plant-breeding techniques used for centuries.[61] The Academy noted that microbes have been used by mankind in food processing, waste treatment, and farming. There is no difference in the risks associated with familiar microbes, whether traditional or bioengineered. Unfamiliar microbes should undergo more scrutiny before being used. In fact, because genetic engineers know exactly what traits they are changing, bioengineered plants and microbes are safer.

"We already have almost a century's worth of safe experience with thousands of microbial strains applied to our fields in concentrations of billions of cells per acre," says Brill.[62] For example, nitrogen-fixing bacteria are routinely applied to crops to improve productivity.

Rifkin and other critics often argue that our experience with imported species like kudzu vine and Japanese beetles parallels what might happen when we introduce bioengineered organisms into the environment. Brill dismisses these comparisons as inappropriate. The pests' success in infesting the countryside depends on tens of thousands of unengineered genes. By contrast, bioengineered organisms—only one or two genes will be changed—will not be much different from their unmodified confreres already in the environment. Also, no one complains of infestations of crop plants like wheat, potatoes, and corn, which are the ones likely to be genetically modified. That's because domesticated crops need human protection to survive.

The vast majority (89 percent) of recombinant DNA scientists in a recent survey believe that current regulations governing biotechnology are adequate or overly stringent. Eighty-three percent reject a proposed ban on releasing genetically modified bacteria into the environment.[63]

Biotech researchers' complacency about regulation could, however, be shattered. As safe as biotech has proven to be, no technology is without some risks. "The biotech industry has learned absolutely no lessons from what happened to other industries like pharmaceuticals and nuclear power," warns Peter Huber, a public policy analyst at the Manhattan Institute.[64] Haunted by the specter of the moribund nuclear power industry, Fred Smith of the Competitive Enterprise Institute, a Washington, D.C., public policy group, fears that some minor incident hyped by the media will trigger an already hypersensitive regulatory system into imposing onerous and unnecessary new requirements.

Regulators are never penalized for rejecting a product; they only get into trouble by approving something that later causes problems. The losers will be consumers and patients who never get a chance to learn about the tremendous benefits of new biotech products and medicines rejected by timid, ass-covering regulators. Unless the industry confronts fearmongers like Rifkin head-on, Smith believes that biotech "will go the way of the nuclear industry."[65]

Meanwhile Rifkin waits. His prophecies of doom, like those of astrologers and his fellow apocalypse abusers, are kept deliberately vague, so that when something unexpected happens, he can be quoted in the major media saying, "I told you so."

Future scientific discoveries and technological advances will certainly create new risks and pose new ethical dilemmas, which we must confront and resolve if we are to express fully our nature as human beings. Those people who are optimistic about humanity's capacities will reject Rifkin's views. Ultimately Rifkin is asking us to surrender that most distinctively human faculty, our questing intellect, to his vision of a timid humanity dwelling quiescently in an unexplored universe.

SEVEN

THE DOOMSDAY MACHINE

"We have, by slow and imperceptible steps, been constructing a Doomsday Machine," warned Cornell University astrophysicist Carl Sagan in 1983.[1] A classic "Doomsday Machine" is a device or system that guarantees that if one combatant launches a nuclear assault on its adversary, the attacker is committing suicide. For example, one country could arrange it so that if it was attacked, it would explode a large number of highly radioactive bombs whose fallout would poison the whole earth. The concept of a nuclear Doomsday Machine ("a device whose only function is to destroy all human life") was first developed by the brilliant RAND Corporation analyst Herman Kahn in his book *On Thermonuclear Warfare*[2] and later made notorious by the movie *Dr. Strangelove*.

Presumably, a country would only construct a Doomsday Machine in order to deter an attack. However, for it to be an effective deterrent, potential attackers must know that it exists. A secret Doomsday Machine is extremely dangerous. Sagan and his colleagues Richard Turco, Owen Toon, Thomas Ackerman, and James Pollack (whose study was named "TTAPS" for their initials) claimed that the superpowers already had inadvertently constructed a Doomsday Machine—nuclear winter.

In 1982, Jonathan Schell published his rhetorically powerful *The Fate of the Earth*, in which he considered human extinction as a possible consequence of a nuclear war. To avert the possibility of extinction, Schell called for "at a minimum, a freeze on the further deployment of nuclear weapons . . . [or] [e]ven better would be a reduction in nuclear arms, for example, by cutting the arsenals of the superpowers in half . . ."[3]

The nuclear freeze movement was in 1982 approaching its high-water mark. Despite Schell's passionate call for a freeze and a great deal of political activism on the issue, the Reagan administration resolutely resisted the idea. Something was required to energize the peace activists. "Horror is needed. The peace movement cannot do without it," acknowledged activist Ralph White.[4]

In 1983 Carl Sagan supplied the flagging freeze movement with a new "horror"—nuclear winter.

Using a very simple computer climate model, the TTAPS team calculated that the detonation of thousands of nuclear bombs with an explosive force of 5,000 megatons[5] would loft millions of tons of smoke high into the atmosphere, blocking sunlight from the surface of the earth for months. Land temperatures would plunge by 15 to 25C degrees, killing crops and freezing the hapless human survivors to death.[6] Sagan argued that the nuclear arsenals of the Soviet Union and the United States had already far exceeded the threshold for triggering nuclear winter in the event of war.[7] Sagan estimated the threshold for nuclear winter at "very roughly around 500–2,000 strategic warheads,"[8] and even suggested that a relatively small 100-megaton nuclear war targeting the world's 100 largest cities could provoke a devastating nuclear winter.[9] Reductions in strategic weapons arsenals of 90 to 99 percent would be necessary to get below Sagan's threshold.

Ubiquitous doomster Paul Ehrlich, who joined the crusade as the lead author of a companion paper on the biological effects of nuclear winter, warned that "the population size of *Homo sapiens* conceivably could be reduced to prehistoric levels or below, and extinction of the human species itself cannot be excluded."[10] Characteristically, Ehrlich's team chose an even more implausible worst-case scenario than Sagan's did for their analysis. Sagan's baseline case was a 5,000-megaton nuclear war, while Ehrlich arbitrarily doubled it to 10,000 megatons, which would provoke a nuclear winter with temperatures falling by 40C degrees.[11] Ehrlich's scenario unrealistically targeted every city on earth with a population greater than 60,000 people.[12]

Sagan and Ehrlich alarmed the Third World by arguing that the smoke pall resulting from nuclear war in the Northern Hemisphere could blanket the entire earth, including the nations in the Southern Hemisphere.[13] Noncombatant countries would therefore have a bigger stake in pressuring the superpowers to cut their nuclear arsenals.[14] Ehrlich claimed that the spread of "subfreezing temperatures to the northern tropics is highly likely and to the Southern Hemisphere at least possible."[15] In fact, Ehrlich assumed temperatures in the Northern Hemisphere would remain at about −43C degrees (−45F degrees) for four months. The Southern Hemisphere would experience a month of temperatures below −18C degrees (zero Fahrenheit).[16]

Early on, environmental advocacy groups were deeply involved in promoting the nuclear winter hypothesis. According to Sagan, "beginning in June 1982 a group of environmentalists and foundation executives had concluded that inadequate attention was being given to the potential consequences of nuclear war."[17] Responding to Jonathan Schell's eloquent appeal to abolish nuclear weapons in *The Fate of the Earth*, the activist groups helping Sagan promote nuclear winter included the Union of Concerned Scientists, Physicians for Social Responsibility, and the Federation of American Scientists.[18]

Like *The Limits to Growth* before it, the nuclear winter concept was launched with an enormous amount of media hoopla. A Washington public relations firm was hired for $80,000 to promote and organize a conference on the topic.[19] In October, the public first heard of this new form of atomic doom in an article by Carl Sagan in the popular Sunday supplement *Parade*. In December, a somewhat toned-down version of the nuclear winter hypothesis was published in the prestigious journal *Science* along with Ehrlich's accompanying article on its biological effects. Also in December, an article penned by Sagan aimed at nuclear strategists and policymakers appeared in *Foreign Affairs*.

Many environmental advocacy organizations, including Greenpeace, the Friends of the Earth, and the Natural Resources Defense Council, had joined the Freeze Campaign in the early 1980s (see Chapter Two). Once nuclear winter was unveiled, they quickly applauded it, and the Union of Concerned Scientists was particularly active in publicizing the idea. Sagan and environmental radicals were once again claiming that a certain state of affairs—the possibility of a nuclear winter—required that specific policies—a freeze on deploying nuclear weapons—be adopted.[20] Thus the nuclear winter hypothesis meshed nicely (and metaphorically) with the specific aims of the freeze movement—freezing superpower nuclear weapons arsenals and opposing the deployment of American intermediate-range nuclear weapons in Europe.

However, matters are not that straightforward. Without going into the arcane details of nuclear strategy and deterrence theory, many nuclear strategists and defense intellectuals concluded that nuclear winter had little or no bearing on how to maintain and strengthen deterrence and nuclear stability between the superpowers.[21]

Prior to nuclear winter, nobody had any doubt that the consequences of nuclear war would be horrific—billions of people could die. However, experts strongly disagreed about what was the best way to prevent war from breaking out. Hawks argued that a large nuclear arsenal strengthens deterrence by convincing aggressive adversaries that they will lose any possible fight, while doves believed that a significantly lower number of weapons would be adequate for maintaining deterrence. The chief contribution that the TTAPS team made to the arms control debate was to try to provide Schell's dark meditations on the possibility of human extinction by means of a nuclear holocaust with some sort of firm scientific basis.

In 1984, Ehrlich and Sagan with other collaborators further popularized nuclear winter in *The Cold and the Dark: The World After Nuclear War*. One adoring reviewer gushed that it could be "the most important book ever published." Indeed the book could have a greater effect on human history than "the Odyssey, the Bible, the Koran, or the collected works of William Shakespeare."[22] Its apocalyptic vision was later promoted by ABC Television's dramatization of the aftermath of a nuclear war, "The Day After."

Unlike other alleged environmental crises such as resource depletion, ozone depletion, and global cooling or warming, nuclear winter can *only* be tested in computer models. In the case of limits on nonrenewable resources, we can see whether resources are in fact becoming scarce, or with regard to global warming, whether temperatures are rising catastrophically. The only reality check for nuclear winter is nuclear war. There are only dueling computer models, and given the huge uncertainties that routinely crop up in computer climate models, it is very difficult to end definitively the debate on the subject.

However, scientists and defense experts were far from unanimous in accepting Sagan's nuclear winter hypothesis. In 1985, a prestigious panel of scientists convened by the Scientific Committee on Problems of the Environment (SCOPE) ruled out the possibility of human extinction due to climatic effects of nuclear war.[23] Even perennial climate doomster Stephen Schneider and his colleague Starley

Thompson attacked Sagan's outlandish conclusions. Using a much more sophisticated climate model than Sagan's, the two showed that the "global apocalyptic conclusions of the initial nuclear winter hypothesis can now be relegated to a vanishingly low level of probability."[24]

Russell Seitz, a visiting scholar at Harvard's Center for International Affairs and a severe critic of nuclear winter, dismissed the defects of the TTAPS climate model in blistering terms: "Instead of a planet with continents and oceans, the TTAPS model postulated a featureless bone-dry billiard ball. Instead of nights and days, it postulated twenty-four-hour sunlight at one-third strength. Instead of realistic smoke emissions, it simply dumped a ten-mile-thick soot cloud into the atmosphere instantly. The model dealt with such complications as east, west, winds, sunrise, sunset, and patchy clouds in a stunningly elegant manner—they were ignored."[25]

When Thompson and Schneider included all these factors in their model, they found that Sagan's predicted drastic drop in temperature moderated substantially. They calculated that the TTAPS team was off by a factor of three to five—summertime temperatures over the United States would drop by 8C to 12C degrees for a few days, not by 25C degrees for months as predicted by Sagan.[26] "These temperature changes more closely describe a nuclear 'fall' than a nuclear winter," the two concluded.[27] Schneider and Thompson also determined that the estimates of smoke generated by a nuclear war were off by a factor of two to four. They found that temperatures wouldn't plunge to and persist at subfreezing levels because the vast amounts of heat stored in the oceans would keep the planet warm and because 75 percent of the smoke would be removed from the atmosphere over the course of a month.[28] Others contradicted the claim that the northern tropics and the Southern Hemisphere would suffer subfreezing temperatures.[29]

MIT political scientist George Rathjens is one of the harshest critics of nuclear winter. Rathjens, a former president of the Council for a Livable World and a past executive of SANE, groups not known for their tolerance of nuclear weapons, denounced nuclear winter as "the worst example of the misrepresentation of science to the public in my memory."[30]

Eventually, Sagan's colleague Turco admitted that he never thought the extinction of human beings by nuclear winter was a real possibility. "That was a speculation of others, including Carl Sagan," he said. "My personal opinion is that the human race wouldn't become extinct, but civilization as we know it certainly would."[31] Of course, the crucial contribution of the nuclear winter hypothesis was the claim that the human race was in danger of extinction. That nuclear war could destroy civilization is a contention no one ever doubted. However, in the 1990 book *A Path Where No Man Thought: Nuclear Winter and the End of the Arms Race*, Turco and Sagan continue doggedly to insist that nuclear winter could cause human beings to become extinct.[32]

The torching of several hundred Kuwaiti oil wells by the retreating armies of Saddam Hussein in 1991 provoked some climate catastrophists and environmentalists into reviving nuclear winter.[33] For example, a British environmental engineer and vice president of the Campaign for Nuclear Disarmament, John Cox, suggested that the smoke could lower temperatures over a quarter of the world's surface.[34] *Scientific American* solemnly declared that optimists believed that oil well firefighters "would complete their task in nearly two years. Pessimists . . . say the job could take seven years."[35] In fact, dousing Kuwait's oil fires took less than a year.

Sagan evidently could not resist making lurid nuclear winter doomsday pronouncements about the Kuwaiti fires, including the prediction that smoke from the fires could cause droughts in India and Bangladesh.[36] When it became clear that the effects of the oil well fires were far from apocalyptic, Sagan complained about having his statements characterized as "doomsday scenarios" by *Science*.[37] But what else could one call his assertion on ABC's "Nightline":

"We think the net effects will be very similar to the explosion of the Indonesian volcano Tambora in 1815, which resulted in the year 1816 being known as the year without a summer. There were massive agricultural failures in North America and in Western Europe, and very serious human suffering, and, in some cases starvation. Especially for South Asia, that seems to be in the cards, and perhaps for a significant fraction of the Northern Hemisphere as well."[38] For good measure, Sagan told CBS's "60 Minutes" that the smoke from Kuwaiti fires could obscure the sun over 10 percent of the Northern Hemisphere. "You might have massive agricultural failures in the United States as a result," he added.[39] Sagan's obsession with nuclear winter has become so loony that other scientists now quip behind his back, "Where there's smoke, there's Sagan."

By the way, instead of suffering a drought as predicted by Sagan and company, India and Bangladesh saw unusually high rainfall during the 1991 monsoon season.[40] And based on their analyses of the smoke from the Kuwaiti oil fires, atmospheric scientists Peter Hobbs and Lawrence Radke concluded that the smoke had "insignificant effects on a global scale."[41] They also calculated that Sagan's estimates of the amount of sunlight that oil fire soot would block after a nuclear war are two to five times too high.[42] This tragic real life experiment casts further doubt on the validity of Sagan's version of nuclear winter.

In 1983, Sagan declared, "Apocalyptic predictions require, to be taken seriously, higher standards of evidence than do assertions on other matters where the stakes are not as great."[43] Succumbing to his desire to bolster the Nuclear Freeze Campaign by means of a "technological fix," Sagan failed to meet the normal standards of scientific evidence, much less the "higher" ones required of apocalyptic predictions. Nuclear winter, like the other environmental dooms analyzed in this book, is just a "scientifically generated fiction" designed to scare the public and policymakers into accepting certain drastic policy prescriptions.[44]

"In the final analysis, we must recognize that whatever

our level of understanding of the effects of nuclear weapons, and whatever our ability to apply technical fixes to weapons, defenses or doctrines, the problem of avoiding nuclear war is not amenable to scientific solution. This problem arises more from political differences than from the latest technical capabilities," concluded Schneider and Thompson in 1986.[45] The truth of this proposition has been fully borne out by the rapid pace of nuclear arms negotiations that followed the collapse of Soviet communism. Deep reductions in nuclear arsenals are coming about not because we were frightened into cuts by apocalyptic scenarios, but because the political differences between the superpowers were vastly lessened. The West no longer confronts a powerful, aggressive totalitarian enemy, so now we can let down our guard and lend a neighborly hand to a friendly democratic regime in Russia.

EIGHT
THE HOLE IN
THE SKY

A full-blown "ozone hole" rivaling the one that appears over Antarctica might open up over the United States, zapping Americans with damaging ultraviolet sunlight during the spring, warned NASA scientists at an ominous early February 1992 press conference. *Time* showcased the story on the front cover of its February 17 issue, warning that "danger is shining through the sky ... No longer is the threat just to our future; the threat is here and now."[1] Then-Senator Albert Gore thundered, "We have to tell our children that they must redefine their relationship to the sky, and they must begin to think of the sky as a threatening part of their environment."[2]

Spooked by NASA, the Senate hastily passed by 96 to 0 an amendment demanding that President Bush order the chemicals implicated in ozone destruction be phased out earlier than scheduled. Stung by the vote, Bush rushed the ban of the refrigerants known as chlorofluorocarbons (CFCs) forward from the year 2000 to the end of 1995.

Although NASA did not acknowledge it, the "danger" of an ozone hole opening over the Northern Hemisphere had already passed in less than a month after the existence of the putative crisis was announced. By late February, satellite data showed that the levels of ozone-destroying chlorine monoxide had dropped significantly and provided absolutely no evidence of a developing ozone hole over the United States. NASA waited until April 30, 1992, to announce at a press conference that a "large arctic ozone depletion" had been "averted." In other words, no ozone hole had opened up over the United States. *Time*, far from featuring the story on its cover, buried NASA's admission that there was no ozone hole over the northern hemisphere in four lines of text in its May 11 issue.[3]

One NASA atmospheric scientist averred that his agency "really jumped the gun," while another drily commented that "it was perhaps premature for NASA to say that something drastic was about to occur."[4] What was the rush? Why did NASA bureaucrats and scientists feel that they needed to frighten the American public?

The NASA revelations were exquisitely timed to bolster the agency's budget requests for its global climate change program, whose funding is slated to double by fiscal 1993. One NASA atmospheric scientist even wondered if it was only a coincidence that Senator Gore's new book of apocalyptic environmentalism, *Earth in the Balance*, was published just days before NASA held its ozone press conference. After all, Gore chaired the subcommittee on Science, Space and Technology, which oversees NASA's budget.

"What you have to understand is that this is about money," Melvyn Shapiro, the chief of meterological research at a National Oceanic and Atmospheric Administration laboratory in Boulder, Colorado, told *Insight* magazine. He added, "If there were no dollars attached to this game, you'd see it played on intellect and integrity. When you say the ozone threat is a scam, you're not only attacking people's scientific integrity, you're going after their pocketbook as well. It's money, purely money."[5] Shortly after Shapiro's frank comments appeared, he was muzzled. He stopped talking to the press and told colleagues that he had been told to shut up by his superiors.

And NASA had another reason for jumping the gun. Environmental activists and their sympathizers in Congress and the bureaucracy were anxious to push President Bush into attending the big United Nations "Earth Summit" in June 1992. Senator Gore likened the alleged ozone crisis to global warming and urged the president to sign the global climate change treaty that was the centerpiece of the "Earth Summit."

By now everyone (94 percent of Americans according to one poll[6]) has heard that the earth's protective ozone shield is wearing thin and even has a hole in it over the South Pole. The looming ozone catastrophe will purportedly bring humanity withered crops, collapsing terrestrial and marine ecosystems, skin cancer epidemics, and populations whose immune systems have been seriously compromised. The culprits in this drama are a group of industrial chemicals purveyed by greedy corporations to pampered and spoiled consumers.[7] Ozone depletion is the perfect ecological morality play.

In a morality play, unfortunately, there is no place for ambiguity. Yet the impact of man-made chlorofluorocarbons (CFCs) on the ozone layer is a complex question that turns on murky evidence, tentative conclusions, conflicting interpretations, and changing predictions. It is tempting to ignore these complications, abandon critical thinking, and join in the apocalyptics' call for *drastic action now*. But humanity would do so only in defiance of reality, for it turns out that ozone depletion, like the other environmental dooms analyzed here, is less a crisis than a nuisance, one that can and should be dealt with in a calm, deliberate, and scientific way.

"It's terrifying," exclaimed an overwrought John Lynch. The program manager for polar aeronomy at the National Science Foundation added, "If these ozone holes keep growing like this, they'll eventually eat the world."[8] As usual

Paul Ehrlich is also alarmed. He warns, "Pure luck may have saved civilization from a catastrophic threat closely related to global warming—ozone depletion."[9] Ehrlich calls ozone depletion "our worst near miss so far."[10]

The ozone layer and the chemical mechanisms that sustain it were first discovered in the 1930s. Ozone, which consists of three oxygen atoms, is produced when ultraviolet rays from the sun split an oxygen molecule in two and one of the resulting atoms combines with another ordinary two-atom oxygen molecule. Ozone is found in the stratosphere, some twelve to forty kilometers above the earth's surface, where it is continuously produced and destroyed. This cycle of creation and destruction prevents the energetic ultraviolet sunlight from reaching the surface where it could damage the delicate proteins and DNA in living organisms.

Ozone is chiefly produced over the sunlight-drenched tropics, from which global air circulation transports it toward the poles. If all the ozone in the stratosphere were compressed to surface air pressures, it would make up a layer only one-eighth of an inch thick.[11]

This vaporous veil floated serenely overhead with no one giving it much thought for years. Then in the 1960s, antinuclear activists urged that atmospheric nuclear testing be banned because nitrous oxide blasted into the stratosphere by the tests damaged the ozone shield. After the Nuclear Test Ban treaty was signed in 1963, the issue temporarily died down. In the early 1980s, the damage to the ozone layer that could be caused by nuclear war was resurrected during the debate over "nuclear winter."

Anxiety over the fate of the ozone layer were rekindled in the late 1960s during the struggle over whether the U.S. government should subsidize the building of two supersonic transport (SST) airplane prototypes. SSTs would fly in the stratosphere fifteen miles above the earth, bridging continents in only hours. Some scientists, like University of California at Berkeley chemist Harold Johnston, claimed that the nitrogen oxides and water vapor in the exhaust gases of a fleet of five hundred SSTs would erode the ozone layer.

Environmental activists pounced on these fears and organized a campaign to oppose government support for the SST program. Congress eventually killed the program, giving the newly emerging environmental movement its first major victory. But scientists later discovered that the SSTs posed no great danger to the ozone layer.[12]

The SST controversy also led the U.S. Department of Transportation to fund the first intensive scientific study of humanity's impact on climate. The $50 million Climatic Impact Assessment Program (CIAP) marks the beginning of the politicization of meteorology and climatology. From this seed sprouted an ever-expanding federal global climate change bureaucracy, which spent over $1.1 billion in 1991 and is slated to spend nearly $1.4 billion by 1993.

The current version of the ozone "crisis" began in 1974, when chemist Sherwood Rowland and his postgraduate fellow Mario Molina at the University of California at Irvine calculated that substances called chlorofluorocarbons (CFCs) had the potential to seriously deplete the sheltering ozone layer. Rowland even quipped to his wife, "The work is going well, but it looks like the end of the world."

In 1928, at about the same time scientists originally discovered the ozone layer, a Du Pont chemist named Thomas Midgely was looking for new coolants to replace the dangerous toxic ones, like ammonia and sulfur dioxide, then in use in refrigerators. He invented a new family of nontoxic, nonflammable, and very stable compounds by combining chlorine and fluorine with carbon and called them chlorofluorocarbons. CFCs were very nearly perfect for the job. Du Pont formed a joint venture with General Motors to manufacture the new miracle compounds, giving them the trade name Freons. Scientists using bromine later invented similar stable chemicals called Halons for use in fire extinguishers.

In 1973, Rowland asked Molina to find out where CFCs went once they escaped from industrial processes, refrigerators, and air conditioners. Since CFCs are extremely stable compounds, no known chemical processes near the earth's surface seemed capable of degrading them into simpler compounds. Molina discovered that other scientists were measuring a steady increase in CFCs over the years in the atmosphere. Molina concluded that CFCs must eventually percolate into the stratosphere, where energetic ultraviolet light would strike them and break the molecular bonds that held them together. But this presented a problem since that is where the ozone shield is located.

Molina and Rowland figured that the highly reactive elements chlorine and bromine, once released from the superstable CFC and Halon molecules, would take part in a complicated chemical chain reaction in which one chlorine or bromine atom could dismember thousands of ozone molecules. They predicted increasing levels of CFCs in the atmosphere could lead to a 7 to 13 percent decline in stratospheric ozone in the next one hundred years.[13] In turn, this would lead to more harmful ultraviolet radiation reaching the earth's surface. This was not news the multibillion-dollar CFC industry would want to hear.

At academic and industry meetings, scientists on both sides hotly debated whether Rowland and Molina could be correct. Environmental pressure groups, notably the Natural Resources Defense Council, quickly adopted ozone depletion as a cause and began to push for a ban on "frivolous" uses of CFCs. Since CFCs were a popular propellant in aerosol spray cans, environmentalists began a campaign stressing the idea that spraying under one's arms with antiperspirant could destroy the planet. The campaign was effective and the sales of aerosol products declined drastically.

Congress held hearings on the issue and the Environmental Protection Agency began to push for a CFC ban. In 1978, the United States became the first nation in the world to ban CFCs as aerosol propellants. In the meantime, the predicted reductions in ozone fluctuated wildly as scientists calculated and recalculated what the effects of CFCs might be. In fact, by 1984, the National Academy of Sciences reported that total ozone might *increase* by 1 percent.[14]

Then from out of the blue came the Antarctic "Ozone

Hole" which so terrified the National Science Foundation's John Lynch. The existence of the ozone hole was announced in 1985 by scientists working for the British Antarctic Survey who had been monitoring declines in the ozone over Halley Bay, Antarctica, since the mid-1970s. Led by Joseph Farman, the British team detected a 50 percent decline in ozone just when spring came to the frigid continent in late September and early October 1984. Ozone levels are measured by ground-based Dobson spectrophotometers, named after their inventor Sir G. M. B. Dobson. These machines measure how much ultraviolet (UV) light reaches the surface, and since ozone absorbs UV, more UV means less ozone. Previously, the British scientists had measured ozone levels of more than 300 Dobson units. In late September and early October of 1984, ozone rapidly dipped to half that—150 Dobson units. None of the atmospheric models had predicted reduced ozone over Antarctica. What could be causing this drop?

Many environmentalists and scientists believed that the "ozone hole" was a smoking gun pointing directly at the CFCs. However, it was not at all clear how CFC chemistry could account for such a rapid and dramatic decline. In the years that followed atmospheric scientists proposed a variety of explanations for the "hole." Some argued it was a normal and transitory phenomenon, others that it was the result of anomalies in wind patterns, or that sunspot activity caused it.

Rowland and Molina still championed their CFC-ozone theory, and began devising and testing chemical theories of how CFCs could destroy ozone in the polar stratosphere. Chlorine floating free in the atmosphere simply could not destroy enough ozone fast enough to cause the hole. The current hypothesis of how the ozone hole opens for a couple of months each year in the Antarctic is based on a long chain of inference leading from the laboratory test tubes through computer models to the skies above the South Pole.

Scientists eventually focused on the thin and very cold ice clouds that waft above Antarctica. These polar stratospheric clouds (PSCs) of water and nitrogen compounds form only in the months-long and exceedingly cold polar night. Every winter a strong and stable wind pattern, called the polar vortex, swirls around the outer margins of the Antarctic land mass. Because the air in the vortex is isolated from warmer air outside the region it is chilled to below −80C degrees.

Nitrogen oxides, which inhibit chlorine chemistry, freeze out of the stratosphere, leaving chlorine and bromine atoms and chlorine monoxides free to attack ozone when the returning sun peeks over the horizon at the beginning of the Antarctic spring in September and October. The clouds are highly effective miniature chemical laboratories in which chlorine and bromine reactions powered by sunlight catalytically destroy huge quantities of ozone. In the spring, nearly all of the ozone between twelve and twenty-five kilometers is destroyed, allowing increased amounts of UV light to reach the surface. As summer approaches, the clouds disappear, the hole is filled with newly produced ozone and ozone flowing down as usual from the tropics, and UV levels return to normal.

In 1987, concern about the ozone hole led thirty-four countries to reach an agreement in Montreal to cut world CFC production in half by the end of the century.

Meanwhile, scientists began to look at other data to see if they could detect any reductions in ozone over regions other than the South Pole. Until 1986, atmospheric scientists had found no evidence for ozone decline globally. NASA set up a panel chaired by a presumably neutral Rowland to analyze data from Northern Hemisphere Dobson stations, and the agency also reanalyzed some of its satellite data. In March 1988, the day after the U.S. Senate ratified the Montreal Protocol on Ozone, NASA issued the report from its Ozone Trends Panel which indicated that ozone levels over the Northern Hemisphere had declined by 0.2 percent per year over the past seventeen years.[15] Depending on latitude, the ozone had allegedly decreased between 1.7 percent and 3 percent between 1969 and 1986. (In 1992, satellite and ground-based data broadly confirmed this trend.[16]) Environmental activists and Congress were further alarmed because these decreases were touted as being twice as deep as the computer models had predicted.

Spurred by reports from the Ozone Trends Panel, negotiators returned to the conference table in London in June 1990 where they hammered out an agreement among ninety-three nations to phase out the production of most CFCs, Halons, and carbon tetrachloride by the end of the century.[17] The agreement also created a $240 million fund to which the industrialized nations must contribute and which is designed to help the developing world adopt new non-CFC-based technologies. The U.S. portion will total $40 to 60 million.

Since 1990, the rate of increase in CFCs in the atmosphere has begun to slacken, and atmospheric chlorine will peak at a little over five parts per billion at the turn of the century.[18] Chlorine density is expected to return to two parts per billion, the level at which the ozone hole first opened, after the middle of the next century.[19]

Despite these projections, a sense of impending doom pervades discussions of the ozone layer. Alarmists warn that the damage has already been done, and public expectations about the impact of ozone depletion are tinged with panic. Accounts in the mainstream news media ignore several key facts that would help to put the supposed hazards into perspective.

First, remember that it is not ozone that we need, but protection against ultraviolet sunlight. Rowland and Molina's original crude calculations suggested that CFCs could destroy 7 to 13 percent of the ozone layer in the course of a century. This would lead to increased UV in the 290- to 330-nanometer range (billionths of an inch) reaching the earth's surface. However, the decline had very strong regional components and over the years these figures have shifted constantly—first up, then down. For example, even if CFCs had not been banned, the tropics would have seen no significant decline in ozone at all.

The ozone layer is not evenly distributed over the planet—its depth is least over the equator where UV is strongest and deepest over the poles where UV is weakest. Generally there is twice as much ozone over the high latitudes than at the tropics. To gain a bit of perspective, consider that a 5 percent decline in the ozone layer would increase UV exposure about as much as moving a mere sixty miles south—the distance from Palm Beach to Miami.[20] Furthermore, UV intensity increases at higher elevations, so people who live in mile-high Denver are exposed to much more UV than people who live in Philadelphia, which is at the same latitude. Yet few people factor the risk of UV exposure into their decisions about where to live. In addition, Goddard Space Flight Center scientist Arlin Krueger, who is in charge of the Total Ozone Mapping Spectrometer (TOMS), points out that ozone levels over the United States fluctuate naturally by as much as 50 percent.[21] These periodic wide swings in ozone have no apparent effect on people, plants, and animals.

"There is no question that terrestrial life is adapted to UV," says Dr. Alan Teramura, a professor of botany at the University of Maryland, and probably the world's leading expert on the effects of UV on terrestrial plants. He adds, "Even at a 20 percent decline in ozone we are not going to burn up all the plants on the surface of the earth or kill all of the people. We wouldn't see plants wilting or fruits dropping unripened from their vines."[22]

What would occur would be "subtle shifts" among plants—those less sensitive to UV would outcompete the more sensitive species. More UV would lead to a gradual shift in the plant communities we would see around us. The impact on plants, if any, of a 5 percent decline in ozone would be masked by other climate effects like drought, pests, and frosts, whose impacts are much greater.

Some crop varieties are sensitive to UV and lower yields could result. For example, Teramura found a 25 percent reduction in yield after exposing one very sensitive variety of soybeans to a UV level corresponding to a 16 percent decrease in ozone. Apocalyptic environmentalists repeat this finding endlessly as evidence of the dire effects we can expect from a thinner ozone layer. But they fail to mention that Teramura also found several types of soybeans actually increased their yields under increased UV, while others were unaffected.

Teramura has discovered that there are large variations in UV sensitivity among different types (cultivars) of soybeans, corn, rice, and wheat. He tested 100 different cultivars, including 40 types of soybeans, and found that 41 were unaffected or tolerant of UV.[23] Teramura tested his plants at UV levels corresponding to 16 percent and 25 percent reductions in ozone—decreases that few responsible scientists predicted would ever occur. Teramura's results mean that crop yields could be maintained by selecting UV-tolerant varieties should a thinning ozone layer ever become a real problem. Famine would not result from reduced ozone.

This conclusion is bolstered by the fact that in Minnesota UV levels are half those of Georgia and Florida, yet corn and soybean yields in the South generally exceed those in the North. The U.S. breadbasket was not on the verge of being blasted out of existence by UV leaking through a newly porous ozone layer.[24] In fact, corn, wheat, rice, and oats all grow in a wide variety of UV environments now.

This is Teramura's bottom line: "I would start getting concerned at a 10 percent decline in ozone." But not panicked. And he means a sustained 10 percent reduction, not transient fluctuations.

Even Teramura's concerns may be exaggerated. Experiments at the Brookhaven National Laboratory have recently shown that the calculations used to predict UV damage to plants have been greatly overstated: "Our results indicate that plants are not among the most sensitive biological targets."[25] Thus another apocalypse dissipates in the face of good science.

So a small decline in the ozone layer poses no terrific problems for the world's ecosystems, but what about the Antarctic ozone hole? Isn't UV frying the penguins and phytoplankton, bringing the "ecosystem of the Southern Hemisphere to the verge of collapse"? Marine ecologist Susan Weiler testified in 1991 at a hearing held by environmental apocalyptic Senator Gore that scientists had measured phytoplankton reductions of 6 to 12 percent around Antarctica.[26]

Marine ecologist Osmond Holm-Hansen of the Scripps Institute of Oceanography gently dismisses Weiler as "more of a politician than a scientist." Since 1988, Holm-Hansen has been intensively investigating the effects of UV on phytoplankton, the tiny marine plants at the base of Antarctica's food chain. He found that the increased UV may reduce total phytoplankton growth in the full water column at most 5 percent during the Antarctic spring.[27] Holm-Hansen adds that even if there were 6 to 12 percent reductions in phytoplankton growth rates, this would mean a 2 to 4 percent overall reduction in the course of a year, which is well within natural variations in the Antarctic ecosystem.[28]

He also points out the Antarctic phytoplankton naturally tolerate similar levels of UV during the Antarctic summer and that most phytoplankton are able to adapt to higher UV levels.[29] With reduced springtime ozone, Antarctica experiences UV levels typically seen over cities like Chicago.[30]

"All the ozone hole does is bring summerlike ultraviolet radiation levels a couple of months early," says John Frederick, an atmospheric scientist at the University of Chicago. "It's not as if there's some god-awful thing called ultraviolet radiation that's getting you for the first time."[31]

"Unlike the scare stories you hear some scientists spreading, the Antarctic ecosystem is absolutely not on the verge of collapsing due to increased ultraviolet light," insists Holm-Hansen.[32] Even oceanographer Raymond Smith, who reported the 6 to 12 percent phytoplankton growth rate declines, acknowledges that "the whole ecosystem does not appear to be collapsing."[33]

One of the most effective scare tactics deployed by the apocalyptics during the ozone controversy was to predict massive increases in skin cancer as a consequence of reduced ozone. Most of us are familiar with the damage that UV light can cause through sunburns. The incidence of nonmelanoma skin cancer is strongly correlated with exposure to UV. The U.S. Environmental Protection Agency (EPA) predicts that for every 1 percent reduction in the ozone layer there will be a 3 percent increase in nonmelanoma skin cancers. The fact is that the incidence of skin cancer increases by 1 percent every 12 to 18 miles closer to the equator or every 150 feet higher up a person lives.[34]

How trustworthy are the EPA's calculations? Not very, according to Temple University dermatologist Dr. Frederick Urbach, who is a consultant on the U.N. Environmental Assessment of ozone reductions. "You can crunch numbers in a computer and get whatever results you want to come out," says Urbach, laughing. He concedes that skin cancer rates have been going up dramatically in recent decades, but adds that "the increases are due to people spending more time outside, not more UV."[35] The death rate for nonmelanoma skin cancer is negligible, less than 1 percent. Dr. Urbach notes, "It takes real talent for someone to die of nonmelanoma skin cancer. You basically have to ignore a hole in your skin for years."[36]

It should be noted that light-skinned people are far more susceptible to UV-induced nonmelanoma skin cancer than are darker-skinned people. It is not an evolutionary accident that peoples who live closer to the equator tend to have darker skins whose melanin protects them from the higher levels of ultraviolet light found naturally in the tropics. As for the far more deadly melanoma, the main risk factor appears to be severe sunburns in childhood rather than frequent exposure to UV.[37]

The weak evidence that UV may slightly lower the body's immunological defenses (after all, sunburn damages the body's largest organ, the skin) has also been greatly exaggerated. Vice-president Gore and Ehrlich even hint that increased UV may make the AIDS epidemic more virulent.[38]

By contrast, Johns Hopkins University dermatologist Dr. Warwick Morison calls the evidence for UV immunosuppression in human beings "very incomplete."[39]

Apocalyptics are also fanning fears of UV-induced epidemics. But the United Nations Environmental Program report admits, "It should be stressed that the activation of viruses by UV is unlikely to result in an increased rate of infection."[40]

People can (and already should) avoid the consequences of excessive exposure to natural levels of UV by using sunscreen, sunglasses, hats, and body-covering clothes despite the contemptuous dismissals of environmental activists of these activities as merely half-measures.

In any case it is not even clear that global ozone is really declining. University of Virginia environmental scientist S. Fred Singer notes that extracting tiny trends from the data is fraught with difficulty because the "natural variability [in ozone levels] is hundreds of times larger than the alleged steady change."[41] In the 1960s the ozone layer "thickened" by 5 percent over the United States. The "thinning" in the 1980s just about brings ozone down to earlier levels, which were not thought to be harmful at the time.

In March 1992, meteorologists Dirk De Muer and his colleagues at the Belgian Meteorological Institute published a study showing that the instruments used to measure ozone have probably mistaken reductions in atmospheric sulfur dioxide (due to air pollution controls) for declines in global ozone. The reduced sulfur dioxide, they wrote, "has induced a fictitious Dobson total ozone trend of -1.69% per decade." The researchers found that, once the sulfur dioxide trends are taken into account, there appears to be a small *upward* trend in global ozone.[42]

If ozone has declined globally, we should already be able to measure an increase in ultraviolet light at the surface. However, scientists find no evidence of increased UV reaching the surface in the Northern Hemisphere. In fact, the network of Robertson-Berger meters that measure UV showed "an average surface ultraviolet radiation trend of

–8% from 1974 to 1985 using RB-meter data from eight stations located in the mainland United States."[43] Paradoxically, UV over the United States is declining although the ozone layer is supposedly thinning. Climate apocalyptics typically dismiss the data by saying that the RB meters "drifted" or are located in polluted areas which mask UV increases. John DeLuisi, at the National Oceanic and Atmospheric Administration, rigorously checked the RB meters and found "little or no drift."[44]

Furthermore, the intensity of UV in the *rural* midlatitude Northern Hemisphere (the U.S.) has declined by between 5 percent and 18 percent during this century, according to National Oceanic and Atmospheric Administration scientist Shaw Liu. He attributes the lessened UV to an increase in clouds and low-level haze resulting from industrial activities.[45] University of Virginia climatologist Patrick Michaels suggests that in the eastern U.S., water vapor and volatile organic compounds released by vegetation actually contribute more to the UV-obscuring haze.[46] Michaels points out that if we were somehow to eliminate the haze, "the increase in skin cancer would far outweigh anything caused by what we may have done in the midlatitude stratosphere."[47]

Moreover, it is wrong to draw conclusions about what might happen to the atmosphere over the United States based on the Antarctic ozone hole. "It's a purely localized phenomenon," says Guy Brasseur at the National Center for Atmospheric Research in Boulder, Colorado. The polar vortex limits its size. The ozone hole occurs in the cold dark stratospheric ice clouds that form over the Antarctic in winter. Such clouds and chemistry can exist only when temperatures fall below – 80C degrees. Brasseur points out that the ozone hole started only after chlorine concentrations had risen above a threshold of two parts per billion in the 1970s. He expects the hole to disappear when chlorine levels drop below that in the next century.[48]

Conditions are less conducive to ozone destruction at the North Pole than at the South. In contrast to Antarctica, the Arctic polar vortex tends to break up before sunlight can reach it, owing to atmospheric turbulence caused by the more variable geography of the Northern Hemisphere. The Arctic is warmer than the Antarctic, so ice clouds there are smaller or don't form at all. Moreover, cold air over the Arctic is dispersed before the sunlight needed to fuel the chlorine reactions reaches it in the spring. Consequently, scientists have detected only some small wintertime reductions in ozone over the Arctic.[49]

So why the furor over a possible ozone hole in the Northern Hemisphere in the spring of 1992? The chief reason was that atmospheric scientists detected elevated levels (1.5 parts per billion) of ozone-destroying chlorine monoxide. Despite the crisis atmosphere generated by NASA's publicity campaign in February 1992, scientists had been predicting since the summer before that global ozone might decline substantially in 1992.[50] Why?

In June 1991, the Mount Pinatubo volcano in the Philippines blasted up to twenty million tons of sulfur into the skies. In the atmosphere, volcanic sulfur is transformed into sulfuric acid droplets, which act like polar stratospheric clouds by sequestering the nitrogen compounds that inhibit the formation of chlorine monoxide.[51] The evidence strongly suggests that the 1992 chlorine monoxide peak in the Northern Hemisphere resulted from the sulfurous Pinatubo eruption. Linwood Callis, a scientist in the Atmospheric Sciences Division at NASA's Langley Research Center, found that after the El Chichón volcano erupted in the early 1980s, ozone was significantly reduced worldwide. In August 1991, Guy Brasseur predicted "a substantial ozone decrease especially in the mid- and high-latitudes, and especially in winter." He predicted wintertime ozone losses due to the volcano of up to 15 percent.[52] NOAA's renowned atmospheric chemist Susan Solomon predicted even more dramatic reductions might occur, perhaps as much as 30 percent in the spring in the midlatitudes.[53] So when NASA created a Northern Hemisphere ozone hole scare, it wasn't exactly a secret that the ozone layer might become a bit frayed in 1992.

"I couldn't understand why NASA didn't come out and say that this could be a very unusual year because of the volcanic eruptions, that maybe what we're seeing is something we'll never see again," mused David Hofmann, an ozone expert at NOAA. "Instead, they seemed to imply that this is the start of something really big. That really wasn't very wise. If there's a major ozone depletion seen this year, it's quite likely that it is related to the volcano."[54] Of course, Hofmann failed to factor in NASA's budget considerations.

Despite elevated levels of chlorine monoxide and the attendant NASA hype, scientists found no evidence of an ozone hole opening up over the Northern Hemisphere in 1992. However, sulfur from Mount Pinatubo and some Southern Hemisphere volcanoes did hasten the opening of the annual Antarctic ozone hole in 1992.

A small Arctic ozone hole could develop during an exceptionally cold, still winter, but it would be a very rare and transitory occurrence.[55] Also, if it ever did appear, it would be in February and early March, when plants and animals in the Northern Hemisphere are dormant and when people are generally indoors or are well covered and sunlight is weak.

While currently the scientific consensus is that the higher levels of CFCs are responsible for the Antarctic ozone hole,[56] some distinguished scientists still think that it may turn out to be a natural and transitory phenomenon. University of Virginia environmental scientist Fred Singer points out that Sir G. M. B. Dobson, the inventor of the machine that measures ozone, reported very low ozone values—only 150 Dobson units—over Halley Bay, Antarctica, in 1956 and 1957.[57] (By contrast, in the 1960s and 1970s, the level was over 300 Dobson units.) Two French scientists recently republished data showing pronounced ozone decreases, down to 120 Dobson units, during the Antarctic spring in 1958.[58] These measurements were taken years before CFCs could have caused any such decline.

The creation of the hole is not dependent solely on the presence of chlorine, but also on intensely cold temperatures. NOAA meteorologist Walter Komhyr links both Antarctic ozone depletion and global declines to sea surface temperatures in the eastern equatorial Pacific Ocean.[59] Analyzing data from the past twenty-five years, Komhyr and his colleagues found that when the eastern equatorial Pacific cooled between 1962 and 1975, global ozone increased. Conversely, when temperatures warmed between 1976 and 1988, ozone declined worldwide.

Warm sea surface temperatures dampen the circulation patterns that replenish ozone supplies at the poles with the huge quantities of ozone produced in the tropics, and also retard the winds that generally break up the circumpolar vortex at the beginning of the Antarctic spring. A stable vortex lasting through September and October prevents stratospheric warming that would short-circuit the ozone-destroying chlorine chemistry, which can only take place in sunlight at temperatures below − 80C degrees.

Timing is crucial to Komhyr's analysis. He notes that the British Antarctic Survey first saw small declines in ozone in the mid-1970s. This is important, because that is also exactly when Pacific sea surface temperatures rose, which Komhyr explains leads to springtime stratospheric temperatures below − 80C degrees. He has observed the correlation of cold sea surface temperatures followed by high levels of ozone in the Antarctic spring in twenty-one of the twenty-seven years between 1962 and 1988.[60]

As further evidence, Komhyr points out that Pacific sea surface temperatures fell drastically in 1988, which would lead, if his analysis is correct, to less ozone loss over Antarctica. In fact, stratospheric temperatures warmed quickly in 1988 and ozone declined to only 250 Dobson units, a level found periodically in the 1960s and 1970s, and higher than the level of 150 Dobson units and below found when ozone loss is greatest.[61] One implication is that if sea surface temperatures should fall and stay low, the ozone hole could disappear, despite the chlorine.

After publishing these data, Komhyr says that a number of angry atmospheric chemists called him on the carpet, arguing that his findings threatened the funding for further research on CFCs.

If the Antarctic ozone hole may not be due solely to CFCs, what about global reductions in ozone levels? The U.N.'s *Scientific Assessment of the Stratospheric Ozone, 1991* acknowledges that "there is not a full accounting of the observed downward trends in global ozone." The panel nevertheless insists on attributing global ozone loss chiefly to chlorine and bromine reactions apparently because they "are the only ones for which direct evidence exists."[62] In other words, we'll blame CFCs because it's the only explanation we have right now.

As noted earlier, however, NOAA's Komhyr thinks that some of the decline in global ozone is due to changes in global circulation. Since the mid-1970s, he explains, weaker tropical winds have failed to transport ozone-rich air from the equator to the higher latitudes.[63]

Linwood Callis analyzes the destructive effects on ozone of highly energetic electrons, the sunspot cycle, volcanic eruptions, the dilution effect from the Antarctic ozone hole, and changing tropical wind patterns. He calculates that fully "73% of the the global O_3 declines between 1979 and 1985 are due to natural effects related to solar variability. . . ."[64] "CFCs come in a very poor last as the cause for lower levels of global ozone," says Callis.[65] He also points out that satellites show global ozone made "a significant recovery between 1985 and May of 1990."[66] Since we passed the solar maximum in 1991, we can expect ozone levels to decline naturally until the buildup to the next solar maximum begins later in the decade.

Radical environmentalists often decry the fourteen years supposedly lost to inaction after Rowland and Molina first made their predictions about CFCs and ozone. But it's not as if there was nothing to lose by imposing an immediate ban on the chemicals. Environmentalists tend to discount the real and substantial contribution to human well-being that CFCs have made.

Cheap refrigeration made possible by CFCs has been a tremendous boon. For millennia humans died because they could not prevent food from rotting or becoming contaminated with disease-carrying organisms. Cheap refrigeration permits fresh and healthy foods to be transported by truck, train, and boat to markets thousands of miles from where they are grown and harvested. While primitive methods of long-term food preservation such as salting and smoking filled foods with huge quantities of potent carcinogens, CFC-based refrigeration saved millions of lives and enabled billions of people to enjoy a much higher quality diet of fresh meats, fruits, and vegetables.

Crusading environmentalists can now point to new substitutes for CFCs. But many are toxic and flammable, making them far less safe to handle. In addition, the substitutes cost three to five times more. The extra cost will delay the spread of desperately needed refrigeration to the developing world where food spoilage is a huge problem. It is probably inevitable that many people will continue to go hungry because of the CFC ban.

"The costs to the country for the termination of CFCs are going to be phenomenal," says NOAA's Melvyn Shapiro. "Globally, it will cost hundreds of billions of dollars. They have alternative substances, but they're flammable. Do I have to worry about the air-conditioning unit in my car turning into a grenade? About my refrigerator blowing up?"[67]

Aside from the cost of a ban, governments and companies have had to contend with ambiguous data and shifting conclusions about the impact of CFCs on the ozone layer. How many times have theories, put forth in good faith, been shown later to be wrong? Recall that in 1972, a very distinguished group of scientists, including Jay Forrester and Dennis and Donella Meadows, predicted in the Club of Rome's *The Limits to Growth* that we would run out of oil in only twenty years. Our government acted on that prediction, making energy conservation the "moral equivalent of war," and ended up wasting billions of dollars on subsidies for synthetic fuels programs.

138

Or consider the dire predictions of activists like Jeremy Rifkin, who warned that biotechnology would let deadly new microbes run amok and upset the balance of nature. Had we acted on such fears and banned biotechnology in the 1970s, humanity would have foregone the new miracle drugs and agricultural products that now promise to alleviate the suffering of the sick and the hunger of the poor. Today scientists agree that early concerns about the hazards of biotechnology were overblown, and the Bush administration moved in 1992 to speed up the approval of foods and drugs produced through genetic manipulation.

There is ample reason to doubt similarly catastrophic warnings about CFCs and the ozone layer. It's instructive to recall that climate catastrophists like Stephen Schneider and Carl Sagan claimed that CFCs were particularly potent greenhouse gases, adding as much as 25 percent to increased global temperatures.[68] But they failed to take into account the first law of ecology: Everything is connected to everything else. Ozone, too, is a potent greenhouse gas and so when CFCs destroy it the atmosphere tends to cool. According to NASA, ozone decreases largely offset predicted increases in global temperatures due to CFCs.[69] "What had been thought was a major greenhouse gas turns out to be having a cooling effect," noted EPA Administrator William Reilly.[70]

Nevertheless, despite a great deal of continuing scientific uncertainty, it appears that CFCs do contribute to the creation of the Antarctic ozone hole and perhaps to a tiny amount of global ozone depletion. If CFCs were allowed to build up in the atmosphere during the next century, ozone depletion might eventually entail significant costs. More ultraviolet light reaching the surface would require adaptation—switching to new crop varieties, for example—and it might boost the incidence of nonfatal skin cancer. In light of these costs, it makes sense to phase out the use of CFCs.

But ozone depletion is certainly not the "global emergency" that environmentalists like Friends of the Earth's Elizabeth Cook say it is.[71] Ozone depletion is not part of some generalized, overarching environmental crisis. It is a nuisance caused by specific chemicals, which are even now being replaced.

The normal processes of science and democratic decision-making have proved adequate to correct what might have become a significant problem. In 1990 our national and international institutions hammered out an agreement to control CFCs, the London Agreement to the Montreal Protocol, which takes the interests of all affected groups into account (though imperfectly). Calls to abandon a moderate course of action and push up the deadline for the CFC ban are based on exaggerated fears and unrealistic predictions. On the evidence so far, despite the lurid crisis-mongering of radical environmentalists, waiting for more information on CFCs and ozone did not cause any great harm to people or to earth's ecosystems, nor will it.

Radical environmentalists, like Ehrlich and Michael Oppenheimer of the Environmental Defense Fund, argue that the experience with ozone depletion should teach us to respond swiftly and dramatically to the threat of global warming. Rafe Pomerance of the World Resources Institute says the international negotiations over CFCs were merely a dress rehearsal for drastic reductions in carbon dioxide emissions aimed at preventing global climate change.[72] While replacing CFCs eventually will cost billions, the price tag for abating carbon dioxide could run as high as $600 billion a year.[73]

The environmentalists are right to suggest that the example of ozone depletion is relevant to the debate over global warming. But the example bolsters the conclusion that humanity should be highly skeptical of environmental apocalypses. The relevant lesson is not "He who hesitates is lost," but rather, "Look before you leap."

NINE
THE SKY IS FALLING

"The beginning of the end," warns Paul Ehrlich.[1] "The mother of all environmental scares," says University of California at Berkeley political scientist Aaron Wildavsky.[2] Both men are talking about "global warming," the latest and greatest apocalypse being peddled by environmental doomsters.

Global warming first caught the public's attention on a sweltering 99F-degree day in June 1988 when Goddard Institute for Space Studies scientist James Hansen told a U.S. Senate Energy Committee that he was "99 percent confident" that the warmer weather in the 1980s was due to an enhanced "greenhouse effect," which he said is caused by rising levels of carbon dioxide in the atmosphere produced by—what else?—industrial civilization. Hansen's work at Goddard was funded in part by the Environmental Defense Fund.[3]

Hansen's dramatic testimony was carefully choreographed by one of the Senate's leading environmental zealots, Senator Timothy Wirth (D-Colo.). Wirth chose to hold the hearing on June 23 because it once had been the hottest day on record in Washington. It was a very propitious bit of timing—just as the temporary success of the Arab oil embargo in the 1970s convinced many that *The Limits to Growth* was true, so too did the summer drought of 1988 convince skeptics that global warming was real. The global warming story hit the front page of *The New York Times*. "Journalists loved it. Environmentalists were ecstatic," crowed born-again global warmer Stephen Schneider.[4]

In America, no crisis is without its literary popularizer. A former "Talk of the Town" writer at *The New Yorker*, Bill McKibben, in his book *The End of Nature*, spelled out the horrors that purportedly will attend the imminent increase in worldwide temperatures. According to McKibben, the "greenhouse effect" will bring about the end of nature. Earth is doomed to heat up by as much as 10F degrees as a consequence of heedless economic growth and industrialization. He predicts rising seas, longer droughts, withered crops, more powerful hurricanes, and hotter weather.

At the Earth Summit in 1992, most of the world's nations signed the Convention on Global Climate Change. By signing this treaty the world's governments officially endorsed the scientifically controversial notion that the earth faces the prospect of catastrophic warming.

This most recent apocalypse fits the classic pattern for millenarian doomsaying. Humanity has brought impending doom down upon itself. Some might escape if we repent and sacrifice. A small self-appointed vanguard of volunteers offer to lead us to the promised land in a postcrisis egalitarian utopia. "Warming (and warming alone), through its primary antidote of withdrawing carbon from production and consumption, is capable of realizing the environmentalist's dream of an egalitarian society based on the rejection of economic growth in favor of a smaller population eating lower on the food chain, consuming a lot less, and sharing a much lower level of resources much more equally," notes Wildavsky.[5]

Not surprisingly, leading the global warming parade are the customary crowd of notorious apocalypse abusers like Paul Ehrlich, the Club of Rome, Lester Brown, Jeremy Rifkin, Carl Sagan, Barry Commoner, and Stephen Schneider.

The public has once again been stampeded by lurid stories on television and in the press into believing that doom is just around the corner. A recent poll showed that 74 percent of Americans think the greenhouse effect is a serious problem. Forty-one percent believe that it is a "very serious problem."[6]

The science underlying greenhouse warming is straightforward. Without its atmosphere, earth would be a lifeless iceball with an average temperature of 0F (-18C) degrees. The earth reflects much of the heat from the sun back toward space. Fortunately for us, some of the reflected heat is trapped by gases in the lower atmosphere, especially water vapor, which reradiate enough of it back toward the surface, warming the atmosphere and providing us our equable climate. In fact, if all other greenhouse gases other than water vapor, like carbon dioxide and methane, were to disappear, the earth would still be left with over 98 percent of the current greenhouse effect.[7]

(The "greenhouse effect" is actually a misnomer. Greenhouses keep warm by preventing outside breezes from cooling the air inside them, not by trapping and reradiating heat.)

Swedish scientist Svante Arrhenius identified carbon dioxide (CO_2) as a greenhouse gas at the end of the nineteenth century. He calculated that a doubling of atmospheric CO_2 could mean a 7- to 10F-degree increase in temperature worldwide. Arrhenius's work lay largely ignored until it was revised in the late 1950s by Roger Revelle and Hans Suess. However, since global temperatures were then declining, Revelle and Suess's work did not cause much of a stir, although a permanent observatory was set up during the International Geophysical Year 1957–58 on Mauna Loa in Hawaii to monitor atmospheric carbon dioxide.

Throughout the global cooling period stretching from 1940 to 1975, atmospheric scientists often mentioned the greenhouse effect as an aside. This turns out to be the obverse side of the climate catastrophists' loaded coin toss, "Tails I win, heads you lose." If the climate continued to cool, then humanity would have been to blame because of the particulates we inject into the atmosphere. If the climate warmed, then we would be culpable because of the CO_2 we emit. Freeze or fry, industrial civilization is at fault.

Human activity has increased the amount of CO_2 and other greenhouse gases (chiefly methane and chlorofluorocarbons) in the earth's atmosphere, largely through burning coal and oil and cutting down forests. Annual CO_2 emission from burning fossil fuels is about 5 billion metric tons, and forest clearing may contribute another 1 to 2 billion tons, although this is now being questioned. While environmental activists rush to claim that "accelerating" deforestation is adding substantial amounts of carbon dioxide to the atmosphere, recent measurements of the ratio of carbon isotopes in ocean water by a team of American, Canadian, and Australian scientists indicate that "there has been no significant net CO_2 released from the biosphere during the last 20 years."[8] They conclude that global deforestation and forest regrowth must be nearly in balance.[9] In fact, expanding temperate forests in Europe and North America are probably acting as "sinks" to sequester carbon dioxide released through tropical deforestation.[10] Forest cover in the United States has expanded from its low of 464 million acres in the 1920s to more than 728 million acres today.[11]

Nevertheless, only half the amount emitted—3 billion tons—ever appears in the atmosphere.[12] Many scientists think that the world's oceans absorb the missing carbon dioxide.[13] Other scientists believe that earth's land plants may be absorbing as much 3.4 billion tons of surplus carbon dioxide.[14] The earth's preindustrial atmosphere, around 1850, is thought to have contained about 275 to 290 parts per million of CO_2[15] while today's atmosphere contains about 355 parts per million.[16]

Attempting to predict the behavior of the earth's climate, some climatologists have created complicated computer models, called General Circulation Models (GCMs). Today, the leading climate models calculate that doubling carbon dioxide to 600 parts per million should increase average global temperatures between 1.5C and 4.5C degrees (2.7F and 8.1F degrees). Note that the higher figure is very close to the values calculated by Arrhenius a century earlier. However, recent projections made by German and British GCMs lowered predicted global warming to only 1.8 to 3.4F (1 to 1.9C) degrees.[17]

The models are far from perfect—they must be "tuned" in order to achieve global warming. The researchers cannot predict climate from first principles, but must instead put information in "by hand." Some move earth closer to the sun, while others change sea surface temperatures from their actual measurements to get the "right" results—global warming. Nearly all the models would melt the polar ice caps, even during the last ice age.[18] Even now, the models can not calculate correctly either the present average temperature of the earth or the equator-to-pole temperature distribution.[19]

The tuning adjustments to the models are greater than the effects which they are supposed to predict. The distinguished MIT climatologist Richard Lindzen pointedly notes, "The computer climate models are a case of GIGO—'garbage in, garbage out.' " The models' arbitrary parameters are carefully calibrated to provide the desired answer: catastrophic global warming.[20] Andrew Solow, a climate statistician from Woods Hole Oceanographic Institution, concurs: "These models have a hard time reproducing current climate from current data. They cannot be expected to predict future climate with any precision."[21]

One telling example of how the models go awry is the case of chlorofluorocarbons. CFCs, which are implicated in destroying stratospheric ozone (see Chapter Eight), are also greenhouse gases. In fact, 20 to 25 percent of the greenhouse effect had been attributed to the buildup of CFCs.[22] How-

145

ever, ozone is also a potent greenhouse gas. Taking the rise of CFCs into account along with the simultaneous reduction in ozone, CFCs produce no net increase in global warming. "It's a net wash to zero," says Dan Albritton of the National Oceanic and Atmospheric Administration.[23] Getting the net effect of CFCs wrong means that climate model projections of future greenhouse warming were greatly exaggerated. Projected global temperatures plunged once the models correctly accounted for CFCs.

With regard to global warming, the environmental apocalyptics again happily ignore the "first law of ecology," which says that "everything is connected to everything else."[24] The earth's atmosphere/ocean system is a dynamic process that is far from being completely understood. Characteristically, apocalyptics search for positive (destabilizing) feedback loops which would accelerate temperature increases, while more careful scientists point out that there are also negative (stabilizing) feedbacks which may well mitigate increases in temperature as we will see below.

The current GCMs depend on a destabilizing feedback loop in which higher surface temperatures increase upper tropospheric water vapor (five to twelve kilometers up), which is the major greenhouse gas. "Without this feedback, no current model would predict warming in excess of 1.7C (3F) degrees," says climatologist Lindzen. The physics of upper tropospheric water vapor is simply unknown, and some models actually produce regions of *negative* water vapor—a physical impossibility. He adds that each destabilizing feedback loop included in the models might actually be stabilizing feedback.[25]

Outside of the models, what has the earth's temperature actually been doing? The answer is, changing. Scientists have barely a century's worth of scanty global temperature data which indicate that over the last century earth's temperature apparently increased by less than one degree Fahrenheit. Between 1890 and 1940 the planet warmed by 0.9F degrees and afterward cooled about one half a degree until 1975, when it warmed up again. Most of the recent warming occurred between 1976 and 1980, with little change since then despite the numerous scare headlines about how x number of the hottest years on record occurred during the 1980s.[26] Andrew Solow dismisses these stories, noting that the largest values in any alleged trend will *always* by definition occur in the most recent years.[27] "We must be prepared to accept the idea that weather and climate records, like those in sports, are always being broken—everywhere, in any season . . . This is the way the ball bounces climatologically: I would be more concerned if records stopped falling by the wayside,"[28] says Harvard researcher Peter Rogers.

According to the headlines, 1990 was the "warmest year on record." But NASA space scientist Roy Spencer, using extremely precise satellite global temperature data, showed that 1990 was actually only the third warmest year of the last thirteen years for which we have satellite data. In 1990, just by chance according to Spencer, it was relatively warmer over those areas of the globe where most of the land-based thermometers are located. Temperature data from these thermometers in North America, Japan, and Europe skewed the results, leading to claims that 1990 was especially warm.[29]

To the dismay of the apocalypse boosters, their data, on which the headlines are based, appear to be simply wrong. Satellites orbiting the earth for the last thirteen years that detect atmospheric temperature differences as small as 0.01C degrees confirm that there has been only a statistically insignificant upward trend of 0.06C degrees in global atmospheric temperatures during the 1980s.[30] This is only a fifth of the 0.3C degrees rate of decadal change predicted by the Intergovernmental Panel on Climate Change report.[31]

Atmospheric scientist John Christy at the University of Alabama in Huntsville notes that even this minor upward trend will turn negative as the sulfate pall caused by the eruption of the Mount Pinatubo volcano in 1991 cools in the earth over the next couple of years. Christy points out that the satellite data also call into question the accuracy of the century-long temperature trends obtained chiefly from land-based thermometers. At the end of 1990, the satellite data detected only a 0.06C-degree increase while land-based thermometers often cited by global warmers showed a 0.19C-degree decadal rise. Given the precision of the satellite data, the land-based thermometers may have been overestimating warming by 300 percent over the last thirteen years.[32] Based on this data, Spencer and Christy both conclude that there is not much scientific basis to fear catastrophic global warming.

The century-long pattern of warming, cooling, and then warming again also presents the climate alarmists with a big problem. According to the climate models, warming should occur in step with increases in greenhouse gases, but it hasn't. As we have seen, most of the warming found in the temperature record occurred between 1890 and 1940. This is a problem because greenhouse gases were at significantly lower levels in the first half of the twentieth century than they are now, yet most of the warming occurred then. Some scientists argue that the pre-1940 warming represents the earth's recovery from the Little Ice Age (A.D. 1400–1890). Such a natural recovery would wipe out the warming attributable to an enhanced greenhouse effect.[33]

The view that the earth's temperatures are bouncing back from a recent global cold snap is bolstered by the findings of two Canadian scientists, Kevin Wang and Trevor Lewis. Past surface temperatures migrate into the ground and can be detected through measurements in deep boreholes. Using the data from three boreholes, Wang and Lewis concluded that "the recent warming might be partially or mostly a return from a cold period" which occurred at the end of the nineteenth century.[34]

The models exhibit other problems as well. University of Virginia climatologist Patrick Michaels calculates that according to the models, the earth should have warmed up in the last fifty years by at least 2.2F (1.2C) degrees.[35] The oceans absorb huge quantities of heat, causing a delay in atmospheric temperature changes. If this ocean lag were removed, then the global average temperature should already have risen by 2.1C degrees (3.7F degrees). Instead temperatures have increased by a negligible 0.45F (0.25C) degrees in the last fifty years. Even arch–global warmer and would-be planetary savior Stephen Schneider acknowledges that the models predict 1.8F (1C) degrees warming over the last century while the temperature record shows only half that, that is, a 0.9F (0.5C) degree increase.[36]

Even that half-degree-centigrade increase may be too great, according to Arizona State University climatologist Robert Balling. He calculates that if the urban heat island effect, desertification trends, and stratospheric aerosol variations, all of which tend to increase temperatures, are taken into account, "at least half of the global warming of the past century can be explained by non-greenhouse phenomena."[37]

The predicted warming trend is an average for the whole globe—the models predict some dramatic regional differences. For example, the models forecast that the temperatures around the North Pole should already have increased significantly, by as much as 4.1F (2.3C) degrees. In fact, if ocean lag time is eliminated, most models predict that polar wintertime temperatures should already have increased by as much as 32F (18C) degrees.[38] However, temperatures in the north polar region have instead *dropped* by 1.8F (1C) degrees during the past fifty years.[39]

Greenhouse alarmists warn that global warming could melt the massive continental glaciers on Antarctica and Greenland, causing sea levels to rise by scores of feet, inundating New York, London, Houston, and Washington, D.C., and low-lying areas like Florida, Bangladesh, and the Maldive Islands.[40] "Sea level rise seems the most probable and perhaps most globally uniform consequence of warming projected into the next century," concluded Schneider.[41] In 1990, Paul Ehrlich reported on NBC's *Today* show that rising temperatures could cause the West Antarctic ice sheet to slip, raising the level of the sea by twenty feet in only a few years. He warned, "The Supreme Court would be flooded. You could tie your boat to the Washington Monument. Storm surges would make the Capitol unusable."[42]

New Yorkers, Londoners, and Bangladeshis can relax. Recent evidence shows that instead of melting away, there has been a "significant increase" in the accumulation of snow and ice in Antarctica. In addition, the West Antarctic ice sheet is stable and still reacting to the changes that occurred at the end of the last ice age.[43] The Greenland ice cap is also growing.[44] So instead of sea levels rising, the accumulation of ice should lower them by a little over one millimeter per year.[45] Another apocalypse avoided.

All of the climate models predict that the Northern Hemisphere should warm up much faster than the Southern Hemisphere. The idea is that the Northern Hemisphere contains most of the world's land, which heats up faster than water, while 90 percent of the Southern Hemisphere is covered with water. The climate record shows that in the last fifty years there has been no net warming in the northern half of our planet, while temperatures have increased 0.45F (0.25C) degrees in the southern part—just the opposite of what the models predict.[46]

The measurements of carbon dioxide trapped in ice cores from Antarctica and Greenland, which the climate catastrophists use to bolster their claims for global warming, have been seriously called into question. According to previous analyses of the ice cores, global temperatures and carbon dioxide levels seem to fluctuate in tandem. There has always been some question of which comes first, higher temperatures followed by increases in CO_2 or vice versa. Now, however, two Norwegian scientists and a Japanese colleague find that pervasive chemical reactions within glaciers greatly change gas concentrations within glacial ice. Consequently, gases obtained from ice cores do not represent the gas concentrations of ancient atmospheres. Also, between 36 and 100 percent of air recovered from old ice is contaminated by recent atmospheric air during field and laboratory operations and thus is useless for determining CO_2 concentrations in earlier times.[47] The Norwegian and Japanese researchers conclude that glaciological studies were "not able to provide a reliable reconstruction of neither [sic] the CO_2 level in the pre-industrial and ancient atmospheres nor paleoclimates. Instead these studies led to a widely accepted false dogma on man-made climatic warming."[48]

As discussed earlier, doomsayers indiscriminately latch on to and publicize just about any natural anomaly or local disaster as evidence to bolster their predictions of impending worldwide catastrophe. The global warming scare has proven to be no different. For example, global warmers regularly cite shrinking sea ice and snow cover, algae blooms in the ocean,[49] bleaching coral reefs, and warming detected in the Arctic tundra's soil as purported evidence for impending catastrophic warming.

Since 1979, sea ice and snow cover in the Northern Hemisphere have been shrinking slightly. Recall, however, that scientists were very worried because sea ice and snow cover were expanding dramatically during the 1960s and 1970s when the planet was cooling. Unless the earth is entering a new ice age, one would expect some natural decrease in both after a heavy buildup. By choosing to begin an alleged trend from a maximum value, the climate catastrophists are simply engaging in one of their characteristic distortions. If a longer period of the records is taken into account, it is readily apparent that the amount of snow cover and ice fluctuates naturally.[50]

Global warming could not be responsible for algae blooms or coral bleaching since there has been no net change in the ocean temperatures for fifty years and mean ocean temperatures of the warmest months have actually *fallen*.[51] Scientists have discovered that large algae blooms occurred regularly more than one thousand years ago when there were no enhanced greenhouse gases.[52] U.S. Geological Survey scientist James Lachenbruch drilled test holes in Arctic permafrost and found there had been warming in the region sometime during the last hundred years. According to British temperature records, the Arctic did warm by 2 to 4C degrees earlier in the century. But the warming occurred before greenhouse gases accumulated to significant levels.

Contrary to the models' predictions, the Arctic has experienced a net cooling in the past fifty years.[53] One prediction is certain to come true: in the future climate apocalyptics will assiduously press every slightly out-of-the-ordinary natural event into service as further evidence of the impending greenhouse catastrophe.

Other than the model predictions, is there any hard evidence for global warming caused by mankind's changes in the atmosphere's chemistry? In a bit of misleading intellectual sleight of hand, Schneider and fellow global warmers ceaselessly point to the 0.9F (0.5C) degree increase during the last century, while very quietly acknowledging there is no evidence that the increase can be attributed to accumulating greenhouse gases. "At the level of global temperature change to date (about 0.5C degrees), the noise in the natural climate variability is simply too large to be able to clearly detect a greenhouse effect signal," concedes Schneider.[54] In 1990, even the United Nations Intergovernmental Panel on Climate Change (IPCC), a group strongly biased toward supporting the greenhouse effect hypothesis, admitted, "It is not possible to attribute all, or even a large part, of the observed global-mean warming to the enhanced greenhouse effect on the basis of observational data currently available."[55]

If James Hansen is 99 percent sure that he has detected global warming, how sure are other scientists? "We have no evidence whatsoever that greenhouse warming has begun," says Richard Lindzen. "When you look at the record of climate you see this kind of fluctuation going on all the time, and to say that a few warm decades mean something significant is just ridiculous," notes Andrew Solow.[56] Even the IPCC does not believe that Hansen has detected the "global warming signal," pronouncing that "the unequivocal detection of the enhanced greenhouse effect from observations is not likely for a decade or more."[57]

Many climatologists believe that there may eventually be some warming associated with increased atmospheric CO_2, but nothing like the climate disaster predicted by the apocalyptics. Lindzen thinks that over the next century "a virtually undetectable rise of a few tenths of a degree might occur."[58] Robert Balling says, "the temperature record of the past century suggests that a doubling of carbon dioxide will produce a global temperature response at the lowest end of the model predictions, probably not more than 1.0C degrees."[59] Patrick Michaels also believes global temperature might rise as much as 1.0C (1.8F) degrees.

Even the Intergovernmental Panel on Climate Change (IPCC) in its 1992 report lowered its estimates of global temperature increases and sea level rise by 20 to 30 percent under its 1990 projections.[60] These reductions occurred because the climate models now take into account the CO_2 fertilization effect and the lower net warming effects of chlorofluorocarbons. While these predicted increases are still beyond the limits of natural variability, it should be kept in mind that as the climate models are refined, the greenhouse catastrophe recedes. Now, the IPCC's best guess is that global temperatures might rise by 2.5C degrees—half of the original projections—and ever closer to the 1C degree predictions of the greenhouse skeptics.[61]

Several feedback mechanisms may actually cool the planet. As temperatures rise, more water evaporates and some of it becomes clouds. Depending on the type, clouds can act as blankets keeping the earth warm or as mirrors that cool it by reflecting heat back into space. On balance it seems that "clouds have a global *cooling* effect."[62] A 5-percent increase in clouds would completely offset all of the greenhouse warming predicted by the models.[63] And the world is becoming cloudier[64]: both the U.S. and Europe are considerably cloudier than they were at the beginning of the century.[65]

As the world becomes cloudier, precipitation worldwide should also increase.[66] In fact, the 1980s were the wettest decade on record for the United States, according to the National Climatic Data Center. This bodes well for American agriculture because a lack of water limits agricultural productivity far more than temperatures do. After all, rain forests are renowned for their biological productivity despite high average temperatures. Paleoclimatologists also point out that six to eight thousand years ago when the earth was substantially warmer, the Sahara Desert was a well-watered grassland supporting a huge variety of animal and plant life.

Cloudiness also reduces temperature differences between day and night. During the day clouds cool the surface by reflecting heat back into space, while at night they keep the surface warm by acting as blankets. The National Climatic Data Center's Tom Karl and his colleagues recently confirmed this effect. Karl found that since 1951 the average nighttime temperatures in China, the former Soviet Union, and the U.S. increased while average daytime temperatures show "little or no warming."[67] Virtually all of the warming in the Northern Hemisphere can be attributed to increases in average nighttime highs. Average maximum daytime temperatures in China and the U.S. actually fell.[68] "The evidence suggests that changes in cloud cover played a direct role" in causing these temperature trends.[69] The computer climate models fail to account for this effect.

Since growing seasons are limited by the last spring frost and the onset of the first autumn frost, warmer nights mean that crop-damaging freezes will start later in the fall and end earlier in the spring. Cooler days and warmer nights would also mean that water would be conserved because plants would suffer less overall evaporation.[70] This is hardly a recipe for a climate disaster.

Another consequence of increased cloudiness is that winters should be warmer and summers cooler in midlatitude countries like the United States or those in Europe. This is because clouds will shade long summer days while long winter nights will be warmed by their cloud blankets. If whatever warming that may occur turns out to be largely confined to the nights, that means the bitterly cold polar nights, when the sun remains below the horizon for months, may warm. Winter temperatures at the poles often hover around −40C degrees, so even the wildest warming predicted by the models, say 18C degrees, could not cause drastic sea level rises due to catastrophic glacial melting.[71]

If warming occurs primarily at night, Patrick Michaels thinks humanity "might be facing the prospect of longer growing seasons, substantially warmed winters with little change in the summers (except, perhaps, a lengthening), and a greener world."[72]

The oceans may harbor another natural "thermostat" tending to cool the planet. Under warmer conditions, certain microscopic marine organisms (phytoplankton) create a gas called dimethyl sulfide (DMS), which acts as condensation nuclei for highly reflective clouds. The clouds cool the surface, which reduces the amount of DMS produced by the phytoplankton, thus regulating surface temperatures.[73]

Despite the accumulating evidence against it, ardent greenhouse proponents continue to prophesy that impending increases in global temperatures will bring on flooded cities, drought-ridden agriculture and famines, more violent hurricanes, prolonged heat waves, and devastated ecosystems. They claim global warming "the most serious threat we have ever faced."[74]

As in the case of the earlier nonrenewable resource depletion and the famine apocalypses, the climate catastrophists claim two things—first that there is a consensus among scientists that what they are predicting is true, and second that the situation is so urgent that we haven't time to quibble over minor uncertainties; we must act immediately.

The apocalyptics are particularly anxious to silence or discredit anyone who disagrees with them. For example, then-Senator Gore tried mightily to force notable greenhouse skeptics, like MIT atmospheric scientist Richard Lindzen, to recant. Gore calls skeptics before his committee and grills them until they cry uncle—the experience is somewhat like good old-fashioned Maoist self-criticism sessions during the Cultural Revolution—and goes so far as to claim in his own recent addition to the literature of apocalyptic environmentalism, *Earth in the Balance,* that Lindzen has recanted. (In 1989, fellow doomster Paul Ehrlich, anxious to claim Lindzen's support for global warming, said that Lindzen had "put his number at a 25 percent chance of big climate change."[75]) Lindzen, for his part, vigorously denies these assertions, and insists that greenhouse warming has not been shown to be a problem.

Gore also is impatient with those who dare to question the approach of the looming apocalypse, stating that "their views sometimes carry far too much weight."[76] He flatly asserted to *Time* magazine in its notorious "Planet of the Year" issue: "That we face an ecological crisis without any precedent in historical terms is no longer a matter of any dispute worthy of recognition." He savagely dismissed greenhouse skeptics, complaining that "those who, for the purpose of maintaining balance in the debate adopt the contrarian view that there is significant uncertainty about whether it's (global warming) real are hurting our ability to respond." Gore in his new book reiterates that press attention (as minuscule as it has been) to greenhouse skeptics "undermines the effort to build a solid base of public support for the difficult actions we must soon take."[77] Simply put—shut up and get with the program. My program.

Gore also implies that 98 percent of atmospheric scientists believe in enhanced greenhouse warming[78]—that figure is probably an accurate reflection of how he has packed his Senate hearings with greenhouse doomsters while excluding more skeptical scientists. A recent Gallup poll conducted for the Institute of Science, Technology and Media found that of those scientists actively involved in global climate research, 53 percent do not believe that global warming has occurred and 30 percent don't know, leaving only 17 percent who believe that global warming has begun—a far cry from Vice-president Gore's near-unanimity. Even global warming propagandist Stephen Schneider admits, "Most climatologists do not yet claim beyond a reasonable doubt that the observed temperature records have been caused by the greenhouse effect."[79] According to Philip Abelson, the distinguished former editor of *Science*, if global warming "is analyzed applying the customary standards of scientific inquiry one must conclude there has been more hype than solid facts."[80]

Nevertheless, Lester Brown calls for a "wholesale reordering, a fundamental restructuring of the world's economy."[81] And Barry Commoner declares, "The increasingly acute global environmental crisis can only be resolved by a comprehensive transformation of the present systems of production."[82] Gore asserts the looming global environmental crisis means we must "change the very foundation of our civilization."[83]

Such demogoguery is what Richard Hofstadter identified as the "paranoid style in politics." Like past political paranoids, they "traffic in the birth and death of whole worlds, whole political orders, whole systems of human values. . . . Time is forever just running out."[84]

But are we running out of time?

No, according to University of Illinois climate modeler Michael Schlesinger. He and his colleague Xingjian Jiang recently calculated that "the penalty is small for a ten year delay in initiating the transition to a regime in which greenhouse-gas emissions are reduced."[85] In other words, we do not now need to make the kind of drastic changes in the world's economy contemplated by the climate catastrophists. We can study the problem for a decade more without making our situation, under even the most apocalyptic assumptions, worse. Roger Revelle, the former director of the Scripps Institution of Oceanography who revived the greenhouse theory in the 1950s (and who first taught Gore about the greenhouse effect), concluded in a recent coauthored article: "*The scientific base for a greenhouse warming is too uncertain to justify drastic action at this time* [emphasis his]."[86]

Gore ignores his old teacher and offers a "global Marshall plan" while calling for just such drastic action. His plan embraces the full policy agenda pushed by the greenhouse doomsters. Gore calls for the massive redistribution of wealth and technology from the industrialized world to the developing world. As we have seen, millenarian

157

environmentalists always want to globalize or internationalize the solutions to the impending apocalypse. Characteristically, Gore advocates creating a United Nations "Stewardship Council," modeled on the Security Council, to deal with global environmental concerns. (This is similar to the Club of Rome's recent U.N. Environmental Security Council proposal.)

Gore also wants to slow economic and population growth and to reduce CO_2 emissions by levying a worldwide "carbon tax" on fossil fuels. Environmentalists constantly assert that a carbon tax would encourage energy efficiency, and surely that must be good, right? A tax, by making something more expensive, forces consumers to use less of it, but how is that more efficient? To use less of just one input, such as energy, by no means automatically improves efficiency as implied by the environmentalists. Which is more efficient—plowing fields with a team of horses or a tractor? With horses the farmer is certainly "saving" gasoline, but he will be unable to plant and harvest nearly as much land.

In June, 1992, at the U.N.'s Earth Summit most of the world's countries signed the Convention on Global Climate Change that committed signatories to devise national plans to reduce their carbon dioxide emissions. The original version of the treaty would have required every nation to freeze its emissions at 1990 levels and gradually cut them back by 20 percent.[87] Is such a treaty enforceable?

The Worldwatch Institute has counted a total of 170 international environmental treaties, two-thirds of which have been adopted since the first U.N. environmental conference at Stockholm in 1972. Are they worth the paper they are printed on? One recent study shows that Norway, a country known for its devotion to environmental causes, has violated 12 of the 28 environmental treaties it signed.[88]

Not surprisingly, environmental millenarians interpret the failure of nations to abide by their agreements as evidence that international governance must be "strengthened."[89] Weak treaty enforcement, of course, dovetails nicely with their globalist ambitions. In order to enforce environmental treaties they argue for a "redefinition of sovereignty." The march toward something like world government remains for the most part unacknowledged by the apocalyptics since they don't want to alarm the public.

"Drastic, precipitous—and, especially unilateral—steps to delay the putative greenhouse impacts can cost jobs and prosperity and increase the human costs of global poverty, without being effective," according to Revelle.[90] Lowering CO_2 emissions would not be cheap. The price tag for abating carbon dioxide could rise as high as $600 billion per year, according to Maurice Strong, the Canadian oilman who served as the secretary-general of the Rio Earth Summit. Strong adds that the industrial nations will have to provide $125 billion more in aid to developing countries to help them lower their CO_2 emissions.[91] At home, it would cost U.S. taxpayers $290 billion per year to reduce CO_2 emissions by 71 percent over the next forty years according to one estimate.[92] Yale economist William Nordhaus estimates that it would cost $200 billion per year to achieve a 50 percent reduction in greenhouse gas emissions.[93]

To achieve the relatively modest goal of capping CO_2 emissions at 20 percent of 1990 levels, the U.S. Department of Energy calculates that it would take a $500 per ton carbon tax. Such measures would cost $95 billion per year and reduce U.S. economic growth rates by 1.4 percent, while more than doubling the price of gasoline and heating oil.[94]

Interestingly, in 1990 global carbon dioxide emissions fell and are likely to continue to fall through 1992. The drop in CO_2 is largely due to the collapse of the centralized economies in Eastern Europe and the former Soviet Union. Furthermore, as former communist countries modernize, they will become far more energy efficient. By the mid-1990s their total emissions could be 30 percent lower, which means that global CO_2 emissions should remain level for the next decade.[95]

Another issue is that many governments are still distorting energy markets in order to encourage the burning of fossil fuels. Recently the World Bank estimated that fossil fuel use is currently subsidized by developing countries to the tune of $139 billion annually. This is equivalent to a *negative* carbon tax of $25 per ton. If the subsidies were cut, higher market prices would lead to an 8 percent reduction in global carbon dioxide emissions. To achieve a similar reduction in the United States, Western Europe, and Japan would require these countries to enact a $50 per ton carbon tax.[96]

Besides, what's the rush? Why immediately reorganize the whole world to meet a crisis that only a few fallible computer models are predicting? We know now how far off the mark the old *Limits to Growth* computer program was. University of Illinois climatologist Michael Schlesinger tells us that we at least have a grace period of ten years in which we can do further research in order to determine whether global warming will be a catastrophe or not. Further research is called for, not massive and disruptive transfers of wealth, changes in technology, and the enlargement of international bureaucracies.

Unfortunately, the fate of acid rain research does not bode well for any future global climate change research program. The federal government's National Acid Precipitation Assessment Program (NAPAP) spent over ten years and $500 million to study the alleged destruction being wrought by acid rain on forests, crops, and lakes in the northeastern United States and southern Canada. "There is no evidence of widespread forest damage from current ambient levels of acidic rain in the United States" was the report's succinct conclusion.[97] NAPAP also found no evidence that acid rain had harmed crops[98] or had caused measurable human health problems.[99] NAPAP soil scientist Edward Krug notes, "We found that the average Adirondack lake is no more acidic now than prior to the Industrial Revolution—not 100-fold more acidic as claimed by the EPA."[100]

Scientific research proved overwhelmingly that acid rain was at most an environmental nuisance, not the environmental catastrophe it was portrayed as being by the apocalyptics. Nevertheless, Congress ignored the NAPAP findings, and under intense pressure from environmental advocacy groups, passed the new Clean Air Act, which will cost the country scores of billions of dollars over the next decade to correct this nonproblem.

Just as in the earlier acid rain controversy, radical environmentalists are demanding that the world's governments act before research can resolve the enormous uncertainties about the consequences and magnitude of global warming. The apocalyptics might succeed in stampeding the world needlessly into adopting stringent limits on carbon dioxide emissions. Such limits would lead to reduced standards of living and wrenching social changes. As shown earlier, many climatologists seriously doubt that global warming will ever be a problem. Unnecessary acid rain regulations will cost only billions, but carbon dioxide controls may cost trillions. The environmentalists who propose sweeping changes in the way the world works have a moral responsibility to prove that the sweeping reforms they advocate are absolutely necessary before humanity is forced to accept them.

What if the prophets of doom turn out to be right about future temperature increases? Does greater warming necessarily spell disaster for humanity? No. Humanity can easily adapt to the projected changes in climate during the next century, according to the National Academy of Sciences (NAS).[101] Humanity's ever-increasing store of knowledge and technology enables us to adjust to changing circumstances faster and more easily as the years pass. Human beings thrive in climates ranging from the Sahara to Sarawak and from the Amazon to Alaska. Therefore, adaptation to any future climate change will most likely be the same as for more familiar climate variations. "The technologies, small and large, that buffer human activity over the long-term will be the same ones that mollify the difference between daytime and nighttime temperatures, protect against normal variability between days, shield from storms and hail, adjust to seasons, and adapt to the wide range of climates where people already live," says Rockefeller University researcher Jesse Ausubel.[102] He notes—and it should be obvious to anyone who considers the matter for a moment—that technology has enormously reduced humanity's vulnerability to climate variation and will continue to do so in the future. We've exchanged smoky campfires for central heating, precarious dependence on local harvests for the abundance of the world's grain markets, and the shaman's rattles for modern medicine.

The NAS report points out that the variations in temperatures predicted by the proponents of disaster are "much smaller than that from day to night, from summer to winter, or between airports that one might leave and reach in an hour."[103] The NAS rejected the notion that climate change means the collapse of natural ecosystems or agriculture. According to the doomsters, significant global warming could take fifty years, but the creation of new crop varieties adapted to various climatic conditions takes far less time than the projected climate change—typically between six and nine years—and costs about $1 million to develop.[104] As bioengineering techniques improve, crop development time will certainly be substantially reduced.

Wild plants and animals dwell successfully in habitats as different as the Himalayas are from Death Valley, and Greenland from the Congo. The NAS recognized that some species might become extinct, but noted that species and entire ecosystems have the ability to migrate to more congenial climates. The NAS advised the creation and preservation of natural corridors to facilitate ecosystem migration.[105]

Even Barry Commoner writes in *Making Peace with the Planet*, "Judged only in ecological terms, global warming can be regarded merely as a change in the structure of the global ecosystem similar to the warming that accompanied that last postglacial period, albeit more rapid. Viewed this way, there is no more reason to oppose global warming than to be unhappy about the last ice age and the rise in global temperature that ended it."[106]

If we choose to stabilize global climate, geo-engineering to reduce CO_2 or reflect sunlight may be possible. The National Academy of Sciences considered several possible ways to reflect sunlight away from the earth including orbiting mirrors in space, injecting dust into the stratosphere using guns, floating billions of aluminized balloons in the stratosphere, and burning sulfur at sea to boost cloud formation.[107] One clever suggestion offered by John Martin of the Moss Landing Marine Laboratory and dubbed the "Geritol Fix" involves fertilizing the oceans with iron. Martin estimates that dumping 300,000 tons of this nutrient in the iron-poor southern oceans would trigger massive phytoplankton blooms which would soak up two billion tons of carbon dioxide. Other scientists figure ocean fertilizing would cost one billion dollars to remove up to two billion tons of CO_2 per year.[108] If feasible, this would be far cheaper than the draconian "global economic restructuring" plans being pushed by the apocalyptics.

The prospect of easy human adaptation to climate change makes environmental mystics melancholy. "So three cheers for us. By dint of our powerful intellects we may have a way out . . . It's not certain that genetic engineering and macromanagement of the world's resources will provide a new cornucopia, but it certainly seems probable. We are a talented species," laments Bill McKibben.[109]

Whether or not the "greenhouse effect" raises average global temperatures significantly, atmospheric carbon dioxide is going to increase, unless the apocalyptics persuade the world to make draconian efforts to reduce it. The National Academy of Sciences noted that doubled CO_2 offers substantial benefits to the environment and to humanity.

Carbon dioxide may be a waste gas to us, but it is food to plants. Experiments show that increased CO_2 dramatically enhances the growth of trees and crops while tempering the effects of heat, drought, and soil salinity.[110] Plants breathe in carbon dioxide through leaf pores which unfortunately also allow water to evaporate when open. In a CO_2-enriched environment, plants conserve water because they do not have to open their pores as wide to absorb ample carbon dioxide.

Scientists estimate that doubled carbon dioxide would raise crop yields by more than a third[111] while perhaps doubling tree growth.[112] Others believe that the increases in crop yields over the past four decades are in part due to already higher levels of CO_2.[113] U.S. Agriculture Department scientist Sherwood Idso thinks that rising carbon dioxide levels may well presage the "greening of the Earth." He points out that the "greening" may already be happening. Idso rejects the findings of a recent Swiss experiment which suggests that tropical plants grown for three months in an enhanced CO_2 atmosphere might suffer from overfertilization.[114] "Trees need to grow at least a year and a half in an enhanced CO_2 atmosphere before the beneficial effects are fully evident," he explains. "They are not being overfertilized."[115]

The Mauna Loa Observatory CO_2 record shows the earth literally breathes carbon dioxide in and out as the seasons alternate. Terrestrial plants in the Northern Hemisphere, which contains most of the world's land, take up huge amounts of carbon dioxide to fuel their growth in the summer and release it in the winter. Idso notes that the *difference* between each winter's peak in atmospheric carbon dioxide and each summer's low is growing—each summer ever greater amounts of carbon dioxide are being absorbed from the atmosphere. He interprets the increasing difference as evidence that earth's plant cover is already becoming more robust as the result of a CO_2-enriched atmosphere.[116]

In November 1991, two scientists, Eigil Friis-Christensen and Knud Lassen of the Danish Meteorological Institute, startled climatologists by showing a remarkably close correlation between the length of the sunspot cycle and global temperature changes over the past 130 years. Sunspots are huge energetic storms that appear as dark blotches on the sun's surface. Their numbers rise and decline in regular nine to 13-year-long cycles. The Danes show that shorter nine-year cycles correlate with hotter global temperatures while longer eleven-year cycles signal cooler weather. For example, when global temperatures declined from 1940 to 1975, solar activity decreased and the sunspot cycles lasted longer. When temperatures began to rise in the 1970s, the sunspot cycle shortened to nine and a half years. The two scientists conclude that their findings may mean the greenhouse effect plays a smaller role in warming than asserted by environmentalists.[117]

Of course, people have been trying for decades to link sunspots to everything from stock market returns to hemlines. The relationship uncovered by Friis-Christensen and Lassen is only a statistical correlation and does not describe any mechanism for how sunspots could physically affect earth's climate. Nevertheless, arch–global warmer James Hansen says, "My gut feeling is that they're at least partly right."[118]

Recall that in 1988, Hansen was sure that he had already detected human-induced greenhouse warming. However, Hansen and his colleagues now claim in work published in early 1992 that sulfate aerosols injected by human activities into the atmosphere have cooled the earth down by the same amount that carbon dioxide emissions would have warmed it up.[119] This leaves open the question, then—how did Hansen detect greenhouse warming as he testified before Congress in 1988 if aerosols had cooled the planet, and thus had masked any global warming?

With echoes of the global cooling scare of the 1970s, some scientists have recently concluded that increased atmospheric CO_2 might trigger a new ice age. Gifford Miller at the University of Colorado and Anne de Vernal of the University of Quebec found that at the beginning of the last ice age 122,000 years ago, global temperatures were a little higher than they are now. They speculate that higher surface temperatures due to the "greenhouse effect" will evaporate more water, which will fall as excess snow in the polar latitudes. The excess snow may eventually grow into vast continental ice sheets, such as those that reached their maximum extent 18,000 years ago.[120] Once again, humanity is caught in the apocalyptics' abiding "Catch-22"—whatever we do, we bring the world's end closer.

The immediate climate prospect for the early 1990s envisions a bit of global cooling owing to the massive eruption of the Mount Pinatubo volcano in the Philippines in 1991. As noted in the chapter on the earlier global cooling crisis, volcanic eruptions can have substantial effects on the world's climate. The eruption of Mount Tambora led to the "year without summer" in 1816, when it snowed in June in New England.

Mount Pinatubo blasted nineteen million tons of sulfur[121] into the atmosphere which will linger as a haze blocking sunlight until the mid-1990s. At the end of 1991, there were ten to one hundred times the normal level of sulfate aerosols in the atmosphere.[122] Calculations indicate that substantial cooling, perhaps 1F degree, will begin in 1992, leading to colder winters and cooler summers worldwide.[123] Also ozone levels will decline temporarily since atmospheric sulfur (in the form of sulfuric acid) enhances the processes that deplete ozone.[124] Pinatubo aerosols are also expected to deepen the annual Antarctic "ozone hole" in 1992.[125] Michaels warns that when the skies clear and temperatures return rapidly to normal later this decade, we can expect unscrupulous prophets of doom to tout the natural reversion to higher temperatures as evidence of catastrophic greenhouse warming.

Why does this misuse of science continue? In any scientific discipline, there are only a few genuine apocalypse abusers. The motives are the usual ones—the quest for prestige and money. Harvard's Peter Rogers notes, "Very rarely is the public informed that these predictions are based on elaborate research models that have not been fully validated and that the future funding of these model studies is subject to being cut off at any moment. This leads to the unconscious desire to present the model results in the best (i.e., most frightening) light to Congress and the federal government, which are ultimately the sole source of funding for this research."[126] Rogers adds, "Because everyone else is crying 'crisis,' responsible scientists are forced to join the chorus or risk losing their research programs."

NASA's Roy Spencer, whose satellite data show only a negligible warming trend since 1979, is more forthright: "Global warming is the new McCarthyism. If you don't jump on the environmental bandwagon to stop the inevitable warming that the earth is going to undergo, you're going to be ostracized from the scientific community because it is not fashionable to disagree with the environmentalists nowadays."[127]

"A lot of people are getting very well known and very well funded as a result of promoting the disastrous scenario of greenhouse warming," says Sherwood Idso.[128] Spencer agrees. "It's easier to get funding if you can show some evidence for an impending climate disaster. In the 1970s it was the coming ice age and now it's the coming global warming. Who knows what it will be ten years from now. But sure, science benefits from some scary scenarios."

And climatologists have benefited. The federal government is funding a multiyear, multibillion-dollar research program on global climate change. In 1992, climate change programs will receive $1.1 billion in federal monies and nearly $1.4 in 1993.[129]

After the balloon bursts on global warming and it has been incorporated like overpopulation, resource depletion, biotech plagues, and the ozone hole into the conventional wisdom of doom, to what new doom will the environmental millenarians turn next? What new crisis can be conjured up and used to promote their sociopolitical engineering schemes while enhancing their power and influence over the world's governments?

TEN

THE MEDIA AND THE MESSIAHS

"No problem, no news," runs one old maxim of journalism. As we have seen throughout this book, many players have a strong interest in hyping environmental problems into "global emergencies" or "worldwide crises." Crises keep donations flowing to environmental advocacy groups, advance the careers of certain bureaucrats and politicians, attract funds to scientists' laboratories, and sell newspapers and TV airtime. This natural process of highlighting bad news is bad enough, but now some journalists are proudly throwing off the professional constraints of objectivity and becoming environmental advocates themselves.

"The media's renewed interest in the environment has made it *the* topic of this new decade, heralded by *Time*'s decision to name the Earth its 'Planet of the Year' for 1988," says Sharon Friedman, chair of Lehigh University's journalism department.[1] The chief inspiration for the "Planet of the Year" issue was the hot summer of 1988 in the United States. *Time*'s managing editor Henry Muller declared, "The new journalistic challenge was to help find solutions, and that by definition meant international solutions."[2] Although he later backpedaled in embarrassment, *Time*'s science editor Charles Alexander added at a conference at the Smithsonian Institution, "I would freely admit that on this issue [environmentalism] we have crossed the boundary from news reporting to advocacy."[3]

An even more egregious example of advocacy journalism is the Cable News Network. CNN producer Barbara Pyle makes no bones about her environmental advocacy: "I switched from being an 'objective journalist' to an advocate in July 1980," after reading the gloomy Global 2000 presidential report.[4] Pyle added, "We [CNN] didn't become the environmental network overnight." Her colleague at the "environmental network," Teya Ryan, producer of CNN's "Network Earth" program, has jettisoned all pretense of objectivity.

"The 'balanced' report, in some cases, may no longer be the most effective, or even the most informative. Indeed, it can be debilitating. Can we afford to wait for our audience to come to its own conclusions? I think not," wrote Ryan.[5] Clearly Ryan is convinced that she knows far better than her viewers what the real truth is about environmental issues and therefore she does not need to bother presenting ideas, information, and solutions with which she, in her wisdom, disagrees.

And leading environmentalists certainly agree with Ryan that the situation is so desperate that we simply have to overlook quaint niceties like objectivity. "The communications industry is the only instrument that has the capacity to educate on the scale needed in the time available," intones the Worldwatch Institute's Lester Brown. "We don't have time for the traditional approach to education—training new generations of teachers to train new generations of students—because we don't have generations, we have years."[6]

Recall that climate catastrophist Stephen Schneider outlined (see Chapter Five) a plan to broadcast government-subsidized environmental programming on television. In fact, the Public Broadcasting System has done a fair job of doing just that. For example, uncritical programs promoting the notion of disastrous global warming, such as the ten-part series "The Race to Save the Planet" and "After the Warming," have been standard fare on PBS. In "The Race to Save the Planet," the narrator warned that humanity faced "enormous calamities in a very short time," concluding that "only an environmental revolution can save the planet from this fate."[7] In 1991, PBS refused to air "The Greenhouse Conspiracy," an award-winning British documentary that questioned the scientific basis of the greenhouse-effect theory, on the grounds that it failed to meet PBS's standards. Yet, unlike "The Race to Save the Planet" and "After the Warming," the producers of "The Greenhouse Conspiracy" had featured their opponents—several prominent global warming advocates, including Stephen Schneider and Thomas Wigley.

Commercial television and the movie industry have also joined the environmental crusade. In the 1950s, many Hollywood stars joined SANE's nuclear disarmament crusade. In the 1990s, much of Hollywood turned decidedly "Green." There is "an extraordinary sea change in the entertainment industry both here and abroad: a Great Awakening at last to ecological woes, and a grim determination to use the power of movies, television, and the press to make the nineties the decade of the environment," writes Michael Schnayerson.[8]

One sign of the greening of Hollywood was the creation of the Environmental Media Association, whose goals are to "reach out and engage the creative community, encouraging them to combat the environmental crisis through their work" and to "encourage films, television programs and other creative projects to incorporate environmental themes."

And the EMA packs clout—the presidents of the four television networks support it as do a number of studio heads and independent producers. EMA's executive director Andy Spahn claims that more than forty prime-time programs have incorporated pro-environmentalist messages, including "L.A. Law," "The Simpsons," "Golden Girls," "Knots Landing," "thirtysomething," and "MacGyver."[9]

Reporters and readers should keep firmly in mind the fact that every institution has its own self-interest and acts to defend it. Environmental activists tend to think of themselves as planetary saviors. Many honestly believe what they are saying, but like everyone, they are inclined, some consciously and others unconsciously, to put their own "spin" on the information.

"On the one hand, as scientists, we are ethically bound to the scientific method, in effect promising to tell the truth, the whole truth, and nothing but—which means we must include all the doubts, caveats, and ifs, ands, and buts," says Stephen Schneider. He then revealingly adds, "On the other hand, we are not just scientists but human beings as well. And like most people we'd like to see the world a better place, which in this context translates into our working to reduce the risk of potentially disastrous climatic change. To do that we need to get some broad-based support, to capture the public's imagination. That, of course, entails getting loads of media coverage. So we have to offer up scary scenarios, make simplified, dramatic statements, and make little mention of any doubts we might have. This 'double ethical bind' we frequently find ourselves in cannot be solved by any formula. Each of us has to decide what the right balance is between being effective and being honest. I hope that means being both."[10] Sara Vickerman of the Defenders of Wildlife puts it more succinctly: "The best way to get on TV is to take an extreme position."[11] Make sure you can distinguish when a scientist is speaking as an expert and when he is speaking merely as a concerned citizen.

Of course, people who are skeptical of or oppose particular environmental policies or proposals are looking out for their self-interests as well. However, they think of themselves as "saviors" of other important values, such as economic progress, and the alleviation of poverty and hunger. Although it is wise to maintain a healthy skepticism, many people who support economic progress are not just promoting higher corporate profits, but are honestly trying to supply needed goods and services to their fellow human beings. As George Gilder, the modern prophet of the spirit of democratic capitalism, reminds us, for the most part people get rich in our economy by helping their fellow citizens—that is, by supplying goods and services at ever lower prices to their customers. The reason business scandals or shoddy products—like instances of environmental harm—make the news is because of their comparative rarity. Just as corporate rip-offs are not characteristic of the American economy—billions of transactions take place every day in which both producers and consumers walk away satisfied—similarly instances of real environmental degradation are rare. Unfortunately the process of reporting the news gives readers and viewers the erroneous impression that corruption and damage are pervasive features of our economy and our environment.

Social critic Witold Rybczynski sums up the situation well:

> The media have a tendency to focus on bad news rather than on good, on the aberration rather than on the norm. In this they probably do no more than reflect public taste. But the result of this emphasis is that the failures of technology tend to receive considerably more of the public's attention than its successes. Thus the accusation of the consumer advocate activist Ralph Nader that the Corvair was an unsafe automobile received much more publicity than the finding of the National Highway Traffic Safety Administration, a decade later, that the Corvair was no less safe than the average car of the day. It is the electrical power failure, the man-made disaster, and the factory recall that catch the baleful eye of the news commentator. Though this bad

news does not alone create a distrust of technology—the failures are, after all, real—it does promote the stereotype of technology as a threat to society, a benevolent despot who, more often than not, runs amok.[12]

Also, journalists sometimes treat factual scientific disagreements as though they were reporting election results or describing a political debate. Given the growing politicization of science it is difficult to avoid this pitfall, but there remains a core of scientific objectivity that can be reached if the reporter works hard enough. Reporters shouldn't allow themselves to become merely the conveyor belt of predigested views embodied in carefully crafted press releases issued by the headquarters of advocacy groups or government agencies. Former EPA press officer Jim Sibbison pointedly notes that "reporters take too much on faith what the government tells them."[13]

The NASA "ozone crisis" in February 1992 is a good example of this. The Mount Pinatubo volcano, whose eruption was the proximate cause of elevated stratospheric chlorine levels and consequent ozone depletion, was mentioned only as an afterthought by NASA's official press release, downplaying its significance. Why?

The NASA ozone press conference is also a wonderful example of how the media can be misled by crafty "media scientists." As it happens, I called up Jim Detjen, the veteran environmental reporter for The Philadelphia Inquirer and president of the Society of Environmental Journalists, to ask him some general questions about how the media treat environmental issues. In the course of our conversation, I mentioned that I had just read the reports of the NASA press conference in The Washington Post and The New York Times. "Why don't you take a look at our coverage?" he asked me. I mentioned that I hoped the Inquirer had presented the other side of the debate over ozone depletion. Apparently quite taken aback, he blurted out, "What debate? There are no skeptics on ozone."

What then of the numerous atmospheric scientists who questioned NASA's rush to judgment on global ozone depletion and an Arctic ozone hole? Why weren't NASA Langley's Linwood Callis, Goddard Space Flight Center's Arlin Krueger, National Oceanic and Atmospheric Administration's Walter Komhyr, and NOAA's Melvyn Shapiro consulted? Scientific critics of NASA's ozone findings weren't all that hard to find.

"The press already knows what it wants to hear," says a bitter Melvyn Shapiro, chief meteorologist at NOAA's Boulder, Colorado laboratory. "Perhaps the NASA news conference [on ozone] was premature, and maybe it wasn't all really all that bad. But then the press calls up the media darlings in the scientific community and they give the press the line. Reporters already know who is going to give them the doomsday scenario."[14]

Regarding the media coverage of global warming, the Center for Media and Public Affairs determined that between 1985 and 1991, the majority of stories in leading news magazines and TV networks "presented global warming in cataclysmic terms as a catastrophe in the making. Stories emphasizing a disaster scenario outnumbered those dismissing such a scenario by a margin of 16 to 1."[15] *Newsweek* contributing editor Greg Easterbrook, who says he's not convinced global warming is really happening, decries what he sees as the "contest among journalists to see who could use the gloomiest words" when reporting about the environment.[16]

Now, I would like to offer some unsolicited advice to my fellow reporters in the hope that they will be able to avoid being taken in by apocalypse abusers in the future.

Political reporting skills come in handy when threading one's way through interagency conflicts and battles. Always remember the rule of financial and business reporting—*follow the money.* This determines which agency, congressman, or advocacy group wins by pushing the policy under consideration. Whose budget staff and media presence will be enlarged due to the alleged crisis?

Although the garden variety test tube jockey is still a good source of information, journalists must never forget that lab directors are keenly aware of how the media can influence their government funding. Individual scientists can be forgiven for thinking that *their* work is of vital importance to humanity, but journalists must not unskeptically share their views. Of the scores of scientists I interviewed for this book, I could count on the fingers of one hand the number who did not mention funding and the scarcity of research monies. Lab directors are not only scientists; they are also public relations officers and politicians who must navigate the dark byways of Congress and government agencies in search of the wherewithal to keep their organizations going. Consequently, they feel enormous institutional pressure to hype the work of their laboratories and to tie it to the solution of some looming mediagenic crisis. Typically, reporters ignore the careful caveats that a scientist might couch his findings in and try to get to the heart of the matter—the terrible crisis that is menacing us all. How many reporters highlight the highest number, the greatest cost, the most terrible possibility as a way of getting the attention of their readers? We are all guilty of this sin.

While this book deals only with alleged global-scale threats—remember how Alar, dioxin, Love Canal, Three Mile Island, and asbestos all turned out—the threats from each were vastly overblown and the public was unnecessarily alarmed. These crises were hyped to further the interests of specific agencies and advocacy groups. Some journalists console themselves with the thought that by reporting a looming disaster which then is later disproved, they can always argue that they were merely demonstrating proper concern for the gravity of the situation. But have they served their readers and viewers well?

Also, why not get mad when you get taken? Follow-up reports of what really happened, while not completely repairing the damage caused by early alarmist articles, can somewhat ameliorate the harm. Why not embarrass in public those who led you down the garden path with their canned crises? It might even serve to make other advocacy groups and agencies more careful in their claims in the future.

Although there are those who urge journalists to throw aside the "blinders" of objectivity—especially in the area of environmental reporting—remember that the public relies on the objectivity of the press. Just as in science, public trust depends on maintaining standards of objectivity. Most good reporters and editors already know these rules and follow them, but don't forget them in the fight to get the news. Don't let yourself get co-opted by your sources. It is especially difficult to resist the temptation to be on the side of those claiming to save the earth. After all, who wants to stand for the destruction of our home?

It is difficult enough for a democratic society to decide how to handle the critical issues that it will confront in the coming century. The media are the senses of a democratic society, its eyes and ears, and if the sights and sounds we convey to our public are distorted, the polity, like a near-sighted man or deaf woman, is in danger of walking off a cliff or being run over by a howling ambulance.

Paraphrasing G. K. Chesterton, if people lose faith in the objectivity of science, they will not then believe in nothing; instead they will believe in everything. Americans are well down the road to believing in everything, as the growing popularity of New Age pseudo-science attests.

The ongoing politicization of science is especially dangerous to a secular liberal society such as ours. If scientific truth and facts are thought to be mere opinions, then the last remaining standards of objectivity on which liberal consensus can be reached will be gone. If everything is up for grabs all the time, including the law of gravity, then our society is completely without moorings. In one recent apocryphal story, a child was asked why oil floats on water. The child, properly schooled in the latest environmentally correct thinking, with all seriousness replied, "I guess it's because people just don't care anymore."

One personally very disheartening experience occurred

after a television program on which I was debating the seriousness of the "ozone crisis" with an environmental activist in front of an audience of high school seniors. A young woman came up to me after the program and told me that even if the ozone "crisis" was not so bad, it was all right to exaggerate the situation to get people's attention. Incredulous, I asked, "So then you're saying it's all right to lie in what you think is a good cause?" With complete earnestness, she replied, "Yes, sometimes you have to lie in a good cause."

Below are some tips on how the public and reporters can tell that they may be dealing with a false prophet of doom.

1 The first indication is flat-out claims that the end of the world is impending due to whatever crisis they are citing.

2 Next, does the proponent assert that certain facts "impel," "require," or "demand" that a specific course of action be followed? Good scientists rarely propose radical social and economic plans in conjunction with releasing scientific research results.

3 Is the proposed program clearly identified with any particular political ideology, party, or interest group?

4 Look at the proponents' past predictive records—have the dooms they flog ever come true? Do they couch the hypothesized doom in "could," "should," "perhaps" language? Conditional language in making dire claims may signal that apocalypse abuse is going on.

5 Think about how a scientist would go about testing the truth of the assertions being made. Do they more closely resemble the vacuities of astrologers, or testable hypotheses like "what goes up must come down"? This process will give you some idea of the real scientific content of the statement.

6 Be especially skeptical about "scientific" reports that are

177

being handled by public relations firms, for example, *The Limits to Growth*, nuclear winter, and the Alar scare.

7 Scientific findings and conclusions are generally highly caveated and nuanced—rarely flat-out one way or the other. Beware of absolute certainty.

8 Find out who funded the work being reported—what agency or foundation, and what is its agenda? Remember that advocacy organizations' personnel need to justify their jobs and perquisites.

9 Beware of moral fervor and high levels of righteous indignation. Just because people are willing to put their lives on the line for their beliefs, à la Greenpeace, doesn't mean that they are right. After all there were hundreds of thousands of convinced Nazis and communists who died for their causes.

10 Talk with scientists—other than those who are pushing the alleged crisis. Be aware, however, that scientists are often reluctant to criticize their fellow scientists and may even fear that their criticisms might endanger the funding for their own work if they speak up in opposition. No one wants to sound like they *favor* nuclear war or destroying the ozone layer.

A. A. Hodge once wrote: "It is easier to find a score of men wise enough to discover the truth, than to find one intrepid enough, in the face of opposition, to stand up for it."

It's a reporter's job to find that one.

NOTES

Notes to Chapter One

1 Paul Ehrlich, *The Population Bomb* (New York: Sierra Club–Ballantine, 1968), i.

2 Donella Meadows, et al., *The Limits to Growth* (New York: New American Library, 1972), 29.

3 Liebe Cavalieri, "New Strains of Life—or Death," *The New York Times Magazine* (Aug. 22, 1976), 67.

4 Michael Oppenheimer, "From Red Menace to Green Threat," *The New York Times* (Mar. 27, 1990), A27. Oppenheimer holds the Barbra Streisand research chair at the Environmental Defense Fund.

5 Nigel Calder, "In the Grip of a New Ice Age?" *International Wildlife* (June 1975), 33–35.

6 Derek Freeman, *Margaret Mead and Samoa: The Making and Unmaking of an Anthropological Myth* (Cambridge,

Massachusetts: Harvard University Press, 1983). See especially 95–109, 282–293.

7 Michael Barkun, *Disaster and the Millennium* (New Haven: Yale University Press, 1974), 205.

8 Witold Rybczynski, *Taming the Tiger: The Struggle to Control Technology* (New York: Viking, 1983), 77.

9 Robert Nisbet, *History of the Idea of Progress* (New York: Basic Books, 1980), 97.

10 Paul Johnson, *The Enemies of Society* (New York: Atheneum, 1977), 88.

11 Ibid., 89.

12 Steve Chase, ed., *Defending the Earth: A Dialogue Between Murray Bookchin and Dave Foreman* (Boston: South End Press, 1991), 57–59.

13 Ibid., 58.

14 Barkun, *Disaster*, 185.

15 Aaron Wildavsky, interview, Oct. 30, 1991.

16 Aaron Wildavsky, *The Rise of Radical Egalitarianism* (Washington, D.C.: American University Press, 1991), 74.

17 Murray Bookchin, *Remaking Society: Pathways to a Green Future* (Boston: South End Press, 1990), 155.

18 Barry Commoner, *The Poverty of Power: Energy and the Economic Crisis* (New York: Knopf, 1976), 262.

19 David Foreman, cited in Chase, *Defending the Earth*, 73–75.

20 Richard Hofstadter, *The Paranoid Style in American Politics and Other Essays* (New York: Knopf, 1965), xii.

21 Ibid., 29.

22 Anna Bramwell, *Ecology in the 20th Century: A History* (New Haven: Yale University Press, 1989), 16.

23 S. Fred Singer, "Lowering the Gloom," *Time* (Sept. 14, 1987), 12.

24 Bill McKibben, *The End of Nature* (New York: Random House, 1989), 174.

25 Wildavsky, *Radical Egalitarianism*, 238–239.

26 Brian Tokar, "The Greens: To Party or Not?" *Z Magazine* (Oct. 1991), 42.

27 Paul Ehrlich and John P. Holdren, "Impact of Population Growth," *Science* 171:1212–1217 (Mar. 26, 1971): 1215.

28 Paul Ehrlich and Anne Ehrlich, *Healing the Planet: Strategies for Resolving the Environmental Crisis* (New York: Addison-Wesley, 1991), 242.

29 Denis Hayes, "Earth Day: A Beginning," *The Progressive* (Apr. 1970), 7.

30 "Action for Survival: A Prologue by the Editors," *The Progressive* (Apr. 1970), 3.

31 Ibid., 5.

32 Tokar, "The Greens," 42.

33 Randolph Viscio, cited in Keith Schneider, "Student Group Seeks Broader Agenda for Environmental Movement," *The New York Times* (Oct. 7, 1991), A12

34 John Cushman, "Environmental Hazards to Poor Gain New Focus at E.P.A.," *The New York Times* (Jan. 21, 1992), C4.

35 Dave Foreman, cited in John Fayhee, "Earth First! And Foremost," *Backpacker* (Sept. 1988), 23.

36 Dave Foreman, "Only Man's Presence Can Save Nature," *Harper's* (Apr. 1990), 48.

37 Thomas Berry, quoted in Murray Bookchin, "Will Ecology Become 'the Dismal Science'?", *The Progressive* (Dec. 1991), 20.

38 Ibid.

39 Christopher Manes, *Green Rage: Radical Environmentalism and the Unmaking of Civilization* (Boston: Little, Brown, 1990), 237.

40 Bill Devall and George Sessions, *Deep Ecology: Living As If Nature Mattered* (Layton, UT: Gibbs Smith, 1987), 14.

41 Ibid., ix.

42 Chase, *Defending the Earth*, 3.

43 Devall, *Deep Ecology*, 65.

44 Charles Cushman, director of the National Inholders Association, cited in *The New York Times* (Dec. 23, 1991), A12.

45 Lynn White, Jr., "The Historical Roots of Our Ecologic Crisis," *Science* (Mar. 10, 1967), 1206.

46 Ibid., 1207.

47 Victor Scheffer, *The Shaping of Environmentalism in America* (Seattle: University of Washington Press, 1991), 7.

48 Archie Ruprecht, "Ask Not for Whom the Owl Hoots," letter to the editor, *The New York Times* (Mar. 14, 1992), 24.

49 Ehrlich and Ehrlich, *Healing the Planet*, 251.

50 Lester Brown, et al., *State of the World 1992* (New York: Norton, 1992), 175.

51 Witold Rybczynski, *Paper Heroes: A Review of Appropriate Technology* (Garden City, N.Y.: Anchor, 1980), 182.

52 Ehrlich and Ehrlich, *Healing the Planet*, 238.

53 Devall, *Deep Ecology*, 35.

54 McKibben, *The End of Nature*, 194.

55 Alexander King and Bertrand Schneider, *The First Global Revolution: A Report by the Council of the Club of Rome* (New York: Pantheon, 1991), 127.

56 Anita Gordon and David Suzuki, *It's A Matter of Survival*, cited by Daniel Kevles in "Some Like It Hot," *The New York Review of Books* (Mar. 26, 1992), 32.

57 Ehrlich and Ehrlich, *Healing the Planet*, xiii.

58 Ibid., 258.

59 Edith Efron, *The Apocalyptics: How Environmental Politics Controls What We Know About Cancer* (New York: Simon & Schuster, 1984), 44.

60 Edward Teller, cited by Starley Thompson and Stephen Schneider, "Nuclear Winter Reappraised," *Foreign Affairs* (Summer 1986), 983.

61 Scheffer, *The Shaping*, 180.

62 Terry Anderson and Donald Leal, *Free Market Environmentalism* (San Francisco: Westview Press, 1991), 94.

63 Bramwell, *Ecology in the 20th Century*, 39.

64 Marion Edey, cited in Scheffer, *The Shaping*, 139.

65 Riley Dunlap, "Public Opinion in the 1980s: Clear Consensus, Ambiguous Commitment," *Environment* (Oct. 1991), 32.

66 George Mitchell, *World on Fire: Saving an Endangered Earth* (New York: Macmillan, 1991), 225.

67 Albert Gore, *Earth in the Balance: Ecology and the Human Spirit* (Boston: Houghton Mifflin, 1992), 14.

68 Ibid., 269.

69 Ibid., 295–360.

70 John Cushman, "Federal Regulation Growing as Quayle

Panel Fights It," *The New York Times* (Dec. 24, 1991), A1.

71 Ibid., A14.

72 Christina Lamb, "Summit in danger of crashing to earth," *Financial Times* (Nov. 7, 1991), 21.

73 Hillary French, Worldwatch Institute Press Conference, Jan. 15, 1992.

74 Bramwell, *Ecology in the 20th Century*, 31.

75 Peter Rogers, "Climate Change and Global Warming," *Environmental Science and Technology* 24:4 (1990), 429.

76 Robert Norris, et al. "History of the Nuclear Stockpile," *Bulletin of the Atomic Scientists* (Aug. 1985), 108.

77 Alice Kimball Smith, *A Peril and a Hope: The Scientists' Movement in America 1945–47* (Chicago: University of Chicago Press, 1965), 522.

78 Colin Norman, "Science Budget: Selective Growth," *Science* (Feb. 7, 1992), 672; William Broad, "Swords Have Been Sheathed But Plowshares Lack Design," *The New York Times* (Feb. 5, 1992), A12.

79 Norman, "Science Budget," 673; Edward Rubin, et al., "Keeping Climate Research Relevant," *Issues in Science and Technology* (Winter 1991–92), 50.

80 Boyce Rensberger, "Science Panel Cites Research Fraud Problem," *The Washington Post* (Apr. 23, 1992), A11.

81 Daniel Cohen, *Waiting for the Apocalypse* (Buffalo, N.Y.: Prometheus, 1973), 248.

82 Eric Zencey, "Apocalypse and Ecology," *North American Review* (June 1988), 55, 57.

83 Cohen, *Waiting for the Apocalypse*, 166.

Notes to Chapter Two

1 Alice Kimball Smith, *A Peril and a Hope: The Scientists' Movement in America 1945–47* (Chicago: University of Chicago Press, 1965), ii.

2 Edward Shils, *The Torment of Secrecy: The Background and Consequences of American Security Policies* (Glencoe, Illinois: Free Press, 1956), 71.

3 J. Robert Oppenheimer, cited in Peter Beckman, et al., *The Nuclear Dilemma: Nuclear Weapons in the Cold War and Beyond* (Englewood Cliffs, N.J.: Prentice Hall, 1992), 10.

4 Jonathan Schell, *The Fate of the Earth* (New York: Knopf, 1982), 188.

5 Bertrand Russell, cited in William Poundstone, *Prisoner's Dilemma* (New York: Doubleday, 1992), 72.

6 Smith, *A Peril and a Hope*, 475.

7 C. P. Snow, "The Moral Un-neutrality of Science," *Science* (Jan. 27, 1961), cited in Herman Kahn, *Thinking about the Unthinkable* (New York: Avon, 1966), 27.

8 Schell, *The Fate of the Earth*, 183–84.

9 Bernard Feld, "Forty Years of Muddling Through," *Bulletin of the Atomic Scientists* (Aug. 1985), 30.

10 Winston Churchill, cited in Schell, *The Fate*, 197.

11 Kahn, *Thinking about the Unthinkable*, 30.

12 Ibid., 101.

13 Dexter Master and Katherine Way, *One World, or None* (New York: McGraw-Hill, 1946).

14 Milton Katz, *Ban the Bomb: A History of SANE, the Committee for a Sane Nuclear Policy, 1957–1985* (New York: Greenwood Press, 1986), 2–3.

15 Leo Marx, cited in Victor Scheffer, *The Shaping of Environmentalism in America* (Seattle: University of Washington Press, 1991), 171.

16 Smith, *A Peril and a Hope*, ii.

17 Solly Zuckerman, *Nuclear Illusion and Reality* (New York: Viking, 1982), 25.

18 Smith, *A Peril and a Hope*, 203, 236.

19 Ibid., 236.

20 Ibid., 237.

21 Katz, *Ban the Bomb*, 2.

22 Smith, *A Peril and a Hope*, 324.

23 Ibid., 445–74.

24 Ibid., 502.

25 "Topics of the Times," *The New York Times* (Oct. 7, 1945), E8; cited in ibid., 176.

26 Poundstone, *Prisoner's Dilemma*, 80.

27 Smith, *A Peril and a Hope*, 294.

28 William Arkin, "History of the Nuclear Stockpile," *Bulletin of the Atomic Scientists* (Aug. 1985), 107.

29 Ibid.

30 Katz, *Ban the Bomb*, 26.

31 Ibid., 16.

32 Ibid., 32.

33 Ibid., 41.

34 Ibid., 43.

35 Ibid., 41.

36 Ibid., 18; Smith, *A Peril and a Hope*, 526.

37 Katz, *Ban the Bomb*, 35.

38 Zuckerman, *Nuclear Illusion*, 120.

39 Scheffer, *The Shaping of Environmentalism*, 16.

40 Bryce Nelson, "Scientists Plan Research Strike at M.I.T. on 4 March," *Science* (Jan. 24, 1969), 373.

41 Gregory Fossedal, "Beware of the Union Label," *Policy Review* (Spring 1985), 47.

42 Marianne Szegedy-Maszak, "Rise and Fall of the Washington Peace Industry," *Bulletin of the Atomic Scientists* (Jan./Feb. 1989), 18–20.

43 Schell, *The Fate*, 111.

44 Carl Sagan and Richard Turco, *A Path Where No Man Thought: Nuclear Winter and the End of the Arms Race* (New York: Random House, 1990), 463.

45 Beckman, et al., *The Nuclear Predicament*, 287.

46 Pamela Sherrid, "Peaceniks Packing Up: Reagan Stole Their Thunder," *U.S. News & World Report* (Dec. 7, 1987), 40.

47 John Gaddis, "Hanging Tough Paid Off," *Bulletin of the Atomic Scientists* (Jan./Feb. 1989), 11.

48 Theodore Reuter and Thomas Kalil, "Nuclear Strategy and Nuclear Winter," *World Politics* (July 1991), 603.

49 Owen Harries, "The Cold War and the Intellectuals," *Commentary* (Oct. 1991), 16.

50 John Tirman, cited in Bill Turque and Daniel Glick, "The Thawing of the Freeze Movement," *Newsweek* (Mar. 12, 1990), 30.

51 Ibid.

52 Alliance for our Common Future, 1992 *Focus* Paper. Available from National Peace Foundation.

53 Dr. Robert Jay Lifton, cited in Joel Brinkley, "U.S. Looking for a New Path as Superpower Conflict Ends," *The New York Times* (Feb. 2, 1992), 10.

Notes to Chapter Three

1 Robert Nisbet, *History of the Idea of Progress* (New York: Basic Books, 1980), 52.

2 William Petersen, "Malthus: The Reactionary Reformer," *The American Scholar* (Spring 1990), 280.

3 Nisbet, *History*, 219.

4 Paul Ehrlich, *The Population Bomb* (New York: Ballantine, rev. ed. 1988), 204.

5 Julian Simon, *Population Matters: People, Resources, Environment and Immigration* (New Brunswick, N.J.: Transaction Books, 1990) 343.

6 Paul Ehrlich, *The Population Bomb* (New York: Sierra Club–Ballantine, 1968), i.

7 Paul Ehrlich and Anne Ehrlich, *The Population Explosion* (New York: Simon & Schuster, 1990), 193.

8 Ehrlich, *Bomb* (1968 ed.), 69–80.

9 Paul Ehrlich, "Eco-Catastrophe!," *Ramparts* (1969), 28.

10 Ibid.

11 Ibid.

12 Paul Ehrlich, "Looking Backward from 2000 A.D.," *The Progressive* (Apr. 1970), 23–25.

13 Paul Ehrlich, cited in David Rorvik, "Ecology's Angry Lobbyist," *Look* (Apr. 21, 1971), 44.

14 Ehrlich, *Explosion*, 10.

15 Dennis Avery, *Global Food Progress 1991* (Indianapolis: Hudson Institute, 1991), 80.

16 Lester Brown, *State of the World 1992: A Worldwatch Institute Report on Progress Toward a Sustainable Society* (New York: Norton, 1992), xiii–xiv.

17 Lester Brown, "The World Outlook for Conventional Agriculture," *Science*, 158:604–611 (Nov. 3, 1967), 604.

18 Lester Brown, *On the Fate of the Earth: Peace on and with the Earth for All Its Children* (San Francisco: Earth Island Institute, 1984), 141.

19 Lester Brown, *State of the World 1989*, (New York: Norton/Worldwatch, 1989), 41.

20 D. Gale Johnson, *Population, Food and Wellbeing*, Paper No. 90:13, University of Chicago Office of Agriculture Economics Research (July 9, 1990), 24.

21 Brown, *Fate*, 143.

22 Kenneth Frederick and Roger Sedjo, eds., *America's Renewable Resources: Historical Trends and Current Challenges* (Washington, D.C.: Resources for the Future, 1991), 191.

23 Ibid., 195.

24 Ibid., 192.

25 Ibid., 193.

26 Ibid., 196.

27 Avery, *Progress*, 225; Sandra Postel, *State of the World 1990*, chap. 3, "Saving Water for Agriculture" (New York: Norton, 1990), 54.

28 Postel, *State of the World*, 57.

29 Frederick and Sedjo, *America's Renewable Resources*, 27.

30 Ibid., 197.

31 Brown, "World Outlook," 607.

32 Brown, *State 1990*, 75.

33 Winston Harrington, "Wildlife: Severe Decline and Partial Recovery," in Frederick and Sedjo, *America's Renewable Resources*, 221–22.

34 Ehrlich and Ehrlich, *Explosion*, 71.

35 Nick Eberstadt, cited in Ronald Bailey, "Raining in Their Hearts," *The National Review* (Dec. 3, 1990), 33.

36 Ehrlich, *Bomb* (1968 ed.), 24.

37 Kirkpatrick Sale, "Bioregionalism—A New Way to Treat the Land," *The Ecologist* 14:4 (1984), 167–73; idem., "Bioregionalism—A Sense of Place," *The Nation* (Oct. 12, 1985), 336–39.

38 Paul Ehrlich and Anne Ehrlich, *Healing the Planet: Strategies for Resolving the Environmental Crisis* (New York: Addison-Wesley, 1991), 228.

39 Barry Commoner, "The Closing Circle," *Environment* (Apr. 1972), 52.

40 Simon, *Population Matters*, 374.

41 John Tierney, "Betting the Planet," *The New York Times Magazine* (Dec. 2, 1990), 52, 72, 81.

42 Johnson, *Wellbeing*, Table of Real Export Prices for Wheat and Maize in 1982 dollars per ton.

43 *World Development Report 1991: The Challenge of Development* (New York: The World Bank/Oxford University Press, 1991), 74.

44 Johnson, *Wellbeing*, 21.

45 Ibid., 22.

46 Indur Goklany, "Adaptation and Climate Change," presented at the annual meeting of the American Association for the Advancement of Science (Feb. 6–11, 1992), 17.

47 Johnson, *Wellbeing*, 4.

48 Paul Ehrlich, interview, March 1990.

49 Donald Plucknett, "Saving Lives Through Agricultural Research," in Avery, *Progress*, 86.

50 *World Development Report 1991*, 15.

51 Dennis Avery, interview, fall 1991.

52 Goklany, "Adaptation," 11.

53 John Campbell, "The Ongoing Green Revolution: Meeting the Global Food Challenge," in Avery, *Progress*, 110.

54 Plucknett, "Saving Lives," 87.

55 Campbell, "Green Revolution," 110.

56 Brown, *State 1991*, 11.

57 Paul Ehrlich and John Holdren, "Impact of Population Growth," *Science* 171:1212–1271 (Mar. 26, 1971), 1213.

58 *World Development Report 1991*, 74.

59 Avery, *Progress*, 91–93.

60 Dennis Avery, "Mother Earth Can Feed Billions More," *The Wall Street Journal* (Sept. 19, 1991), A14.

61 Robert Kates, "Surprising Reality about Hunger—Hopeful Outlook for the World," *Orlando Sentinel* (May 20, 1990), editorial page.

62 Julian Simon, "Resources, Population, Environment: An Oversupply of False Bad News," *Science* 208:1431–1437 (June 27, 1980), 1433.

63 Nick Eberstadt, manuscript, chap. 8, "Another Look at the World Food Situation," 150.

64 Thomas Poleman, manuscript, "Recent Trends in Food Availability and Nutritional Wellbeing," Professor of International Food Economics, Cornell University, 6.

65 Eberstadt, manuscript, 153.

66 Paul Lewis, "U.N. to Centralize Its Relief Efforts," *The New York Times* (Dec. 18, 1991), A19.

67 Avery, *Progress*, 20.

68 Johnson, *Wellbeing*, 26.

69 David Osterfeld, "Hope for the World Food Situation," *Journal of Economic Growth* (Winter 1989–90), 42.

70 Ibid., 43.

71 Johnson, *Wellbeing*, 28.

72 Steven Sinding and Sheldon Segal, "Birth-Rate News," *The New York Times* (Dec. 19, 1991), A34.

73 Garrett Hardin, "The Tragedy of the Commons," *Science* (Dec. 13, 1968), 1244.

74 *Demographic and Health Surveys: Comparative Studies 2: Fertility*, Institute for Resource Development (Oct. 1990), 15–16.

75 *Demographic and Health Surveys Newsletter*, "DHS Documents Major Fertility Declines," Institute for Resource Development 4:1 (1991), 1.

76 *Demographic and Health Surveys: Comparative Studies 2*, 15.

77 Ibid., 16.

78 Editorial, "Where Family Planning Works," *The Washington Post* (Feb. 22, 1992), A18.

79 World Resources Institute, *World Resources 1990–91: A Guide to the Global Environment* (New York: Oxford University Press, 1990), 257.

80 *World Development Report 1991*, 60.

81 Johnson, *Wellbeing*, 2.

82 *World Development Report 1991*, 30, Table 1.5.

83 Ehrlich and Ehrlich, *Explosion*, 175.

Notes to Chapter Four

1 Donella Meadows, et al., *The Limits to Growth: A Report for the Club of Rome's Project on the Predicament of Mankind* (New York: New American Library, 1972), introductory remarks.

2 Time (Jan. 24, 1972), 32.

3 Lester Brown, *State of the World 1990: A Worldwatch Institute Report on Progress Toward a Sustainable Society* (New York: Norton, 1990), see especially chap. 10, "Picturing a Sustainable Society," 173–90; *Our Common Future: The World Commission on Environment and Development*, chaired by Gro Brundtland (New York: Oxford University Press, 1987), 8–9, 43–65.

4 H. S. D. Cole, et al., *Models of Doom: A Critique of "The Limits to Growth"* (New York: Universe Books, 1973), 175.

5 Robert Gillette, "The Limits to Growth: Hard Sell for a Computer View of Doomsday," *Science* (Mar. 10, 1972), 1092.

6 Robert Reinhold, "Mankind Warned of Perils in Growth," *The New York Times* (Feb. 27, 1972), 1.

7 "Is the Worst Yet to Be?" Time (Jan. 24, 1972), 32.

8 Robert Gillette, *Science*, 1092.

9 Meadows, *Limits*, 29.

10 Jay Forrester, *World Dynamics*, 2 ed. (Cambridge, MA: Wright-Allen Press, 1973, original ed. 1971), 27.

11 Meadows, *Limits*, 180.

12 Ibid., 180–84.

13 Jay Forrester, interview, spring 1990.

14 Meadows, *Limits*, 64–67.

15 *Mineral Commodity Summaries 1991*, U.S. Dept. of Interior, Bureau of Mines.

16 *World Resources 1988–89* and *World Resources 1990–91* (World Resources Institute/New York: Basic Books, 1988), 240–1; (New York: Oxford University Press, 1990), 250.

17 American Petroleum Institute, Charles DiBona interview, fall 1991.

18 *World Resources 1990–91*, 145.

19 John Young, *Worldwatch Paper 109: Mining the Earth* (Washington, D.C.: Worldwatch Institute, July 1992), 6.

20 Forrester interview.

21 Dwight, Lee "The Perpetual Assault on Progress," *The St. Croix Review* (Oct. 1991), 13.

22 Ibid., 14.

23 Martin Wooster, "Selling Shortages Short," *Public Opinion* (Nov./Dec. 1988), 48.

24 Kenneth Frederick and Roger Sedjo, eds., *America's Renewable Resources*, "Forest Resources: Resilient and Serviceable" (Sedjo), (Washington, D.C. Resources for the Future, 1991), 89.

25 Wooster, "Selling," 49.

26 Lee, "Perpetual Assault," 10.

27 D. Gale Johnson, *Population, Food and Wellbeing*, Paper No. 90:13, University of Chicago Office of Agricultural Economics (July 9, 1990), 11.

28 Lee, "Perpetual Assault," 13.

29 Julian Simon, *Population Matters: People, Resources,*

Environment and Immigration (New Brunswick, NJ: Transaction, 1990), 375.

30 *World Development Report 1991*, 26.

31 Forrester interview.

32 Cole, *Models of Doom*, 118.

33 Forrester, *World Dynamics*, 90.

34 Ibid., 113.

35 Ibid., 46.

36 Nick Eberstadt, interview, spring 1990.

37 Forrester, *World Dynamics*, 43.

38 *Environmental Quality: 21st Annual Report of the Council on Environmental Quality* (Washington, D.C.: U.S. Gov't Printing Office, 1991), 311.

39 *National Air Quality and Emissions Trends Report 1990*, U.S. Environmental Protection Agency (Nov. 1991), 1-1 to 1-15.

40 Frederick and Sedjo, *America's Renewable Resources*, 61.

41 *National Water Quality Inventory: 1988 Report to Congress*, U.S. Environmental Protection Agency (Apr. 1990), xi.

42 *Environmental Quality*, 308.

43 *World Resources 1990–91*, 166.

44 Gene Grossman and Alan Krueger, manuscript "Environmental Impacts of a North American Free Trade Agreement" (Oct. 8, 1991), 16–17.

45 Forrester, *World Dynamics*, 41.

46 Nick Eberstadt, *The Poverty of Communism* (New Brunswick, N.J.: Transaction, 1989).

47 Cole, *Models of Doom*, 133.

48 *Our Common Future*, 9.

49 Ibid., 59, 45.

50 Ibid., 60.

51 Ibid., 8, 29.

52 Alexander King and Bertrand Schneider, *The First Global Revolution: A Report by the Council of the Club of Rome* (New York: Pantheon, 1991), 98.

53 D. Gabor, et al., *Beyond the Age of Waste: A Report to the Club of Rome* (New York: Pergamom Press, 1978), viii.

54 King and Schneider, *Global Revolution*, 54.

55 Ibid., 166.

56 Ibid., 173.

57 Ibid., 179–80.

58 Ibid., 204.

59 Ibid., 175–76.

60 Ibid., 158.

61 Brown, *State of the World 1990*, 3.

62 *World Development Report 1991*, 28, Table 1.4; 30, Table 1.5.

63 Ibid., 14, Table 1.1.

64 Ibid., 13.

65 Nicholas Kristof, "In China, A Little Goes a Long Way," *The New York Times* (Dec. 17, 1991), A10.

66 *World Development Report 1991*, 11.

67 Ibid., 27, 30.

Notes to Chapter Five

1 I. S. Rasool and Stephen Schneider, "Atmospheric Carbon Dioxide and Aerosols: Effects of Large Increases on Global Climate," *Science* (July 9, 1971), 138.

2 Lowell Ponte, *The Cooling* (Englewood Cliffs, NJ: Prentice Hall, 1976), xi.

3 Ibid., x.

4 Thomas Crowley and Gerald North, *Paleoclimatology* (New York: Oxford University Press, 1991), 52.

5 Ibid., 54.

6 Samuel Wilson, "The Vikings and the Eskimos," *Natural History* (Feb. 1992), 21; Stephen Schneider, and Randi Londer, *The Coevolution of Climate and Life* (San Francisco: Sierra Club Books, 1984), 111.

7 Crowley and North, *Paleoclimatology*, 94–95.

8 Carl Sagan and Richard Turco, *A Path Where No Man Thought: Nuclear Winter and the End of the Arms Race* (New York: Random House, 1991), 99.

9 James Luhr, "Volcanic Shade Causes Cooling," *Nature* (Nov. 14, 1991), 104.

10 John Douglas, "Climate Change: Chilling Possibilities," *Science News* (Mar. 1, 1975), 138.

11 "Weather Change: Poor Harvests," *Time* (Nov. 11, 1974), 82.

12 Ibid.

13 Ponte, *The Cooling*, 89.

14 "Another Ice Age?" *Time* (June 24, 1974), 86.

15 Kendrick Frazier, "Earth's Cooling Climate," *Science News* (Nov. 15, 1969), 458.

16 Ibid.

17 Douglas, "Climate Change," 139.

18 Ibid.

19 Nigel Calder, "In the Grip of a New Ice Age?" *International Wildlife* (June 1975), 33–35.

20 Ponte, *The Cooling*, 15.

21 Calder, "New Ice Age," 33.

22 Cited by Stephen Schneider and Lynne Mesirow, *The Genesis Strategy: Climate and Global Survival* (New York: Plenum, 1976), 23.

23 Ibid., 36.

24 Ibid., 33.

25 Ibid., 10.

26 Ibid., 312.

27 Ibid., 303.

28 Ibid., 308.

29 Ibid., 42.

Notes to Chapter Six

1 Bernadine Healy, cited in Malcolm Gladwell, "NIH Seeks Patent Protection for Human Genes," *The Washington Post* (Feb. 13, 1992), A16.

2 Winston Brill, "Competitiveness in Biotechnology," speech presented at the Brookings Institution (Apr. 8, 1987), 2.

3 Jeremy Rifkin and Ted Howard, *Who Should Play God?: The Artificial Creation of Life and What It Means for the Future of the Human Race* (New York: Dell Publishing, 1977), 9.

4 Bill McKibben, *The End of Nature* (New York: Random House, 1989), 166.

5 Rifkin, interview, 1985.

6 Industrial Biotechnology Backgrounder Series, "U.S. Biotechnology Industry Fact Sheet" (Washington, D.C.: Industrial Biotechnology Association, Oct. 1991).

7 Charles Warren, U.S. Patent Office, Group 180, interview, fall 1991.

8 Andrew Pollack, "Gene Therapy Gets the Go-Ahead," *The New York Times* (Feb. 14, 1992), D1, D5.

9 Philip Abelson, "Biotechnology in a Global Economy," *Science* (Jan. 24, 1992), 381.

10 Anne Moffat, "Biotechnology in a Global Economy," *Science* (Feb. 21, 1992), 919.

11 Paul Berg, et al., "Potential Biohazards of Recombinant DNA Molecules," letter to editor, *Science* (July 26, 1974), 303.

12 Liebe Cavalieri, "New Strains of Life—or Death," *The New York Times Magazine* (Aug. 22, 1976), 67.

13 Ibid., 9.

14 Alfred Vellucci, cited in John Kifner, " 'Creation of Life' Experiment at Harvard Stirs Heated Debate," *The New York Times* (June 17, 1976), 1.

15 Burke Zimmerman, *Biofuture: Confronting the Genetic Era* (New York: Plenum Press, 1984), 176.

16 Nina Federoff, cited in Gina Kolata, "How Safe Are Engineered Organisms?" *Science* (July 5, 1985), 35.

17 Waclaw Szybalski cited in Ronald Bailey, "Fear and Loathing of Biotech's Bright Future," *Reason* (Nov. 1985), 24.

18 Jeremy Rifkin, *Algeny: A New Word—A New World* (Penguin, 1984), 188.

19 Ibid., 47.

20 Ibid., 252.

21 Ibid., 233.

22 L. R. Batra and W. Klassen, *Public Perceptions of Biotechnology* (Bethesda, Maryland: Agricultural Research Institute, 1987), 213.

23 Arthur Caplan cited in Ronald Bailey, "Fear and Loathing of Biotech's Bright Future," *Reason* (Nov. 1985), 30.

24 Rifkin and Howard, *Who Should Play God?* 223.

25 Ibid.

26 Ibid., 219–20.

27 Jeremy Rifkin cited in Ronald Bailey, "Fear and Loathing of Biotech's Bright Future," *Reason* (Nov. 1985), 24.

28 Ibid.

29 Rifkin interview, 1985.

30 Daniel Callahan, interview, 1985.

31 Jeremy Rifkin and Ted Howard, *The Emerging Order: God in the Age of Scarcity* (New York: Putnam, 1979), x.

32 Rifkin, *Emerging Order*, xi.

33 Rifkin, *Emerging Order*, 47–75.

34 Rifkin interview, 1985.

35 Stephen Jay Gould "Review of *Algeny*," *Discover* (Jan. 1985), 34.

36 Gould, *Discover*, 35.

37 Steven Witt, *Biotechnology: Microbes and the Environment* (San Francisco: Center for Science Information, 1990), 53.

38 Fred Smith, interview, 1988.

39 Ibid.

40 Witt, *Biotechnology*, 54.

41 Rifkin, interview, 1988.

42 Peter Huber, interview, 1988.

43 Albert Heier, interview, 1988.

44 Ronald Bailey, "Fear and Loathing of Biotech's Bright Future," *Reason* (Nov. 1985), 28.

45 Karen Brown, Food Marketing Institute, interview, summer 1989.

46 Gerard Ingenthron, cited in Ronald Bailey, "Spooked Again," *Forbes* (Oct. 2, 1989), 10.

47 Peter Huber, interview, summer 1989.

48 Michael Schnayerson, "Environment: The Hot Issue," *Vanity Fair* (Sept. 1989), 172.

49 Isaac Rabino, "The Impact of Activist Pressures on Recombinant DNA Research," *Science, Technology & Human Values* (Winter 1991), 83.

50 Ronald Bailey, "Brain Drain," *Forbes* (Nov. 27, 1989), 261.

51 Batra and Klassen, *Public Perceptions*, 54.

52 Jeremy Rifkin, press release for *The Global Greenhouse Network First International Conference* (Oct. 5, 1988), 1.

53 Rifkin, *The Greenhouse Crisis Foundation: General Information and 1992 Project Guide*, 2.

54 Rifkin, press release for *The Global Greenhouse Network*, 7–9.

55 Rabino, "Impact," 75–78.

56 Winston Brill, cited in Ronald Bailey, "Ministry of Fear," *Forbes* (June 27, 1988), 139.

57 Alan Goldhammer, interview, fall 1991.

58 Witt, *Biotechnology,* 47–48. See also Winston Brill, "Why Engineered Organisms Are Safe," *Issues in Science and Technology* (Spring, 1988).

59 James Tiedje, et al., "The Release of Genetically Engineered Organisms: A Perspective from the Ecological Society of America," *Ecology* (Apr. 1989), 301.

60 Ibid., 302.

61 National Research Council, *Field Testing Genetically Modified Organisms: Framework for Decisions* (Washington, D.C.: National Academy Press, 1989), 3.

62 Brill, "Why Engineered Organisms," 46.

63 Rabino, "Impact," 83.

64 Huber interview.

65 Fred Smith, interview, summer 1989.

Notes to Chapter Seven

1 Carl Sagan, "Nuclear War and Climatic Catastrophe: Some Policy Implications," *Foreign Affairs* (Winter 1983/84), 285.

2 Herman Kahn, *On Thermonuclear Warfare,* 2d ed. (Princeton, N.J.: Princeton University Press, 1961), 145.

3 Jonathan Schell, *The Fate of the Earth* (New York: Knopf, 1982), 227–28.

4 Ralph White, *The Fearful Warriors,* cited in Russell Seitz, "In From The Cold: 'Nuclear Winter' Melts Down," *The National Interest* (Fall 1986), 3.

5 R. P. Turco, et al., "Nuclear Winter: Global Consequences of Multiple Nuclear Explosions," *Science* (Dec. 23, 1983), 1284.

6 Ibid., 1283.

7 Sagan, "Nuclear War," 284.

8 Ibid., 292.

9 Ibid., 267.

10 Paul Ehrlich, et al., "Long-Term Biological Consequences of Nuclear War," *Science* (Dec. 23, 1983), 1293.

11 Ibid.

12 Starley Thompson and Stephen Schneider, "Comment and Correspondence: The Nuclear Winter Debate," *Foreign Affairs* (Fall 1986), 176.

13 Turco, "Nuclear Winter," 1289–90; Ehrlich, "Long-Term Biological Consequences," 1298–99.

14 Carl Sagan, "Comment and Correspondence: The Nuclear Winter Debate," *Foreign Affairs* (Fall 1986), 168.

15 Ehrlich, "Long-Term Biological Consequences," 1298.

16 Ibid., 1294.

17 Carl Sagan and Richard Turco, *A Path Where No Man Thought: Nuclear Winter and the End of the Arms Race* (New York: Random House, 1990), 463.

18 Seitz, " 'Nuclear Winter' Melts Down," 4.

19 Ibid., 5.

20 Sagan, "Nuclear War," 289.

21 Theodore Reuter and Thomas Kalil, "Nuclear Strategy and Nuclear Winter," *World Politics* (July 1991), 587–607.

22 Cited in Seitz, " 'Nuclear Winter' Melts Down," 7.

23 Mark Harwell, et al., *SCOPE 28: Environmental Consequences of Nuclear War: Ecological and Agricultural Effects, Volume II* (New York: Wiley & Sons, 1985), 490.

24 Starley Thompson and Stephen Schneider, "Nuclear Winter Reappraised," *Foreign Affairs* (Summer 1986), 983.

25 Seitz, " 'Nuclear Winter' Melts Down," 4.

26 Stephen Schneider and Starley Thompson, "Simulating the Climatic Effects of Nuclear War," *Nature* (May 19, 1988), 321; idem, "The Nuclear Winter Debate," 174–75.

27 Idem. "Nuclear Winter Reappraised," 993. See also idem, "Simulating the Climatic Effects of Nuclear War," 221.

28 Idem, "Nuclear Winter Reappraised," 994.

29 George Rathjens and Ronald Siegel, "Comment and Correspondence: The Nuclear Winter Debate," *Foreign Affairs* (Fall 1986), 170.

30 Rathjens, cited in Seitz, " 'Nuclear Winter' Melts Down," 11.

31 Richard Turco, cited in Malcolm Browne, "Nuclear Winter Theorists Pull Back," *The New York Times* (Jan. 23, 1990), C1.

32 Sagan and Turco, *A Path*, 74.

33 Elliot Marshall, " 'Nuclear Winter' from Gulf War Discounted," *Science* (Jan. 25, 1991), 372; John Horgan, "Science and the Citizen: Up in Flames," *Scientific American* (May 1991), 20.

34 Marshall, " 'Nuclear Winter' from Gulf War Discounted," 251.

35 Horgan, "Science and the Citizen," 17.

36 Marshall, " 'Nuclear Winter' from Gulf War Discounted," 372.

37 Carl Sagan, "Letters: Kuwaiti Fires and Nuclear Winter," *Science* (Dec. 6, 1991) 1434.

38 Sagan, cited by Forrest Mims, "Letters: Sagan's Scenario," *Science* (Feb. 14, 1992), 783.

39 Sagan, cited in "Sacred Sagan Scorched," *Media Watch* (Sept. 1991), 8.

40 Michelle Hoffman, "Rainy Forecast for Gulf Area?" *Science* (Aug. 30, 1991), 971.

41 Peter Hobbs and Lawrence Radke, "Airborne Studies of the Smoke from the Kuwait Oil Fires," *Science* (May 15, 1992), 990.

42 Ibid.

43 Sagan, "Nuclear War," 257–58.

44 Thomas Levenson, "Tales of the Future," *Oceanus* (Summer 1989), 73.

45 Thompson, "Nuclear Winter Reappraised," 1005.

Notes to Chapter Eight

1 Michael Lemonick "The Ozone Vanishes," *Time* (Feb. 17, 1992), 60.

2 Albert Gore, *Congressional Record* (Feb. 6, 1992), S1129.

3 Interviews with NASA scientists, Feb. 1992, anonymity requested.

4 *Time*, "The Heat is On" (May 11, 1992), 17.

5 Melvyn Shapiro, cited in Micah Morrison, "Ozone Scare," *Insight* (Apr. 6, 1992), 13.

6 Sharon Roan, *Ozone Crisis: The 15 Year Evolution of a Sudden Global Emergency* (New York: Wiley, 1990), 263.

7 Albert Gore, *Earth in the Balance: Ecology and the Human Spirit* (Boston: Houghton Mifflin, 1992), 81–88; Paul Ehrlich and Anne Ehrlich, *Healing the Planet: Strategies for Resolving the Environmental Crisis* (New York: Addison-Wesley, 1991), 113–29; Lester Brown, et al., *State of the World 1989* (New York: Norton, 1989), 77–96.

8 Malcolm Browne, "Growing Hole in Ozone Shield Is Discovered Over Antarctica," *The New York Times* (Sept. 23, 1989), 2.

9 Ehrlich and Ehrlich, *Healing the Planet*, 113.

10 Paul Ehrlich, interview, 1990.

11 Roan, *Ozone Crisis*, 8.

12 Ibid., 72; Fred Singer, "My Adventures in the Ozone Hole," *National Review* (June 30, 1989), 35; *Executive Summary: Scientific Assessment of Stratospheric Ozone 1991* (Washington, D.C.: NASA Oct. 22, 1991), 6.

13 Roan, *Ozone Crisis*, 32.

14 Ibid., 111.

15 Singer, "My Adventures," 36.

16 Richard Stolarkski, et al. "Measured Trends in Stratospheric Ozone," *Science* (Apr. 17, 1992), 346.

17 Ehrlich and Ehrlich, *Healing the Planet*, 124.

18 Guy Brasseur, chief ozone modeler, NCAR, interview, Jan. 1992.

19 *Executive Summary*, 7.

20 Singer, "My Adventures," 36.

21 Arlin Krueger, Goddard Space Flight Center, interview, Mar. 1992.

22 Alan Teramura, interview, winter 1992.

23 Manfred Tevini and Alan Teramura, "UV-B Effects on Terrestrial Plants," *Photochemistry and Photobiology* (Oct. 1989), 481.

24 Patrick Michaels, *The Satanic Gases: Global Warming and Political Science*, manuscript, 1992, 175.

25 F. E. Qualte, B. M. Sutherland and J. F. Sutherland, "action spectrum for DNA damage in alfalfa lowers predicted impact of ozone depletion," *Nature* (August 13, 1992), 578.

26 Susan Weiler, cited in Keith Schneider, "Ozone Depletion Harming Sea Life," *The New York Times* (Nov. 16, 1991), 6.

27 Osmond Holm-Hansen, Scripps Institute of Oceanography, interview, Jan. and Feb. 1992.

28 Holm-Hansen, interview, Feb. 1992.

29 Ibid.

30 "UV pours through ozone hole," *Science News* (Oct. 5, 1991), 214.

31 John Frederick, interview, summer 1989.

32 Holm-Hansen, interview, Jan. 1992.

33 Raymond Smith, "Ozone Hole Adversely Affecting Antarctic Life," press release, University of California at Santa Barbara (Feb. 21, 1992), 3.

34 Hugh Ellsaesser, "The Holes in the Ozone Hole II," paper prepared for the Cato Institute Conference, "Global Environmental Crises: Science or Politics" (June 5–6, 1991), 7–8.

35 Frederick Urbach, dermatologist, Temple University, interview, Jan. 1992.

36 Urbach, interview, Oct. 1989.

37 Urbach interview, Jan. 1992.

38 Ehrlich and Ehrlich, *Healing the Planet*, 119.

39 Warwick Morison, "Effects of Ultraviolet Radiation on the Immune System in Humans," *Photochemistry and Photobiology* (Oct. 1989), 515.

40 United Nations Environment Program, *Environmental*

Effects of Ozone Depletion: 1991 Update (Nov. 1991), 17.

41 Singer, "My Adventures," 36.

42 Dirk De Muer and H. De Backer, "Revision of 20 Years of Dobson Total Ozone Data at Uccle (Belgium) Fictitious Dobson Total Ozone Trends Induced by Sulfur Dioxide Trends," *Journal of Geophysical Research—Atmospheres* (Apr. 20, 1992), 5921.

43 John DeLuisi, et al., "An examination of the spectral response characteristics of seven Robertson-Berger meters after long-term field use," manuscript, fall 1991, citing Scotto, et al., "Biologically effective ultraviolet radiation: surface measurements in the United States, 1974–1985," *Science*, 293 (1988), 762–64.

44 Ibid., 10.

45 Shaw Liu, et al., "Effect of Anthropogenic Aerosols On Biologically Active Ultraviolet Radiation," *Geophysical Research Letters* (Jan. 3, 1992), 2265.

46 Patrick Michaels, "Intelligence Lost in the Ozone," *Washington Times* (Jan. 14, 1992), F1.

47 Ibid.

48 Brasseur interview.

49 *Executive Summary*, 1.

50 Richard Kerr, "Huge Eruption May Cool Globe," *Science* (June 28, 1991), 1780; R. Monastersky, "Pinatubo's impact spreads around the globe," *Science News* (Aug. 31, 1991), 132; "Volcano could cool climate, reduce ozone," *Science News* (July 6, 1991), 7.

51 David Hofmann and Susan Solomon, "Ozone Destruction Through Heterogeneous Chemistry Following the Eruption of El Chichón," *Journal of Geophysical Re-*

search (Apr. 20, 1989), 5029; Guy Brasseur, Claire Granier, and Stacy Walters, "Future Changes in Stratospheric Ozone and the Role of Heterogeneous Chemistry," *Nature* (Dec. 13, 1990), 626.

52 Guy Brasseur, cited in Monastersky, "Pinatubo's impact," 132.

53 Susan Solomon, cited in John Horgan, "Volcanic Disruption," *Scientific American* (Mar. 1992), 28.

54 David Hofmann, cited in Morrison, "Ozone Scare," 11.

55 Brasseur interview.

56 Linwood Callis, NASA Langley Research Center, interview, Jan. 1992.

57 Singer, "My Adventures," 37.

58 P. Rigaud and B. Leroy, "Presumptive Evidence for a Low Value of the Total Ozone Content Above Antarctica in September 1958," *Annales Geophysicae* 8(11) (1990), 791–94.

59 Walter Komhyr, et al., "Possible influence of long-term sea surface temperature anomalies in the tropical Pacific on global ozone," *Canadian Journal of Physics* 69 (1991), 1093–1102.

60 Ibid., 1094.

61 Ibid.

62 *Executive Summary*, 3.

63 Komhyr, "Possible influence," 1099–1100.

64 Linwood Callis, et al., "Ozone Depletion in the High Latitudes Lower Stratosphere: 1979–1990," *Journal of Geophysical Research* (Feb. 20, 1991), 2931.

65 Callis interview.

66 Callis, "Ozone Depletion," 2925.

67 Melvyn Shapiro, cited in Morrison, "The Ozone Scare," 27.

68 Stephen Schneider, *Global Warming: Are We Entering the Greenhouse Century?* (New York: Vintage, 1990), 21; Carl Sagan, "Croesus and Cassandra: Policy Response to Global Warming," *American Journal of Physics* (Aug. 1990), 725.

69 *Executive Summary,* 7.

70 William Reilly, cited in William Stevens, "Summertime Harm to Shield of Ozone Detected Over U.S.," *The New York Times* (Oct. 23, 1991), 1.

71 Elizabeth Cook, "Close-up," C-SPAN TV, March 1992.

72 Rafe Pomerance, cited in Roan, *Ozone Crisis,* 256.

73 Maurice Strong, interview, April, 1992.

Notes to Chapter Nine

1 Paul Ehrlich and Anne Ehrlich, *Healing the Planet: Strategies for Resolving the Environmental Crisis* (New York: Addison-Wesley, 1991), 72.

2 Aaron Wildavsky, in the foreword to Robert Balling, *The Heated Debate: Greenhouse Predictions Versus Climate Reality* (San Francisco, CA: Pacific Research Institute, 1992), xv.

3 Richard Lindzen, "Some Personal Observations on the Politics of Global Warming," lecture at Tel Aviv University (Jan. 1, 1992), 7.

4 Stephen Schneider, cited in Patrick Michaels, *The Satanic Gases: Global Warming and Political Science,* manuscript, 12.

5 Wildavsky, in Balling, *The Heated Debate,* xv.

6 Riley Dunlap, "Public Opinion in the 1980s: Clear Consensus, Ambiguous Commitment," *Environment* (Oct. 1991), 36.

7 Lindzen, "Some Personal Observations," 3.

8 P. D. Quay, et al., "Oceanic Uptake of Fossil Fuel CO_2: Carbon-13 Evidence," *Science* (Apr. 3, 1992), 74.

9 Quay, *Science*, 78.

10 Pekka Kauppi, et al., "Biomass and Carbon Budget of European Forests, 1971 to 1990," *Science* (Apr. 3, 1992), 70.

11 Kenneth Frederick and Roger Sedjo, editors, *America's Renewable Resources: Historical Trends and Current Challenges* (Washington, D.C.: Resources for the Future, 1991), 92.

12 Fakhri Bazzaz, et al., "Plant Life in a CO_2-Rich World," *Scientific American* (Jan. 1992), 73.

13 P. D. Quay, *et al.*, "Oceanic Uptake of Fossil Fuel CO_2: Carbon 13 Evidence," *Science* (Apr. 3, 1992), 74.

14 Bazzaz, "Plant Life," 73.

15 Stephen Schneider and Randi Londer, *The Coevolution of Climate and Life* (San Francisco: Sierra Club Books, 1984), 309.

16 Ehrlich and Ehrlich, *Healing the Planet*, 73.

17 Patrick Michaels, interview, Jan. 1992.

18 Ibid.

19 Lindzen, "Some Personal Observations," 4.

20 Lindzen, telephone interview, summer 1989.

21 Andrew Solow, "Pseudo-Scientific Hot Air," *The New York Times* (Dec. 28, 1988), A27.

22 Stephen Schneider, *Global Warming: Are We Entering the Greenhouse Century?* (New York: Vintage, 1989), 21.

23 "CFCs, Ozone Depletion, and Climate: What Are the Scientists Really Saying," *Global Environmental Change*

Report, New York: Cutter Information Corp. (Nov. 1, 1991), 5.

24 Barry Commoner, *Making Peace with the Planet* (New York: Pantheon, 1990), 8.

25 Lindzen, "Some Personal Observations," 4.

26 "1991 Is Called '2nd Warmest' Year on Record," *The Washington Post* (Jan. 9, 1992), A4; Carl Sagan, "Croesus and Cassandra: Policy Response to Global Warming," *American Journal of Physics* (Aug. 1990), 726; Fred Singer, Roger Revelle, and Chauncey Starr, "What to Do About Greenhouse Warming: Look Before You Leap," *Cosmos* (1991), 30.

27 Andrew Solow, "The Detection of Greenhouse Warming," paper presented at the Cato Institute Conference on "Global Environmental Crises: Science or Politics" (June 5–6, 1991), 6.

28 Peter Rogers, cited in Jerome Namias, "The Greenhouse Effect as a Symptom of Our Collective Angst," *Oceanus* (Summer 1989), 66.

29 Roy Spencer, interview, Feb. 1992.

30 Roy Spencer and John Christy, "Precise Monitoring of Global Temperature: Trends from Satellites," *Science* (Mar. 30, 1990), 1558; Spencer interview.

31 Spencer interview.

32 John Christy, interview, Feb. 1992.

33 Balling, *The Heated Debate,* 50; Fred Singer, "Global Climate Change: Facts and Fiction," *World Climate Change Report,* Bureau of National Affairs (Dec. 1990), 21.

34 Kevin Wang and Trevor Lewis, "Geothermal Evidence from Canada for a Cold Period Before Recent Climatic Warming," *Science* (May 15, 1992), 1003.

35 Michaels, *The Satanic Gases*, 43.

36 Schneider, *Global Warming*, 117.

37 Robert Balling, "Interpreting the Global Temperature Effect," paper prepared for the Cato Institute Conference on "Global Environmental Crises: Science or Politics?" (June 5–6, 1991), 9–10. See also Balling, *The Heated Debate*, 60, 64, 67.

38 Michaels interview.

39 Balling, *The Heated Debate*, 90; Singer, "Global Climate Change," 22; see also Michaels, *The Satanic Gases*, 43.

40 Schneider, *Global Warming*, 163; Ehrlich and Ehrlich, *Healing the Planet*, 92–94.

41 Schneider, *Global Warming*, 163.

42 Paul Ehrlich, NBC's "Today" show, Jan. 11, 1990, cited in *Mediawatch* (Feb. 1990), 4.

43 Walter Sullivan, "Antarctic Ice Buildup," *The New York Times* (Dec. 3, 1991), C5

44 Jay Zwally, cited in Singer, "Global Climate Change," 23.

45 V. I. Morgan, et al., "Evidence from Antarctic ice cores for recent increases in snow accumulation," *Nature* (Nov. 7, 1991), 58.

46 Balling, *The Heated Debate*, 87; Singer, "Global Climate Change," 22; see also Michaels, *The Satanic Gases*, 53, 59.

47 Zbigniew Jaworowski, Tom Segalstad, and Nobuo Ono, "Do Glaciers Tell a True Atmospheric CO_2 Story?," prepublication manuscript, accepted for publication in the journal *The Science of the Total Environment* (Aug. 18, 1991), 55.

48 Ibid., 2.

49 "Algae Bloom Outbreaks Seen in Oceans," *The Washington Post* (Oct. 31, 1991), A4.

50 Michaels, *The Satanic Gases*, 83.

51 Ibid., 200.

52 "Algae Bloom Outbreaks," A4.

53 Michaels, *The Satanic Gases*, 75.

54 Schneider, *Global Warming*, 216.

55 Intergovernmental Panel on Climate Change, *Scientific Assessment of Climate Change*, June 1990, cited in Science and Environmental Policy Project survey, Washington Institute, Aug. 1991, survey question 3.

56 Andrew Solow, cited in Ronald Bailey, "Raining in Their Hearts," *National Review* (Dec. 3, 1990), p. 36.

57 Singer, "Global Climate Change," 21.

58 Richard Lindzen, "Global Warming and Recantation," manuscript (Nov. 1991), 2.

59 Balling, "Interpreting the Global Temperature Effect," 10.

60 T. M. L. Wigley and S. C. B. Raper "Implications for climate and sea level of revised IPCC emissions scenarios," *Nature* (May 28, 1992), 300.

61 Wigley, *Nature*, 299.

62 V. Ramanathan, et al., "Climate and the Earth's Radiation Budget," *Physics Today* (May 1989), 32; see also Balling, *The Heated Debate*, 45.

63 Michaels, *The Satanic Gases*, 110.

64 Balling, *The Heated Debate*, 79.

65 Bruce Hayden, climatologist, University of Virginia, interview, Jan. 1992.

66 Balling, *The Heated Debate*, 79.

67 Tom Karl, et al., "Global Warming: Evidence for Asymmetric Diurnal Temperature Change," prepublication report (Oct. 17, 1991), 1.

68 Ibid., 5; see also Balling, *The Heated Debate*, 100–104.

69 Associated Press, "Ecology: Does Pollution Cause Global Warming," *The Washington Post* (Dec. 12, 1991), A2.

70 Michaels, *The Satanic Gases*, 123.

71 Ibid., 124.

72 Ibid., 125.

73 "Climate 'Thermostat' Theory Gets Another Empirical Boost," *Global Environmental Change Report*, Cutter Information Corp. (Nov. 1, 1991), 6.

74 Albert Gore, *Earth in the Balance: Ecology and the Human Spirit* (Boston: Houghton Mifflin, 1992), 40.

75 Paul Ehrlich interview, summer 1989.

76 Gore, *Earth in the Balance*, 38.

77 Ibid., 39.

78 Ibid., 38.

79 Schneider, *Global Warming*, 118.

80 Philip Abelson, "Uncertainties About Global Warming," *Science* (Mar. 30, 1990), 1529.

81 Lester Brown, cited in Michaels, *The Satanic Gases*, 10.

82 Commoner, *Making Peace*, 211.

83 Gore, *Earth in the Balance*, 14.

84 Richard Hofstadter, *The Paranoid Style in American Politics and other Essays* (New York: Knopf, 1965), 29.

85 Michael Schlesinger and Xingjian Jiang, "Revised Projection of Future Greenhouse Warming," *Nature* (Mar. 21, 1991), 221.

86 Revelle, et al., "What to Do About Greenhouse Warming," 28.

87 Bruce Babbitt, "Earth Summit," *World Monitor* (Jan. 1992), 29.

88 Worldwatch Institute press conference, Hart Senate Office Building, Jan. 15, 1992.

89 Lester Brown, et al., *State of the World 1992* (New York: Norton, 1992), 155.

90 Revelle, et al., "What to Do About Greenhouse Warming," 33.

91 Maurice Strong, interview, April 1992; see also, Maurice Strong, cited in Paul Lewis, "U.N. Opens Environment Talks: Europe Spurs U.S. to Act Urgently," *The New York Times* (Mar. 3, 1992), A11.

92 "NGO Study Finds U.S. Could Save Trillions by Cutting CO_2," *Global Environmental Change Report*, Cutter Information Corp. (Nov. 1991), 4.

93 William Nordhaus, "The Cost of Slowing Climate Change: a Survey," *The Energy Journal* 12:1, 63.

94 Richard Bradley, et al., *Limiting Net Greenhouse Gas Emissions in the United States: Executive Summary*, U.S. Department of Energy, Office of Environmental Analysis (Sept. 1991, released Dec. 5, 1991), 7, 14–15.

95 Matthew Wald, "Carbon Dioxide Emissions Dropped in 1990, Ecologists Say," *The New York Times* (Dec. 8, 1991), 17.

96 Anwar Shah and Bjorn Larsen, "Global Warming, Carbon Taxes and Developing Countries," presented at the 1992 annual meeting of the American Economic Association (Jan. 3, 1992), 21.

97 National Acid Precipitation Assessment Program: 1990 Integrated Assessment Report, NAPAP Office of the Director (Nov. 1991), 45.

98 Ibid., 46.

99 Ibid., 126.

100 Edward Krug, "The Environmental Party's Bid for Power," speech to the Indiana Electric Power Association's annual meeting (Oct. 1, 1991), 7.

101 National Academy of Sciences, *Policy Implications of Greenhouse Warming: The Synthesis Panel* (Washington, D.C.: National Academy Press, 1991), 45.

102 Jesse Ausubel, "Does Climate Still Matter?" *Nature* (Apr. 25, 1991), 651.

103 National Academy of Sciences, *Policy Implications of Greenhouse Warming: Report of the Adaptation Panel*, prepublication manuscript, Washington, D.C., 104.

104 Ibid., 52.

105 *Policy Implications of Greenhouse Warming*, 35; *Adaptation Panel Report*, prepublication manuscript, 65.

106 Barry Commoner, *Making Peace with the Planet*, 17.

107 *Policy Implications of Greenhouse Warming: The Synthesis Panel Report*, 58.

108 Leslie Roberts, "Report Nixes 'Geritol' Fix for Global Warming," *Science* (Sept. 27, 1991), 1490–91.

109 Bill McKibben, *The End of Nature* (New York: Random House, 1989), 166.

110 *Policy Implications of Greenhouse Warming: Adaptation Panel Report*, prepublication manuscript, 42–46.

111 Sherwood Idso, *Carbon Dioxide and Global Change: Earth in Transition* (Tempe, Arizona: IBR Press, 1989), 68.

112 Ibid., 109.

113 Ibid., 108.

114 Christian Korner and John Arnone, "Responses to Elevated Carbon Dioxide in Artificial Tropical Ecosystems," *Science* (Sept. 18, 1992): 1672–1675.

115 Sherwood Idso, interview, Sept. 1992.

116 Sherwood Idso, "The Greening of Planet Earth: The Effects of Carbon Dioxide on the Biosphere" documentary, 1991.

117 E. Friis-Christensen and K. Lassen, "Length of the Solar Cycle: An Indicator of Solar Activity Closely Associated with Climate," *Science* (Nov. 1, 1991): 700.

118 James Hansen, cited in William Stevens, "Danes Link Sunspot Intensity to Global Temperature Rise," *The New York Times* (Nov. 5, 1991), C4.

119 R. J. Charlson, et al., "Climate Forcing by Anthropogenic Aerosols," *Science* (Jan. 24, 1992), 423.

120 Gilford Miller and Anne de Vernal, cited in William Stevens, "Scientists Suggest Global Warming Could Hasten the Next Ice Age," *The New York Times* (Jan. 21, 1992), C4.

121 Guy Brasseur, National Center for Atmospheric Research, interview, Jan. 1992.

122 Lamont Poole, NASA Langley Research Center, interview, Feb. 1992.

123 William Stevens, "Earth's Temperature Has Dropped a Little After a Warm Spell," *The New York Times* (Dec. 24, 1991), C4.

124 J. K. Angell, National Oceanic and Atmospheric Agency, interview, Dec. 1991.

125 David Hofmann cited in *Volcanism and Climate*

Change (Washington, D.C.: American Geophysical Union, May 1992), 18.

126 Peter Rogers, "Climate Change and Global Warming," *Environment, Science & Technology* 24:4 (1990), 429.

127 Roy Spencer, cited in "The Greenhouse Conspiracy" *Equinox*, Hilary Lawson, Producer, (London, England: TBS Productions, 1991).

128 Idso cited in "The Greenhouse Conspiracy."

129 *Environmental and Energy Study Institute Report*, Special Report (Jan. 30, 1992), 17; Edward Rubin, et al., "Keeping Climate Research Relevant," *Issues in Science and Technology* (Winter 1991–92), 50.

Notes to Chapter Ten

1 Sharon Friedman, "Two Decades of the Environmental Beat," *Gannett Center Journal* (Summer 1990), 13.

2 Henry Muller, cited by Robert Miller, "From the Publisher," *Time* (Jan. 2, 1989), 3.

3 Charles Alexander, cited by Amar Kumar Naj, "Greens and Greenbacks," *Gannett Center Journal* (Summer 1990), 86.

4 Barbara Pyle, speech to the 1990 "Early Warnings" conference sponsored by the *Utne Reader* in Minneapolis. Remarks taken from transcript of her speech.

5 Teya Ryan, "Network Earth: Advocacy, Journalism and the Environment," *Gannett Center Journal* (Summer 1990), 71.

6 Lester Brown, cited in Mark Hertsgaard, "Covering the World; Ignoring the Earth," *Rolling Stone,* reprinted by *Greenpeace News* (May/June 1991), 15.

7 "The Race to Save the Planet," PBS-TV documentary cited in "PBS: Planet Panic," *Mediawatch* (Dec. 1990), 4.

8 Michael Schnayerson, "Environment: The Hot Issue," *Vanity Fair* (Sept. 1989), 166.

9 Richard Bernstein, "Should Stars Set the Agenda?" *The New York Times* (Mar. 10, 1991), B11.

10 Stephen Schneider, cited by Jonathan Schell in *Discover*, "Our Fragile Earth" (Oct. 1989), 47.

11 Sara Vickerman, cited by Tom Arrandale in "The Midlife Crisis of the Environmental Lobby," *Governing* (Apr. 1992), 36.

12 Witold Rybczynski, *Taming the Tiger: The Struggle to Control Technology* (New York: Viking, 1983), 27.

13 Jim Sibbison, "Environmental Reporters: Prisoners of Gullibility," *The Washington Monthly* (Mar. 1984), 28.

14 Melvyn Shapiro, cited in Micah Morrison, "The Ozone Scare," *Insight* (Mar. 22, 1992), 26.

15 Robert Lichter, et al., *Media Coverage of Global Warming 1985–1991*, Center for Media and Public Affiars, 79.

16 Greg Easterbrook, cited in "Special Report: Environmental Journalism 1992," *TFJR Business News Reporter* (Jan. 1992), 6.

INDEX

221

biotechnology (*cont.*)
recombinant DNA, 2, 89–94, 98,
103–04, 108–09
Bookchin, Murray, 6
Borlaug, Norman, 55
Boyer, Herbert, 89, 91
Bramwell, Anna, 7, 16, 19
Brasseur, Guy, 133–34
Brill, Winston, 88, 107–08
British Antarctic Survey, 125, 136
Brookhaven National Laboratory, 129
Brown, Karen, 105
Brown, Dr. Lester, xi, 12, 22, 40, 41,
45–49, 52, 56, 61, 64, 70, 85, 99,
106, 143, 157, 169
Brundtland, Gro, 64, 74
Bryson, Reid, 80, 84
Bulletin of the Atomic Scientists, 26,
32, 36
Bush, George, 36, 38, 119, 121, 139

Calder, Nigel, 84
California (at Berkeley), University of,
6, 89, 101–102, 122, 141
California (at Irvine), University of,
123
Callahan, David, 98
Callis, Linwood, 134, 137, 174
Campaign for Nuclear Disarmament
(CND), 31, 116
Campaign for the Earth, 38
Caplan, Arthur, 96
carbon dioxide emissions, 143–44,
150–53, 158–60, 163–65
Carter, Jimmy, 34, 64
Cavalieri, Liebe, 93
CBS "60 Minutes", 21, 117
chlorofluorocarbons (CFC), 26, 80,
119, 121, 123–27, 135, 137–40,
144
Christy, John, 147–48
civil rights and environmentalists,
8–9, 32–33
Clean Air Act, 161
Climatic Impact Assessment Program
(CIAP), 20, 123
climatology, 20–21, 79–87

See also global cooling; global
warming
Closing Circle, The (Commoner), 53
Club of Rome, 13, 63–64, 74, 76–77,
106, 138, 143, 158
CNN "Network Earth," 169
Cohen, Daniel, 23
Cohen, Stanley, 89, 91
*Cold and the Dark: The World After
Nuclear War, The* (Ehrlich/
Sagan), 114
Cold War, end of, 36–38, 118
Commoner, Barry, 7, 31–32, 53, 99,
143, 162
Competitive Enterprise Institute, 103,
109
computer models, and environmental
research, 13, 63–67, 70, 111–12,
114, 115, 127, 145, 146, 152, 154,
160, 166
Cook, Elizabeth, 139
Cooling, The (Ponte), 80, 83
Council for a Livable World, 35, 115
Cousins, Norman, 28, 31–32
Cox, John, 116
Crick, Francis, 89
Crosson, Pierre, 47–48

Davis, C. Bernard, 98
"Day After, The" (ABC TV movie),
114
De Muer, Dirk, 132
deep ecology, 10–11, 12–13, 15, 75,
96
Defenders of Wildlife, 171
deforestation, 2, 13, 46, 79–80, 144
DeLuisi, John, 133
Detjen, Jim, 173
Devall, Bill, 11, 13
di Fiore, Joachim, 5
Disaster and the Millennium (Bar-
kun), 3
Discover magazine, 100
Dobson, Sir. G. M. B., 125, 135
Dr. Strangelove, 110
Du Pont, 123
Dun's Review, 98

223

225

227

technology (*cont.*)
technophobia, 38–39, 97, 98
See also biotechnology; resources
Teller, Edward, 27
Teramura, Dr. Alan, 128–29
Tertullian, 40
Thinking about the Unthinkable (Kahn), 26
Thompson, Starley, 114–15, 118
Time magazine, 65, 83, 119–20, 156, 168–69
Tirman, John, 38
Toon, Owen, 111
Total Ozone Mapping Spectrometer, 128
"Tragedy of the Commons, The" (Hardin), 60
Turco, Richard, 111, 116

ultraviolet light, 125–33
Union of Concerned Scientists (UCS), 33, 35, 113
United Council of Church Women, 29
United Nations, 77
Atomic Energy Commission, 29
Environment Project, 107
Food and Agriculture Organization, 57
Intergovernmental Panel on Climate Change, 152–53
Sustainable Development Commission, 18
World Commission on Environment and Development, 74
United States
Agency for International Development, 61
Department of Energy, 159
Department of Transportation, 123
Food & Drug Administration, 105, 107
International Agriculture Development Services, 46
Nuclear Regulatory Commission, 93
Public Interest Research Group, 107

Science, Space and Technology subcommittee, 120
United World Federalists, 28
Urbach, Dr. Frederick, 131

Vellucci, Alfred, 93–94
Vernal, Anne de, 165
Vickerman, Sara, 171
Virginia, University of, xi, 132, 133, 135
Viscio, Randolph, 9–10

Waiting for the Apocalypse (Cohen), 23
Wald, George, 39
Wang, Kevin, 148
Watson, James, 89, 91, 94
Wattenberg, Ben, 53
wealth, redistribution of, 9, 18–19, 74–75, 85, 86
Weiler, Susan, 130
White, Lynn, Jr., 11
White, Ralph, 111
Wigley, Thomas, 170
Wigner, Eugene, 27–28
Wildavsky, Aaron, 8, 141
Wirth, Timothy, 142
World Bank, 57, 77, 78, 160
World Dynamics (Forrester), 64, 66, 70
World Federalist Association, 38
world government, 27, 28, 159
World Health Organization, 73
World Hunger Program, 57
World on Fire: Saving an Endangered Earth (Mitchell), 16
World Resources Institute, 57, 67, 73, 107, 140
World Security Institutes, 85–86
Worldwatch Institute, 45, 64, 67, 158, 169

Zencey, Eric, 23
Zero Population Growth, 42
Zimmerman, Burke, 94